ISLANDICA

A SERIES RELATING TO ICELAND AND THE

FISKE ICELANDIC COLLECTION

CORNELL UNIVERSITY LIBRARIES

EDITED BY VILHJALMUR BJARNAR

VOLUME XLIII

The Legend of Brynhild
By Theodore M. Andersson

By the same author

The Problem of Icelandic Saga Origins: A Historical Survey

The Icelandic Family Saga: An Analytic Reading

Co-editor with Larry D. Benson, *The Literary Context of Chaucer's Fabliaux: Texts and Translations*

Early Epic Scenery: Homer, Virgil, and the Medieval Legacy

The Legend of Brynhild

Theodore M. Andersson

ISLANDICA XLIII

CORNELL UNIVERSITY PRESS

Ithaca and London, 1980

First published 1980 by Cornell University Press.
Published in the United Kingdom by Cornell University Press Ltd.,
2–4 Brook Street, London W1Y 1AA.

International Standard Book Number 0-8014-1302-8
Library of Congress Catalog Card Number 80-16008
Printed in the United States of America
*Librarians: Library of Congress cataloging information appears
on the last page of the book.*

Preface

Brynhild is the paramount figure of Germanic legend, but she has been subordinated more often than not to the male object of her passion. Her story is thus normally referred to as the legend of Sigurd or, in German circles, the legend of Siegfried. The title of this book is intended to make the point that the legend sings principally of the woman, not the man, a view that I argue specifically at the beginning of Chapter 2. My task has been to examine the sometimes fragmentary and always refractory medieval accounts of Brynhild with a view to extracting from them a better appreciation of her personality. This task made it necessary to reopen the long-standing debate on the textual relationships of the major literary documents (*Poetic Edda, Vǫlsunga saga, Þiðreks saga,* and *Nibelungenlied*). As a consequence the book has become a general reassessment of the so-called Nibelung question, a good part of which it attempts to summarize and elucidate.

My method will be readily recognizable to scholars in the field as the property of Andreas Heusler, subject to a few limitations noted in the Introduction. *Nibelungenlied* scholars in particular will find this method antiquated because they are currently more concerned with the literary or oral qualities of the poem than with the sources. I ask them to bear in mind that the present study focuses on the Brynhild tradition, not the status of *Nibelungenlied* research, a topic to which I hope to return in the future. Although I have not entered into the *Nibelungenlied* controversy as such, my position will be clear enough. I follow Heusler in believing that Part I is based on a single oral source and that Part II is based on a written epic, the "Ältere Not." The "Ältere Not" in particular has encountered much skepticism in recent years, but, with the exception of Friedrich Panzer, those scholars who have studied the problem closely (Léon Polak, Andreas Heusler, Roswitha Wisniewski) agree on the necessity of assuming an anterior epic. I have not reviewed this aspect of the problem partly because it is peripheral to the subject of Brynhild and partly because I have argued my position fully in a separate paper ("The Epic Source of Niflunga saga and the Nibelungenlied," *Arkiv för nordisk filologi*, 88 [1973], 1–54). The reconstructions of the "Ältere Not" are in fairly good agreement with each other and I believe the burden of disproof rests on the skeptics. They must find an alternative explanation for the massive correspondences in detail and wording between "Niflunga saga" and Part II of the *Nibelungenlied*. Until such an explanation is offered, it is safe to assume that the correspondences derive from a common written source. This assumption underlies Chapters 5 and 6.

The form of Norse proper names appropriate to an English context is always a vexing problem. A frequent practice has been to drop the nominative ending -r (hence Sigurd for Sigurðr, and so forth), but this practice leads to inconsistencies because other nominative endings are retained. Inconsistency no doubt is unavoidable, but I prefer a variety that calls for the retention of all nominative endings with a few exceptions. These exceptions are dictated by my sense that the most important names in the Brynhild legend are sufficiently familiar to the English reader in Anglicized form that a reversion to the Norse form would seem artificial. Hence I write Sigurd for Sigurðr, Sigmund for Sigmundr, Gudrun for Guðrún, Brynhild for Brynhildr, and Grimhild for Grímhildr. In the case of Brynhild it is also useful to adopt a neutral form midway between the Norse Brynhildr and the German Brünhilt. Thus "Brynhild" in the following pages may refer to our heroine as she figures in either the Norse or German legend or in a common antecedent tradition.

This project was completed with the help of a grant from Stanford University and the Lilly Endowment. In a period of shrinking opportunities for humanistic research, I am greatly indebted to Stanford for its generous support. The work was carried out from September of 1978 to June of 1979 and facilitated by the extraordinary resources of Widener Library. I am particularly grateful to Dorothy Boerstler, Dorrit Cohn, and Eckehard Simon for helping with the arrangements and otherwise conspiring to make my year comfortable and convivial. My work was made doubly pleasant by the genial company of such old friends as Larry Benson, Henry Hatfield, and Einar Haugen.

T. M. A.

Berkeley, California

Contents

Editions Cited

Edda   Neckel, Gustav, ed. *Edda: Die Lieder des Codex Re-*
                    gius nebst verwandten Denkmälern. 4th ed. revised by
                    Hans Kuhn. Heidelberg: Winter, 1962.
Nibelungenlied   Boor, Helmut de, ed. *Das Nibelungenlied.* 20th ptg.
                    Wiesbaden: F. A. Brockhaus, 1972.
Snorra Edda   Jónsson, Finnur, ed. *Edda Snorra Sturlusonar.*
                    Copenhagen: Gyldendal, 1931.
Vǫlsunga saga   Olsen, Magnus, ed. *Vǫlsunga saga ok Ragnars saga*
                    loðbrókar. Samfund til udgivelse af gammel nordisk
                    litteratur. Copenhagen: S. L. Møller, 1906–1908.
Þiðreks saga   Bertelsen, Henrik, ed. *Þiðreks saga af Bern.* Samfund
                    til udgivelse af gammel nordisk litteratur. 2 vols.
                    Copenhagen: S. L. Møller, 1905–1911.

All translations included in the text are my own.

Abbreviations

ANF	*Arkiv för nordisk filologi*
Archiv	*Archiv für das Studium der neueren Sprachen und Literaturen*
BGDSL	*Beiträge zur Geschichte der deutschen Sprache und Literatur*
DVLG	*Deutsche Vierteljahrsschrift für Literaturwissenschaft und Geistesgeschichte*
GL & L	*German Life and Letters*
GR	*Germanic Review*
GRM	*Germanisch-romanische Monatsschrift*
JEGP	*Journal of English and Germanic Philology*
MA	*Medium Aevum*
MLR	*Modern Language Review*
MP	*Modern Philology*
NM	*Neuphilologische Mitteilungen*
WW	*Wirkendes Wort*
ZD	*Zeitschrift für Deutschkunde*
ZDA	*Zeitschrift für deutsches Altertum*
ZDP	*Zeitschrift für deutsche Philologie*
ZVL	*Zeitschrift für vergleichende Literaturgeschichte*

The Legend of Brynhild

Introduction

In the words of Hugo Kuhn: "The history of the 'Nibelungs' has been the master problem of German philology since its inception."[1] The richness of the Nibelung transmissions in medieval Scandinavia and Germany, the intrinsic interest of the story, and the status of the *Nibelungenlied* as a German national epic have conspired to make it so. Brynhild's passionate contrivance of Sigurd's murder in the *Edda* and Kriemhilt's passionate revenge for her dead husband in the *Nibelungenlied* have assured an avid readership, and the position of the *Nibelungenlied* as the only indigenous epic from the great flowering of Middle High German literature around 1200 has placed it at the center of the literary historian's concern. At the same time, the abundant traditions handed down in both Old Norse and Middle High German and the intricacies of relating these traditions to one another with the tempting prospect of establishing some ancestral prototype have made the Nibelung question into the North European equivalent of the Homeric question and have engaged scholars in exceptionally subtle and detailed debates. As Andreas Heusler pointed out at the beginning of his celebrated book *Nibelungensage und Nibelungenlied,* the German *Nibelungenlied* holds a place in the epic procession of the Greek *Iliad,* the English *Beowulf,* and the

[1]Hugo Kuhn in *Annalen der deutschen Literatur von den Anfängen bis zur Gegenwart,* ed. Heinz Otto Burger (Stuttgart: Metzler, 1952), p. 152: "Die Geschichte der 'Nibelungen' ist das Königsproblem der deutschen Philologie seit ihrem Anfang." The formulation is also cited by Werner Hoffmann, "Zur Situation der gegenwärtigen Nibelungenforschung: Probleme, Ergebnisse, Aufgaben," *WW,* 12 (1962), 79, and Karl Heinz Ihlenburg, *Das Nibelungenlied: Problem und Gehalt* (Berlin: Akademie-Verlag, 1969), p. 7.

French *Roland*. But none of these epics affords anything like the insight into the prehistory of the legend which can be gleaned from a comparison of the Nibelung texts. These texts provide a unique opportunity for studying the growth of a medieval epic. The opportunity has been welcomed with varying degrees of warmth depending on time and place. In Scandinavia the legend of Brynhild and Sigurd must compete for popular and scholarly favor with other heroic tales and with the most extraordinary literary creation of medieval Europe—the Icelandic sagas. The attention of Scandinavian scholars has therefore been, for the most part, otherwise engaged. In Germany, on the other hand, the contribution has been prodigious. Although some of the earliest important studies were made by the Dutch scholars Barend Symons, Richard Constant Boer, and Léon Polak, and although the great master was the Swiss Heusler, the Nibelung question has traditionally been a special German province. It was debated with vigor and acrimony in the nineteenth century along lines similar to those that divide traditionalists and unitarians in Homeric scholarship, but the lasting work began with Symons' "Untersuchungen ueber die sogenannte Völsunga saga" in 1876 and culminated with Heusler's *Nibelungensage und Nibelungenlied* in 1920. The modern phase of the controversy has thus been in full swing for over a century, but the first two decades of this century, the years between Heusler's "Die Lieder der Lücke im Codex Regius der Edda" (1902) and his *Nibelungensage und Nibelungenlied* (1920) may be described as the golden age. Heusler's book effectively concluded the debate despite adjustments proposed by Heinrich Hempel in 1926, Hermann Schneider in 1928, Per Wieselgren in 1935, and despite a voluminous but fragmentary revision proposed by Dietrich von Kralik in 1941. Unable to make headway on Heusler's own terms since World War II, German scholarship has relegated him to the background with the justification that he was concerned only with the prehistory of the *Nibelungenlied* and not with the text itself. Heusler answered such criticism already in the third edition of *Nibelungensage und Nibelungenlied* (1929) by observing that it could be entertained only by a reader so unfortunate as to possess a copy of the book ending on page 100. Heusler's point is well taken, but the claim that he dealt only with lost versions has become a cherished refrain and continues to be echoed mechanically.[2] It serves to justify a purely descriptive approach to the *Nibelungenlied,* as if it were indeed an *Iliad,* a *Beowulf,* or a *Roland* with no analogues to shed light on the particular form of the story which it embodies. This approach has enabled scholars to interpret the *Nibelungenlied* without the encumbrance of preliminary source studies.

Something can be said for a little neglect of the sources. Scholars now seem agreed that the reconstruction of a legend in the various stages of its growth is a fruitless endeavor; the extant texts are not adequate to document an evolution on which everyone can agree. Heusler's scheme, which established forms of the story from the sixth century down to the thirteenth, is no longer taken to be accurate, and is considered at best approximately representative, perhaps only symbolical of the evolution. Nor is there any confidence that the reconstruction of a prototype does anything to assist our understanding of the literature in hand. Critics now prefer a direct reading without reference to subtexts. It is of course a useful exercise to read the *Nibelungenlied* in the context of Middle High German literature in the period around 1170–1220, that is, in the literary framework provided by Heinrich von Veldeke, Hartmann von Aue, Wolfram von Eschenbach, Gottfried von Strassburg, and Walther von der Vogelweide. Similarly, the *Poetic Edda* and *Vǫlsunga saga* may be read profitably as part of the flowering of Icelandic letters in the thirteenth century. But this is not a full reading. We know that the Nibelung stories antedate the forms and times in which they finally emerged, and we know that they had earlier contexts.

The question is whether the genetic viewpoint has been overcome once and for all or whether it has temporarily receded in the

<hr>

[2]Heusler's sally was in all likelihood provoked by Ernest Tonnelat, *La chanson des Nibelungen: Etude sur la formation du poème épique* (Paris: Société d'Edition: Les Belles Lettres, 1926), p. 5. Symptomatic of current thinking are the following: Werner Schröder, "Die epische Konzeption des Nibelungenlied-Dichters," *WW,* 11 (1961), 194; Gottfried Weber, *Das Nibelungenlied: Problem und Idee* (Stuttgart: Metzler, 1963), p. 2; D. G. Mowatt and Hugh Sacker, *The Nibelungenlied: An Interpretative Commentary* (Toronto: Toronto University Press, 1967), p. 20; and Stephen L. Wailes, "The *Nibelungenlied* as Heroic Epic" in *Heroic Epic and Saga: An Introduction to the World's Great Folk Epics,* ed. Felix J. Oinas (Bloomington and London: Indiana University Press, 1978), p. 120.

cycle of scholarly fashions. In what follows it will be apparent
that I hold the latter view and believe that in the long run a
synthesis of diachronic and synchronic analysis is possible and
desirable. The neglect of legendary history in the past forty years
need not be taken to mean that the pursuit is futile or unproduc-
tive. It is more likely to signal exhaustion, in the sense that
scholars can no longer muster the patience to explore all aspects
of the debate and because too they believe that the attainable has
been attained and that further refinements will only compound
the speculative quality of our conclusions.

We naturally must not ignore caveats of such long standing.
The break with Heusler was occasioned to some extent by his
ambition not only to trace the immediate sources of the
Nibelungenlied, but to recover still earlier forms of the legend
reaching back into the early Middle Ages. The legend of Siegfried
was dissected with almost surgical precision by Heusler's student
Léon Polak and then arranged in successive layers. It is difficult
to fault Polak's logic, but legends subscribe to many logics. Any
particular logic may lead to wrong deductions even for the poems
immediately underlying our extant texts. For each anterior poetic
layer such deductions become progressively more doubtful. We
must therefore retrench and content ourselves with the approximate reconstruction of the most obvious sources, that is, those
sources that must have existed because they explain the presence
of German and Norse texts that tell the same story without direct
access to one another. We have an obligation to concern ourselves with these sources not only because they existed, but because they are a valuable instrument for our critical appreciation
of the surviving versions. If we have some idea of the form in
which the *Nibelungenlied* poet received the Siegfried story, we
are in a position to analyze his contribution. We can assess his
interests, his attitudes, and his emphases, and therefore understand his literary achievement in greater detail. If we can reconstruct "The Old Lay of Sigurd" and "The Long Lay of Sigurd"
with some plausibility, we can compare them to the extant "Short
Lay of Sigurd" and say something about the literary development
of the heroic lay in Iceland. Such reconstruction is not otiose, but
a prerequisite for the writing of literary history.

The various forms of the Brynhild legend in Scandinavia and Germany invite comparison to the extent that they are both similar and different. Shared features reveal the shape of the Germanic heroic lay and the solidity of the tradition. Differences illuminate the genius of the individual poets who were drawn to the legend. These perspectives are obscured by a provincial outlook that focuses on the surviving texts to the exclusion of the larger pan-Germanic context. Germanic literature, which did not observe the tribal boundaries and which survives most abundantly in heroic poetry, is itself a historical entity with a claim on our attention. No more important key exists to our understanding of Germanic literature than the legend of Brynhild.

For those readers who are skeptical about the pursuit of literary study beyond the precisely documented confines of the thirteenth century, the present volume may still offer some compensation as a research history. Despite its loss of popularity, the Nibelung question remains a classical problem and has enlisted many of the best scholars in a tradition still fundamental to many of our literary habits. Those who do not believe in the continuing vitality of the problem may nonetheless find it of antiquarian interest. It has not been reviewed in English for forty years and the Scandinavian aspects have never been fully dealt with.[3] The recent spate of books on the *Nibelungenlied* by Gottfried Weber, Bert Nagel, Werner Hoffmann, Karl Heinz Ihlenburg, and Walter Falk has coincided with the period of synchronic study and has skirted source questions. Even Heusler's book is of limited use as an introduction to the problem because, as Hans-Friedrich Rosenfeld pointed out,[4] it dispensed with argumentation and apparatus in favor of a pithy summary of the author's views arrived at in earlier serial publications. The logical recourse would be to Hermann Schneider's *Germanische Heldensage* (1928), but Heusler

[3] Mary Thorp, *The Study of the Nibelungenlied: Being the History of the Study of the Epic and Legend from 1775 to 1937* (Oxford: Clarendon Press, 1940). Elizabeth Edrop Bohning's *The Concept 'Sage' in Nibelungen Criticism: The History of the Conception of 'Sage' in the Nibelungen Criticism from Lachmann to Heusler* (Bethlehem, Penna.: Times Publishing Company, 1944) is a commented bibliography with 844 entries.

[4] H.-Fr. Rosenfeld, "Nibelungensage und Nibelungenlied in der Forschung der letzten Jahre," *NM*, 26 (1925), 146.

noted the refractory nature of the presentation for the beginner and the presupposition of a fully informed readership.[5] I have tried to fill the need for a less demanding introduction by summarizing the texts in some detail and explaining each step in the argument. If the endeavor continues to be judged fruitless, I hope that it may at least be dismissed on a more enlightened basis. A clearly stated hypothesis may serve to clarify the counterarguments.

The initial difficulty in presenting the problem is created by the variety of texts from which the legend of Brynhild must be pieced together. I list the most important under seven headings.

1. A number of poems in the *Poetic Edda*, also known as the *Elder Edda* and formerly referred to as *Sæmundar Edda*, a compilation of gnomic, mythological, and heroic verse transmitted in integral form only in a unique Icelandic manuscript written in the second half of the thirteenth century (Codex Regius 2365,4°). It was long housed in the Royal Library in Copenhagen, but was transferred to the Arnamagnaean Manuscript Institute in Reykjavik in 1971. The pertinent poems fall into three groups: accounts of Sigurd's youthful adventures; descriptions of his betrothal to Brynhild, marriage to Gudrun, and death; and, finally, reflections on the aftermath of his death in a series of elegiac poems. The first group includes four poems entitled *Grípisspá* ("The Prophecy of Grípir"), *Reginsmál* ("The Words of Reginn"), *Fáfnismál* ("The Words of Fáfnir"), and *Sigrdrífumál* ("The Words of Sigrdrífa"). The second group includes three poems, *Brot af Sigurðarkviðu* ("Fragment of the Lay of Sigurd"), also known in its hypothetical full form as *Sigurðarkviða in forna* ("The Old Lay of Sigurd"), *Sigurðarkviða in skamma* ("The Short Lay of Sigurd"), and *Sigurðarkviða in meiri* ("The Long Lay of Sigurd"). Because of a substantial lacuna in Codex Regius, only about half of *Forna* is preserved and the whole of *Meiri* is lost. The third or elegiac group includes *Guðrúnarkviða in fyrsta* ("The First Lay of Gudrun"), *Guðrúnarkviða ǫnnur* ("The Second Lay of Gudrun"), *Guðrúnarkviða in þriðja* ("The Third Lay of Gudrun"), *Helreið Brynhildar* ("Brynhild's Journey to the Underworld"), and *Odd-*

[5] *Anzeiger für deutsches Altertum*, 48 (1929), 164; rpt. in his *Kleine Schriften*, I, ed. Helga Reuschel (Berlin: de Gruyter, 1969), 179.

rúnargrátr ("Oddrún's Lament"). This is a confusing multiplicity, made more confusing by the fact that the tale is told differently in different poems. We must therefore decide how these poems relate to each other, which are older, which retain the more original version of the story, and which betray contamination from other Norse or German versions.

2. *Vǫlsunga saga*, a prose harmonization of the heroic poems in the *Poetic Edda*, including additional details on Sigurd's ancestry and youth. It is preserved in a medieval manuscript from around 1400 and was composed in the middle of the thirteenth century. The special value of *Vǫlsunga saga* lies in a fuller version of the story than the one found in Codex Regius of the *Poetic Edda*. It was worked out at a time when the Eddic collection was still complete and therefore includes the portion of the narrative which fell in the lacuna of Codex Regius. It is thus the primary source for a reconstruction of the partially extant *Sigurðarkviða in forna* and the lost *Sigurðarkviða in meiri*.

3. *Snorra Edda*, a mythological manual composed about 1220 by medieval Iceland's most distinguished man of letters, Snorri Sturluson (1178/1179–1241). In the section on skaldic tropes known as "Skáldskaparmál" ("Discourse on Skaldic Diction"), two of the four main manuscripts (Regius and Trajectinus) contain a brief summary of the legend of Brynhild and Sigurd. Since the summary is not found in the other two manuscripts (Wormianus and Upsaliensis), there is some doubt about whether it belongs to Snorri's original. In any event, it differs slightly from the other sources and must therefore be taken into account.

4. *Þiðreks saga*, a Norwegian translation of a north German amalgam of heroic tales. The tales center on the legendary figure of Theodoric (Dietrich von Bern in German and Þiðrekr in Norse), but the compilation also contains a medley of other heroic traditions, including three separate sections on Sigurd: "Upphaf Sigurðar sveins" ("The Birth of Young Sigurd"), "Kvánfang Sigurðar ok Gunnars" ("The Marriage of Sigurd and Gunnarr"), and "Dráp Sigurðar sveins" ("The Slaying of Young Sigurd"). Although the story in *Þiðreks saga* is originally German, the Norse translator complicated the picture by occasionally introducing features from the Norse version, which was more familiar to him. The dating of *Þiðreks saga* is difficult. It seems

certain that the Norse version was executed before the composition of *Vǫlsunga saga* because the latter borrows a chapter from it. The portion of *Þiðreks saga* that retells the destruction of the Burgundians by Atli (''Niflunga saga'') is based on the source of the *Nibelungenlied* Part II and cannot have been composed much after 1200 when the *Nibelungenlied* would have been available and would presumably have been the preferred model. The German version was most probably set down in written form in Soest (the scene of ''Niflunga saga'' and familiar to the author judging from references to local lore) and translated into Norse during the first half of the thirteenth century. Since the translation of Continental literature was encouraged by King Hákon Hákonarson (1217–1263), *Þiðreks saga* should probably be assigned to this context.

  5. The *Nibelungenlied*, a south German or Austrian heroic epic written around 1200. It combines the story of Siegfried and Brynhild with the destruction of the Burgundians by Etzel's (Attila's) Huns in the same manner as the *Poetic Edda*, *Vǫlsunga saga*, and *Þiðreks saga*. The *Nibelungenlied* is preserved in three differing redactions and a large number of manuscripts from the first half of the thirteenth century on. The account of Brynhild and Siegfried is closest to what we find in *Þiðreks saga*, but it is considerably altered by epic expansion and an overlay of courtly romance in the style of the period in which it was written.

  6. *Das Lied vom Hürnen Seyfrid*, a sixteenth-century version of the story which relates Siegfried's encounter with a giant and a dragon in the course of rescuing an imprisoned damsel (Kriemhilt). Brynhild has disappeared altogether from the scene, but it has often been argued that this fantastic tale preserves older features of the legend.

  7. A group of Faroese ballads under the general title *Sjúrðarkvæði* (''The Romance of Sigurd'') collected in the late eighteenth and nineteenth centuries. The group comprises ''Regin smiður'' (''Reginn Smith''), ''Brynhildar táttur'' (''The Ballad of Brynhild''), and ''Høgna táttur'' (''The Ballad of Hǫgni''). Despite the recent recording of these texts, it has been argued that they shed light on the earlier forms of the legend. Only ''Brynhildar táttur'' has an immediate bearing on our discussion.

  All these sources are interrelated in ways that will be explained

in the following pages, but rather than force the reader to construct the picture piece by piece, I provide a stemma of the main
texts in anticipation of my conclusions (Figure 1):

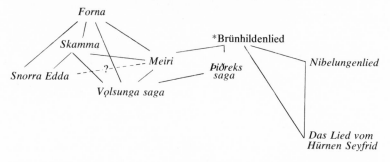

Figure 1.

In analyzing the filiations, I shall deal first with the Norse group
(Eddic poems and *Vǫlsunga saga*), then the German group. By
far the largest part of the book must be devoted to this groundwork. Only when the textual questions are resolved does it become possible to survey the literary history of Brynhild.

CHAPTER 1

The Eddic Sigurd Poems

A start must be made somewhere in the maze of texts before us. One strategy would be to begin with the latest forms and peel back layers gradually to reveal the older forms, but literary evolution is easier to visualize as growth than as atrophy. We could also begin with an approximate prototype and work through successive elaborations, but such a prototype is too remote and elusive to recover accurately. We will therefore choose a middle ground and begin with a text that is partially extant, but is traditionally assumed to be the oldest surviving Brynhild poem.[1] This text is variously titled *Sigurðarkviða in forna* ("The Old Lay of Sigurd") or *Brot af Sigurðarkviðu* ("Fragment of the Lay of Sigurd"), or abbreviated as *Brot* or *Forna*. The second half is found at the beginning of the sixth gathering of Codex Regius, but the first half was lost with the disappearance of the fifth gathering sometime before the manuscript came to public attention in the seventeenth century. Because of this lacuna the beginning of the poem must be reconstructed from a prose harmonization (*Vǫlsunga saga*) made in the latter part of the thirteenth century when the Eddic collection of Codex Regius was still intact. That is, the

[1]Finnur Jónsson, *Den oldnorske og oldislandske litteraturs historie*, I (Copenhagen: Gad, 1920), 284–86, and B. Sijmons, ed., *Die Lieder der Edda*, I (Halle: Verlag der Buchhandlung des Waisenhauses, 1906), CCLXXIV, dated it to the tenth century, but Gustav Neckel ("Zu den Eddaliedern der Lücke," *ZDP*, 39 [1907], 293–302), Friedrich Panzer (*Studien zur germanischen Sagengeschichte*, II: *Sigfrid* [Munich: Beck, 1912], 189–215), and Jan de Vries (*Altnordische Literaturgeschichte*, II, Grundriss der germanischen Philologie, 16 [Berlin: de Gruyter, 1942], 138–41; 2d ed., I, 299–303), detected late features. There is no certainty that the poem antedates the twelfth century.

material from *Forna* absorbed into *Vǫlsunga saga* must be disengaged from the material belonging to a second Brynhild poem, the so-called *Sigurðarkviða in meiri* ("The Long Lay of Sigurd"), with which it was interwoven. This task was performed by Andreas Heusler in 1902 based largely on stylistic observations.[2] Judging from the extant half of *Forna*, he considered it a terse, dramatic lay in the old heroic manner, comparable to the earliest survivals of the genre.[3] Such a style is, however, not characteristic of the prose retelling in *Vǫlsunga saga*, much of which is ample, descriptive, and reflective. On the basis of this discrepancy, Heusler partitioned the prose, assigning the tightly told passages to *Forna* and the loose psychologizing narrative to *Meiri*. Heusler's solution has carried conviction for the last three quarters of a century, and I shall continue to adhere to it, at least in my conception of *Forna*.[4] But weathering does not guarantee

[2]Andreas Heusler, "Die Lieder der Lücke im Codex Regius der Edda" in *Germanistische Abhandlungen, Hermann Paul dargebracht* (Strasbourg: Trübner, 1902), pp. 1–98; rpt. in Heusler's *Kleine Schriften*, II, ed. Stefan Sonderegger (Berlin: de Gruyter, 1969), 223–91. Future references will be to the reprinted version since it is more likely to be available to the reader.

[3]Andreas Heusler, *Die altgermanische Dichtung* (Darmstadt: Wissenschaftliche Buchgesellschaft, 1957), p. 153. Heusler considered that the original form of the heroic lay was best preserved in *Forna, Atlakviða, Hamðismál, Vǫlundarkviða,* and *Hlǫðskviða.*

[4]I have tested Heusler's hypothesis in "The Lays in the Lacuna of Codex Regius" in *Speculum Norrænum: Norse Studies in Memory of Gabriel Turville-Petre,* ed. Ursula Dronke, Guðrún P. Helgadóttir, Gerd Wolfgang Weber, and Hans Bekker-Nielsen (Odense: Odense University Press, forthcoming). My most substantial deviation from Heusler's scheme is the assumption that the narrative in the lacuna assigned by Heusler to his "Falkenlied" and "Traumlied" belonged to *Sigurðarkviða in meiri.* In the partitioning of *Forna* and *Meiri,* I do not differ with him. This part of the argument has in fact never been successfully challenged, though alternatives have been proposed. B. Symons, "Untersuchungen ueber die sogenannte Völsunga saga," *BGDSL,* 3 (1876), 282–85, was inclined to follow Sophus Bugge in positing a single large poem embracing the narrative of the lacuna together with the following fragment of *Forna* and Finnur Jónsson in *Den oldnorske og oldislandske litteraturs historie,* I, 284–85, and "Sagnformen i heltedigtene i Codex Regius," *Aarbøger for nordisk oldkyndighed og historie* (1921), 52–57, persisted in this view. Henrik Ussing, *Om det indbyrdes forhold mellem heltekvadene i ældre Edda* (Copenhagen: Gad, 1910), pp. 106–8, posited three poems, which he called "Grimhildsdigtet," "Aastridsdigtet," and "Tavshedsdigtet." See also Per Wieselgren, *Quellenstudien zur Vǫlsungasaga,* Acta et Commentationes Universitatis Tartuensis, B, Humaniora, 37 (Tartu: K. Mattiesens Buchdruckerei, 1935), pp. 264–67. A differing conception of *Forna* was proposed more recently by Klaus von See, "Die Werbung um Brünhild,"

an argument and even if Heusler's partition is the neatest explanation of the literary materials in hand, it is not necessarily correct; it remains no more than a carefully reasoned surmise. According to Heusler, the story told in *Forna* was the following:

Analysis of the Three Sigurd Poems

Sigurðarkviða in forna

Sigurd comes to the court of the Gjukungs (Gunnarr, Hǫgni, and Gotþormr), swears blood brotherhood with Gunnarr and Hǫgni, and marries their sister Gudrun. He then accompanies Gunnarr on an expedition to woo Brynhild, an independent warrior princess residing in her flame-circled hall. Gunnarr's mount balks at the prospect of leaping the flames and he borrows Sigurd's horse Grani. When Grani too stays rooted to the spot, Sigurd and Gunnarr exchange shapes and Sigurd clears the flames.[5] He presents himself as Gunnarr Gjúkason and lays claim to Brynhild's hand. She alleges her warlike nature and urges him to refrain from his suit unless he is the foremost of men and prepared to slay her wooers. He reminds her of her promise (not previously mentioned) to marry the man who crosses the flame wall and she acquiesces. The couple then spends three nights together, but Sigurd places his sword Gramr between

---

ZDA, 88 (1957–1958), 1–20, and "Freierprobe und Königinnenzank in der Sigfridsage," *ZDA*, 89 (1958–1959), 163–72, but see the reservations expressed by R. G. Finch, "Brunhild and Siegfried," *Saga-Book of the Viking Society*, 17 (1967–1968), 224–60.

[5] Two stanzas on the clearing of the flame wall are cited at this point in *Vǫlsunga saga* (p. 67). Heusler, "Lieder der Lücke," pp. 262–63, assigned them to *Forna* and was followed by Gustav Neckel, "Zur Vǫlsunga saga und den Eddaliedern der Lücke," *ZDP*, 37 (1905), 28–29, "Zu den Eddaliedern der Lücke," pp. 293–94, *Beiträge zur Eddaforschung* (Dortmund: Ruhfus, 1908), p. 346, and Panzer, II, 190. R. C. Boer, "Sigrdrifumál und Helreið," *ZDP*, 35 (1903), 310–12, originally assigned them to *Helreið Brynhildar*, but later changed his mind in *Untersuchungen über den Ursprung und die Entwicklung der Nibelungensage*, I (Halle: Verlag der Buchhandlung des Waisenhauses, 1906), 84–85 and 203, and assigned them to his "Sigurðarkviða in yngri." Sijmons, p. cclxxiv, noted that the stanzas differed stylistically from *Forna*, and they were subsequently assigned to *Meiri* by Hermann Schneider, "Verlorene Sigurddichtung," *ANF*, 45 (1929), 3–4, Wolfgang Mohr, review of Dietrich von Kralik, *Die Sigfridtrilogie*, in *Dichtung und Volkstum*, 42 (1942), 107, and von See, "Die Werbung um Brünhild," pp. 3–4. See also Finch, p. 237. I am inclined to agree with Neckel (1905, p. 29) and Schneider (p. 4) that *Forna* and *Meiri* did not differ greatly at this point.

them, explaining that it is ordained that he should marry in this way or else die.[6] On departing he takes a ring from Brynhild, rides off, and resumes his natural shape. The two couples, Sigurd and Gudrun and Gunnarr and Brynhild, now live in temporary concord at Gunnarr's court, but one day trouble erupts when Brynhild takes precedence as the two queens bathe in the Rhine. She justifies her privilege by claiming that her husband has performed many bold deeds while Sigurd was a thrall (a reference to Sigurd's childhood clarified below). Gudrun disputes the contention and points out that Brynhild is scarcely the right one to vilify Sigurd since he was her first lover. To verify the accusation she exhibits the ring that Sigurd took from Brynhild when he shared her bed as Gunnarr's proxy. Brynhild recognizes the ring, turns pale as death, and lapses into silence. That evening Gunnarr inquires into her grief and she replies that she does not wish to live any longer because Sigurd betrayed them both when Gunnarr caused him to enter her bed. "I do not wish to have two husbands in the same hall and this will be the death of Sigurd or your death or mine, for he has told Gudrun all and she abuses me." Gunnarr accedes to her urging and takes counsel with Họgni, who warns of Brynhild's envy, but is unable to deter Gunnarr. A magic brew is concocted to fortify their brother Gotþormr, then the three of them kill Sigurd (the location is unspecified, but presumably in the forest since a raven calls prophetically from a tree). On their return Gudrun questions them and Họgni proclaims the deed. Brynhild triumphs and Gudrun laments. That night Gunnarr stays awake musing on the raven's prophecy that the Hunnish king Atli will murder them. Brynhild awakens a little before day and at last gives free rein to her sorrow, though before she had exulted. She mourns Sigurd and describes an ominous dream in which she saw Gunnarr riding fettered in the midst of his enemies. She reminds the brothers of their broken oaths of blood brotherhood and reveals that Sigurd was faithful to his oath since he placed a sword between them during the proxy nuptials.

[6]On this motif see Jakob Grimm, *Deutsche Rechtsalterthümer,* 2d ed. (Göttingen: Dieterichsche Buchhandlung, 1854), pp. 168–70; Bernard Heller, "L'épée symbole et gardienne de chasteté," *Romania,* 36 (1907), 36–49, and ibid., 37 (1908), 162–63; Gertrude Schoepperle Loomis, *Tristan and Isolt: A Study of the Sources of the Romance,* 2 vols. (Frankfurt: J. Baer, 1913; rpt. New York: Burt Franklin, 1963), pp. 262–64 and 430–31; Johannes Bolte and Georg Polívka, *Anmerkungen zu den Kinder- und Hausmärchen der Brüder Grimm,* I (Leipzig: Dieterich'sche Verlagsbuchhandlung, 1913), 554; Alexander Haggerty Krappe, "Volsungasaga XXVII 61–64," *ZDA,* 66 (1929), 60–64; and Klaus von See, "Die Werbung um Brünhild," p. 10.

In comparing *Forna* to later versions one should emphasize a few salient features. In the first place, there is no preface. The story begins with Sigurd's arrival at the court of the Gjukungs. We learn nothing of his birth, youth, and early adventures, matters treated at length elsewhere in the legend. There is no account of a prior betrothal between Sigurd and Brynhild, a feature that complicates the relationships in "The Long Lay of Sigurd."[7] In *Forna* Sigurd's crime is not that he jilts Brynhild, but that he participates in her deception and thwarts her determination to have the foremost of men (*Vǫlsunga saga* 68.8–10). The nature of her resentment is more ambiguous. Hǫgni states (in stanza 3 of the extant text) that she envies Gudrun's good marriage and resents being in Gunnarr's possession. The implication is that Brynhild wants Sigurd for herself. That much is borne out by her grief in the early morning, displacing her earlier exultation (stanza 15): "All were silent when she uttered such words; no one grasped the ways of women when she set about telling in tears what she had asked the men laughing." She is plainly suffering from an emotional disjunction and the evidence stuns her listeners. Her grief may stem from her baleful dream about Gunnarr and her envy of Gudrun from a simple desire to have the more distinguished husband, but it all looks suspiciously like jealousy, especially in light of the fully developed jealousy in subsequent versions.[8] Perhaps *Forna* was a transition piece between a form

[7]Christian August Mayer, "Brünhilde: Eine Untersuchung zur deutschen Heldensage," *ZVL*, 16 (1905), 132, seems to have attributed the prior betrothal to *Forna*. Ussing, pp. 98, 106, 126, considered that no poem in the collection other than *Grípisspá* included the prior betrothal. Wilhelm Lehmgrübner, *Die Erwekkung der Walküre*, Hermaea, 32 (Halle: Niemeyer, 1936; rpt. 1973), p. 49, argued that *Forna* was created by combining the figures of the Burgundian legend with the legend of Young Sigurd, but made no explicit mention of the prior betrothal. Klaus von See, "Die Werbung um Brünhild," pp. 5 and 18–19, also appears to attribute the prior betrothal to *Forna*, but see Finch, p. 241. Generally speaking, Heusler's identification of a *Forna* without prior betrothal has stood the test of time.

[8]On traces of jealousy in *Forna* see Heinrich Hempel, *Nibelungenstudien, I: Nibelungenlied, Thidrikssaga und Balladen*, Germanische Bibliothek, Untersuchungen und Texte, 22 (Heidelberg: Winter, 1926), 137; Hermann Schneider, *Germanische Heldensage*, I (Berlin and Leipzig: de Gruyter, 1928; rpt. 1962), 177; Hans Kuhn, "Brünhilds und Kriemhilds Tod," *ZDA*, 82 (1950), 193; rpt. in his *Kleine Schriften*, II, ed. Dietrich Hofmann (Berlin: de Gruyter, 1971), 82; Einar Ól. Sveinsson, *Íslenzkar bókmenntir í fornöld*, I (n.p.: Almenna Bókafélagið, 1962), 414.

of the story in which Brynhild resented Gudrun's title to the better man and a form in which this resentment became erotic jealousy, leading eventually to the idea that Brynhild had a prior claim on Sigurd. Or perhaps *Forna*, which derives from a German source as the location on the Rhine indicates, suppressed but did not eradicate all signs of the prior betrothal, a feature which haunts all German versions of the tale. This German background also shows through in Sigurd's forest death, which contrasts to his death in bed as we find it in *Skamma* and probably in *Meiri*.

Sigurðarkviða in skamma

Forna is truncated at the beginning and ends abruptly with Brynhild's shocking revelation.[9] In turning to "The Short Lay of Sigurd" (*Skamma*), we find no such problems of fragmentary transmission because it is preserved in its entirety in Codex Regius. The story runs as follows:

> Sigurd once came to the court of Gjúki and swore oaths with Gunnarr and Hǫgni. They offered him their sister Gudrun in marriage, together with great treasures, and all lived contentedly until one day they ride out to woo Brynhild. Sigurd accompanies the brothers because he knows the way (the poet adds that Sigurd would have wed Brynhild if he could). The details of the wooing are omitted, and we learn only that Sigurd placed a naked sword between Brynhild and himself to preserve her for Gunnarr. The following scene presupposes the union with Gunnarr because it finds Brynhild sitting alone in the evening vowing to have Sigurd, or else his life. She goes out into the ice and snow at night seething with bitterness when Sigurd and Gudrun go to bed. Bitterness turns to vengefulness, and she threatens to leave Gunnarr and return to her family unless he kills Sigurd and Sigurd's son. Gunnarr is torn by doubt and confers with Hǫgni, inciting him with a promise of Sigurd's gold. Hǫgni protests that they are bound to Sigurd by oath and dependent on his support; he knows precisely that the plot originates with Brynhild. Gunnarr next proposes that they persuade their unsuspecting younger brother Gotþormr to do the deed. An abbreviated stanza of two long lines (stanza 21) reports that this was easily

[9]Heusler, "Lieder der Lücke," pp. 265–66, thought that something was lost at the end of the poem, but Boer, *Untersuchungen*, I, 61; Finnur Jónsson, 2d ed., I, 285; and Wolfgang Mohr, p. 106, thought not. Neckel, "Zu den Eddaliedern der Lücke," p. 301, believed that *Forna* originally concluded with Brynhild's suicide.

accomplished and that Gotþormr plunged his sword into Sigurd's heart. Sigurd avenges himself by hurling his sword after his assailant and cutting him in two. In the meantime Gudrun awakens bathed in the blood of her dying husband. He comforts her with the thought that her brothers are still alive, foresees the death of his son, and recalls that Brynhild loved him above all men, but that he was true to the oaths he had sworn to Gunnarr. With these words he expires.

Brynhild laughs when she hears Gudrun's shrill laments, but Gunnarr understands that the laughter is false and rebukes her: she deserves to have her brother Atli slain before her very eyes. Brynhild brushes his anger aside and recounts the circumstances of her marriage. She had resisted any thought of marriage until the three Gjukungs arrived. Then she betrothed herself (or merely vowed to have?) the rider of Grani (Sigurd), who bore no resemblance to the Gjukungs. But her brother Atli threatened to deprive her of her inheritance unless she allowed herself to be given in marriage (to Gunnarr). She considered donning her byrnie and doing battle, but agreed to a truce. Even so, she loves only one man and Atli will know, when he learns of her bloody exploit, that a spiritless[10] woman should never take another's husband. Gunnarr tries to console Brynhild, but Hǫgni wishes her to the devil. She distributes her treasure and stabs herself with a sword, but before dying she utters a long prophecy: she predicts the birth of Gudrun's daughter Svanhildr, the marriage of Gudrun to Atli, Gunnarr's clandestine affair with Oddrún despite Atli's prohibition, Gunnarr's subsequent death at Atli's hands, Gudrun's slaying of Atli in revenge, her marriage to Jónakr, Svanhildr's marriage to Jǫrmunrekkr, and her death instigated by Bikki's evil counsel, marking the end of Sigurd's lineage. Brynhild's last request is for a common funeral pyre on which she and Sigurd will be separated by a sword as once before when they were titled man and wife.

Compared to *Forna, Skamma* is a curious combination of reduction and expansion. The first forty-one stanzas bring us to about the same point as the total of some fifty stanzas in *Forna,* that is, to Brynhild's confessional words after the death of Sigurd. There follows a long appendix of thirty stanzas comprising additional dialogue, prophetic utterances, and the account of Brynhild's suicide. The brevity at the beginning of the poem is

---

[10]The meaning of "þunngeð" is uncertain. Fritz Mezger, "Aisl. þunngeðr," *Acta philologica scandinavica,* 9 (1934–1935), 313–14, argued for *þung-geð r.*

explained by the omission of certain matters covered in *Forna,* notably details of the wooing sequence (the exchange of shapes and the crossing of the flame wall) and the quarrel of the queens. We may surmise that the proxy wooing at least is presupposed by *Skamma.* As Finnur Jónsson pointed out, there must have been some special difficulty in the suit or Sigurd's presence would not have been required.[11] That he did in fact substitute for Gunnarr on this occasion is confirmed by Brynhild's dying words concerning the sword that separated her from Sigurd when they shared a single bed. Thus *Skamma* presupposes information provided by *Forna* and probably presupposes a knowledge of *Forna* itself, as verbal echoes demonstrate.[12] To this extent it is a variation on *Forna.*

But the variation is not only stylistic. There are substantive departures from the version in *Forna.*[13] We observed that in *Forna* there is no question of a prior betrothal between Sigurd and Brynhild, a commitment that should have taken precedence over Sigurd's marriage to Gudrun. In *Skamma,* on the other hand, there are hints of a prior betrothal, albeit ambiguous.[14] For one thing, Sigurd accompanies the suitors because "he knew the way" (stanza 3).[15] If he knew the way to Brynhild's residence, he

[11]"Sagnformen i Sigurðarkviða en skamma," *ANF,* 34 (1918), 282. Finnur Jónsson's remark is tacitly directed against Boer, *Untersuchungen,* I, 38–41, who thought that there were no impediments in *Skamma.*

[12]On the *Skamma* poet's familiarity with *Forna* see Sijmons, p. cclxxiv; Jan de Vries, "Het Korte Sigurdlied," *Mededeelingen der Koninklijke Nederlandsche Akademie van Wetenschappen,* Afd. Letterkunde, N.R., 2 (1939), no. 11, 17–21, and *Altnordische Literaturgeschichte,* 1st ed., II, 140; 2d ed., II, 147–48; and Einar Ól. Sveinsson, pp. 415 and 517.

[13]These are summarized by de Vries, "Het Korte Sigurdlied," pp. 20–21. Here he takes *Brot* to be a fragment of *Meiri,* but cf. his *Altnordische Literaturgeschichte,* 1st ed., II, 156; 2d ed., II, 150.

[14]Ussing, p. 92, was certain that *Skamma* implied no prior visit or betrothal, but other critics are less decisive. Hempel, p. 137, concluded that the poet referred to a prior betrothal outside the framework of his own poem. Lehmgrübner, p. 24, concluded that the *Skamma* poet did not include the prior betrothal, but must have been aware of it. Hermann Schneider, *Die deutschen Lieder von Siegfrieds Tod* (Weimar: Hermann Böhlau, 1947), pp. 28–29, detected the same veiling of the motif as in *Þiðreks saga* and the *Nibelungenlied.* Klaus von See also argues for a knowledge of the prior betrothal in "Die Werbung um Brünhild," pp. 14–15.

[15]On the verse "er vega kunni" see Finnur Jónsson, "Sagnformen i Sigurðar-kviða en skamma," *ANF,* 34 (1918), 278, and de Vries, "Het Korte Sigurdlied," pp. 30 (note) and 56. Finnur Jónsson interpreted "vega" as a noun ("who knew

must have been there before and the most obvious reason for a prior visit is the betrothal to Brynhild related in *Vǫlsunga saga*. Furthermore, when Brynhild reviews the circumstances of her marriage, she states (stanza 39):

> Þeim hétomc þá,
> er með gulli sat   á Grana bógom;

These lines can be read as a literal mention of a betrothal: "I then betrothed myself to the one who sat with gold (either Fáfnir's treasure or gold adornment) on Grani's back" (namely Sigurd). Or they can be read as something less than a formal betrothal: "I then promised myself (or committed myself) to Sigurd."[16] This

---

the ways") while de Vries interpreted it as a verb ("who knew how to fight"). To the opinions registered in de Vries's note may be added Wolfgang Golther, "Ueber die Sage von Siegfried und den Nibelungen," *ZVL*, 12 (1898), 199, who agreed with Finnur Jónsson. We will see below that this preference is supported by verbatim correspondences in *Þiðreks saga* II.38.14 and the *Nibelungenlied* 378.3.

[16]Finnur Jónsson, the only critic to attempt a detailed analysis of the passage, believed that it implied the prior betrothal ("Sagnformen i Sigurðarkviða en skamma," p. 280). He imagined that the poet had the following sequence in mind (p. 282): Sigurd rides directly to Gjúki's court without visiting Brynhild. He and the Gjukungs then ride to Atli's residence to woo Brynhild for Sigurd and the couple is betrothed. (Jónsson later changed his mind on this point and decided that Sigurd did not participate in the first expedition. The three Gjukungs, Gunnarr, Hǫgni, and Gotþormr, rode alone and Gunnarr's suit was rejected, setting the stage for the later hostilities ["Sagnformen i heltedigtene i Codex Regius," *Aarbøger* (1921), p. 65].) They return home, but Gunnarr has in the meantime fallen in love with Brynhild. To resolve the conflict, Sigurd is given a potion of forgetfulness, loses all memory of his betrothal to Brynhild, and marries Gudrun. Now Sigurd and his sworn brothers ride off once again to Atli's court and we must imagine some form of deception even if it is unstated. Sigurd presumably exchanges shapes with Gunnarr because of a hindrance that can hardly have been anything other than the flame wall. As Jónsson admits (p. 283), this form of the legend corresponds to no known version, but since it is clear that the *Skamma* poet knew *Forna*, good reasons should be offered for such a drastic departure from the form represented by *Forna*. De Vries ("Het Korte Sigurdlied," p. 56, and *Altnordische Literaturgeschichte,* 1st ed., II, 155; 2d ed., II, 149) believed there was no betrothal, but that Atli tricked Brynhild by promising her to Sigurd, then marrying her to Gunnarr. Heusler, without entering into detail, opted for the inner commitment ("Lieder der Lücke," p. 283). Panzer, II, 217–18, took the same view. Klaus von See assumed an explicit reference to the prior betrothal in *Skamma* ("Die Werbung um Brünhild," pp. 14–15) and conjectured: "þeim hétomk þá / á Hindarfialli" ("I betrothed myself to him on Hindarfjall"). Sveinsson, p. 515, expressed uncertainty, but was inclined to agree with Heusler. See also Mayer, p. 133.

could be taken to mean that Brynhild had vowed to marry only the man who cleared the flame wall (Sigurd, as it turns out). It could also mean simply that Brynhild wanted Sigurd, not that she had an official claim on him. In any case no explicit mention is made of a previous trip to Brynhild's residence or of a previous commitment.

How do we explain the ambiguity in *Skamma?* We can argue first of all that there is no ambiguity. Sigurd happens to know the way to Brynhild's residence, perhaps because he is a well-traveled adventurer, and the "hétomc" of stanza 39 expresses a wish rather than an act. If this is so, *Skamma* remains on the same legendary level as *Forna* with respect to the prior betrothal. A second explanation is that the poet of *Skamma* knew very well about the prior betrothal and expected the reader to take it for granted. The ambiguity arises in our minds only because the poet passes lightly and allusively over the event, just as he passes lightly over the details of the wooing in general. If this is true, *Skamma* represents a more evolved form of the legend and shares the prior betrothal, as we will see below, with "The Long Lay of Sigurd." A third possibility is that the poet of *Skamma* was familiar with both legendary forms, with and without prior betrothal. He solved the dilemma by adopting an ambiguous stance that would allow for either interpretation. It seems futile to choose among these explanations. All that can be said with any certainty is that there were two versions of the story in circulation, one including a prior betrothal and the other not. The *Skamma* poet knew one or the other or both.

The impossibility of solving this question impedes our understanding of the poem because Brynhild's motivation remains obscure. The problem is compounded by the absence of the queens' quarrel and the revelations it produces. Without these revelations and without the certainty of a prior betrothal, it is difficult to know in what way Brynhild has been wronged. The poet thus skirts the central issue of the tale, the wronging of Brynhild and the motivation of her vengeance against Sigurd. Perhaps the only wrong she suffers is the thwarting of her desires. She wants Sigurd, fails to get him, and therefore forces Gunnarr to arrange his death. A misfortune that she attributes chiefly to Atli is turned into a vendetta against Sigurd. We cannot of course

decide whether this is psychologically more or less compelling
than the version in *Forna,* according to which Brynhild has
explicitly vowed to wed only the superior man who can cross the
magic flame wall, then finds herself played into the hands of an
inferior by the very man who fits the description. Brynhild's reaction is better rationalized in *Forna* than in *Skamma,* but not
necessarily better justified. Perhaps, in fact, some dissatisfaction
with Brynhild's motivation in *Forna* is at the bottom of the
psychological experimentation that is everywhere evident in the
later analysis of Brynhild. What may strike us as more effective in
Forna is the vivid portrayal of Brynhild's emotions, her shock at
the revelation of Sigurd's deception, her steely arrangement of his
murder by counter deception, and the contrasting and equally
convincing outbursts of satisfaction and grief when the deed has
been done.

There are still other departures from the version established by
Forna. The scene of the murder has been shifted from the forest
to Sigurd's bedchamber in accordance with the references to
Sigurd's death in the Eddic poems *Hamðismál* 6–7 and *Guðrúnarhvǫt* 4.[17] *Forna* leaves the exact identity of the murderer or
murderers unclear, while *Hamðismál* 6 (*Guðrúnarhvǫt* 4) impli-
cates Hǫgni. *Skamma* settles on the younger brother Gotþormr.
The explanation, if one is needed, may be a concern for the hon-
oring of the oaths of blood brotherhood. These oaths were reported in *Forna,* but broken. The *Skamma* poet decided they
should be observed and therefore devised the scheme of a
younger brother who did not participate in the oaths. The trauma
experienced by Gudrun as she awakens in her husband's gore has
no particular relevance in a poem that centers on Brynhild and
must relate in some way to the preoccupation with Gudrun's
psyche in the late elegiac poetry. Our poet resorts to this inten-
sification because he is fond of flamboyant effects.

By far the largest portion of the increased length in *Skamma* is
new dialogue, Brynhild's retrospective view of her marriage
(stanzas 33–41) and her prophecy of the family fate (stanzas 53–

---

[17]Jan de Vries, "Het Korte Sigurdlied," p. 59. For the evidence that the
Skamma poet knew *Hamðismál* and *Guðrúnarhvǫt,* see pp. 11–14.

64), in which the story of Sigurd prefaces the subsequent destruction of the Burgundians by the Huns and the murder of
Svanhildr.[18] Both retrospection and prophecy elaborate what is
already adumbrated in *Forna* 16–19.[19] The cyclical extension
may also help to explain a new family relationship in *Skamma*, in
which Brynhild is cast as Atli's sister. This speculation accords
with the elegiac poetry of the *Edda*.[20] Perhaps it originated in the
idea that Brynhild and Atli were associated with one another by
virtue of their common antagonism toward the Burgundians. Atli's high-handed role in forcing Brynhild to marry may then be
seen in the light of his pecuniary strategy. With a marriage alliance he is laying the groundwork for his later attempt on the
Burgundian gold. His own marriage to Gudrun and invitation of
the Burgundians in the Eddic poem *Atlakviða* pursue the same
strategy.[21]

The last important innovation in *Skamma* is Brynhild's suicide.
Nothing of the sort is reported in *Forna*, though something may
be missing at the end of the poem. As we will see, the conclusion
of *Meiri* can be reconstructed only in the most tenuous way and
does not bear much argument. In *Þiðreks saga* and the
Nibelungenlied Brynhild's fate is left suspended. It is therefore
possible that *Skamma* stood alone with the suicide, but the explanation is not difficult. Both Siggeirr's wife Signý in *Vǫlsunga
saga* (19.30–20.3) and Gudrun herself, according to the most
probable interpretation of *Atlakviða* 43, end their days as heroic

[18]Heusler, "Lieder der Lücke," p. 285, noted the analogy to the expanded
dialogues in *Atlamál*. See also Sveinsson, p. 513, and T. M. Andersson, "Did the
Poet of *Atlamál* Know *Atlakviða*?" in *Edda: A Collection of Essays*, ed. Robert J.
Glendinning and Haraldur Bessason, University of Manitoba Icelandic Studies 4
(Manitoba: University of Manitoba Press, forthcoming).

[19]Heusler, "Lieder der Lücke," pp. 280–81, and Sijmons, p. CCCXXXI.

[20]Brynhild appears as Atli's sister specifically in *Guðrúnarkviða* I.25, *Helreið
Brynhildar* 6 (in the variant reading of *Norna-Gests þáttr*), *Guðrúnarkviða* II.27,
and *Oddrúnargrátr* 21. Jan de Vries, "Het Korte Sigurdlied," pp. 8–11, 14–17,
22–23, compiled evidence that *Skamma* drew on all these poems, but I shall argue
the opposite view in Chapter 3 below. See also Sveinsson, pp. 517–18.

[21]"Dráp Niflunga" (Neckel-Kuhn, p. 223) states specifically that Atli blamed
the Gjukungs for Brynhild's death and got Guðrún's hand in compensation:
"Kendi hann Giúcungom vǫld um andlát Brynhildar. Þat var til sætta, at þeir
scyldo gipta hánom Guðrúno." The object is plainly to keep the family alliance
intact.

suicides and their model may have inspired an extension of the motif to Brynhild.[22]

On the whole, *Skamma* cannot be judged a powerful poem. There are more signs of combination and conjecture than of originality or a firm new conception. The poem is rapid to the point of obscurity at times and unduly long-winded at others. There is, especially toward the end, a disproportionate amount of the reflective and prophetic dialogue characteristic of late Eddic poetry. The detailed forecast of later events has, in particular, no immediate relevance to the drama of the situation.[23]

Sigurðarkviða in meiri

Skamma may be regarded as a transition piece between *Forna* and *Meiri*, though there is no decisive reason for dating *Skamma* earlier than *Meiri*.[24] The principal consideration is that *Meiri* is more fully developed. It is also the centerpiece of the Brynhild legend and the key to everything around it. At the same time, it is a riddle because we have no part of it in the original, only the synthetic retelling in *Vǫlsunga saga* and a few stanzas that may be attributed to it. Heusler deduced large portions from this prose summary beginning with Sigurd's arrival at the court of the Gjukungs, that is, the same point at which *Forna* and *Skamma* begin. He assumed that it was prefaced by two much shorter nonnarrative poems (also lost in the lacuna) which he called the "Falkenlied" ("Falcon Lay") and "Traumlied" ("Dream Lay") and similarly reconstructed from the prose of *Vǫlsunga saga*. On this point I differ with Heusler.[25] "Falkenlied" and "Traumlied"

---

[22]Hans Kuhn, pp. 191–99; rpt. in his *Kleine Schriften*, II, 80–87, argued that Brynhild did not originally commit suicide. Sveinsson, p. 518, suggested that the common pyre shared by Sigurd and Brynhild in *Skamma* is a reflex of *Guð-rúnarhvǫt* 20.

[23]Panzer, II, 220, condemned the conclusion, but Jan de Vries, "Het Korte Sigurdlied," pp. 59–60, tried to justify Brynhild's dying monologue in terms of medieval taste.

[24]Golther, p. 201, believed that the *Skamma* poet made use of *Meiri*, but Heusler, "Lieder der Lücke," p. 289, assembled evidence that *Meiri* is later and composed with *Skamma* in mind. Schneider, "Verlorene Sigurddichtung," p. 14, described *Meiri* as "a curious mixture of Forna and Skamma." Lehmgrübner, p. 24, also considered that *Meiri* was contentually and stylistically later than *Skamma*.

[25]T. M. Andersson, "The Lays in the Lacuna of Codex Regius" (forthcoming).

have such clear contentual and stylistic affinities to *Meiri* that they must be part of the same poem. This poem did not begin with the arrival at the court of Gjúki, but with Sigurd's prior betrothal to Brynhild, which, as Heusler and later critics agree, lies at the heart of the poet's conception. Retreating to this point in the narrative, we must review the story as told in *Vǫlsunga saga* (57.3–80.22).

Sigurd comes to the residence of Brynhild's foster father Heimir and is hospitably entertained. Brynhild herself lives separately in a remote tower, where she busies herself with the pictorial weaving of Sigurd's deeds. One day Sigurd rides to the forest to hunt and one of his hawks perches by a window in Brynhild's tower.[26] While retrieving it, he sees her inside and becomes melancholy at the sight of her beauty, but he learns from Heimir's son Alsviðr that she is devoted to martial pursuits and unreceptive to men. Sigurd woos her notwithstanding. She objects that she is a shield maiden and when Sigurd persists, she declares that he is fated to marry Gudrun the daughter of Gjúki. Sigurd continues to press his suit and Brynhild finally accedes. They swear mutual oaths and he departs.

In the meantime, Gudrun has had ominous dreams. A lady-in-waiting inquires into them and Gudrun tells of seeing a fair hawk on her hand with feathers the color of gold. The woman explains that Gudrun is destined to be wooed by a prince. Gudrun now wishes to consult Brynhild on the identity of this prince and she sets out for Brynhild's residence, where she is well received. Gudrun begins by asking who the greatest kings are (presumably an indirect inquiry into the identity of her future prince). Brynhild names Haki and Hagbarðr and Gudrun asks about the standing of her own brothers. Brynhild judges that they are promising though not much tested, but

---

[26]Heusler, "Lieder der Lücke," p. 245, noted this motif in the story "Sole, Luna e Talia" in Giambattista Basile's *Pentamerone, 5.5.* Jakob Grimm had remarked on the correspondence in his "Einleitung" to Felix Liebrecht's translation *Der Pentamerone oder das Märchen aller Märchen* von Giambattista Basile (Breslau: Josef Max und Komp., 1846), I, xii–xvi. Italian text: Giambattista Basile, *Il pentamerone ossia la fiaba delle fiabe,* trans. (from the Neapolitan) Benedetto Croce (Bari: Editori Laterza, n. d. [1958?]), pp. 498–503. English translation: *The Pentamerone of Giambattista Basile,* trans. N. M. Penzer (London: John Lane the Bodley Head Ltd. and New York: Dutton, 1932), II, 129–33. See also Reinhold Spiller, "Zur Geschichte des Märchens vom Dornröschen," *Programm der Thurgauischen Kantonschule für das Schuljahr 1892–93* (Frauenfeld: Huber, 1893), pp. 24–28.

she lauds Sigurd, the son of Sigmund, who avenged his father while still a child. Gudrun replies that Brynhild's interest is prompted by love and changes the subject: the purpose of her visit is to recount her dreams. She tells of seeing a great stag with a coat of gold, which her companions wished to catch. Only she succeeded, but Brynhild slew the stag at her very feet, then gave her a wolf cub drenched in the blood of her brothers. Brynhild responds by prophesying that Sigurd will come to the Gjukungs. Queen Grimhild will give him a drugged mead, Gudrun will marry him, but lose him soon afterward. Then she will marry King Atli, lose her brothers, and kill Atli. With this forecast Gudrun returns home.

The fulfillment of the prophecy begins without delay when Sigurd comes to the court of Gjúki and Grimhild administers the potion that causes him to forget his betrothal to Brynhild. He subsequently swears blood brotherhood with Gunnarr and Hǫgni and marries Gudrun.[27] The blood brothers travel far and wide performing great deeds, then return home laden with booty. Grimhild now proposes that Gunnarr should woo Brynhild and Sigurd agrees to accompany him.

They interview her father Buðli, who says that Brynhild must make her own decision, and her foster father Heimir, who describes the flame wall and declares that Brynhild will accept only the suitor who crosses it. Gunnarr fails in the enterprise and he exchanges shapes with Sigurd as Grimhild had instructed them. Sigurd clears the flame wall and woos Brynhild on Gunnarr's behalf.[28] The wooing party returns to Gjúki's court and the wedding is celebrated. At the conclusion of the festivities Sigurd remembers his prior oaths, but says nothing.[29]

---

[27]As we will see below, the marriage to Gudrun at this early stage in Vǫlsunga saga 65.29–30 probably corresponds to the order of events in Forna, whereas in Meiri, according to the evidence of Grípisspá 43, it seems to have occurred simultaneously with the later marriage of Gunnarr and Brynhild.

[28]The details of this encounter in Meiri are unclear because the betrothal passage in Vǫlsunga saga 67.27–68.27 appears to be based on Forna. There may, however, be an admixture from Meiri (cf. n. 5 above). Klaus von See, "Die Werbung um Brünhild," p. 2, argues that there was no flame wall in Forna, but see Finch, pp. 236–37. The subsequent passage 68.27–69.4, in which Brynhild leaves her daughter by Sigurd (Áslaug) with Heimir, is the saga writer's own addition to account for the figure of Áslaug in Ragnars saga loðbrókar.

[29]The revelation of the deception in Meiri is unclear because the quarrel of the queens in Vǫlsunga saga 69.13–70.7 is taken from Forna and Grípisspá omits the quarrel altogether. Heusler was uncertain ("Lieder der Lücke," p. 271), Neckel thought there was no quarrel in Meiri ("Zu den Eddaliedern der Lücke," p. 325), but Schneider felt certain that Meiri as well as Forna had the river quarrel ("Ver-

There ensues a long sequence of dialogues. First Gudrun meets with Sigurd and asks why Brynhild is so grieved (the river quarrel taken from *Forna* having ended with a description of her deathly pallor and speechlessness). Sigurd replies that he does not know precisely, but suspects that they will know soon enough. Gudrun asks why she does not enjoy her wealth, good fortune, recognition, and the husband she wanted. Sigurd is curious to know when Brynhild stated that she had the best husband or the one she wanted. Gudrun says she will ask the next day whom Brynhild would rather have. Sigurd advises against such an inquiry and predicts she will regret it.

The next morning the two queens sit in the hall and Brynhild is silent. Gudrun asks why she is so downcast and whether she is troubled by their previous conversation.[30] Brynhild replies that Gudrun is motivated by malice and has a cold heart. Gudrun protests and urges Brynhild to speak openly. Brynhild bids her ask only what it profits her to know and be content with her lot since everything has gone according to her wishes. Gudrun replies that it is too early to make such a claim and asks what Brynhild has to reproach her for since she has done her no injury. Brynhild now admits outright that she begrudges her Sigurd and the gold treasure. Gudrun claims not to have known of the prior agreement and states that her father Gjúki was free to arrange the marriage without consulting Brynhild. Brynhild maintains that they had no secret agreement, but that Gudrun and her brothers knew full well of the oaths they swore and betrayed them knowingly. She vows vengeance. Gudrun retorts that Brynhild has a better marriage than she deserves and that many will suffer the consequences of her arrogance. Brynhild would rest content if Gudrun did not have the more distinguished husband. Gudrun contends that Brynhild has a husband whose distinction makes it unclear who is the greater king; in addition she has a great portion of

lorene Sigurddichtung," p. 5). Klaus von See, pp. 4–5, derived the quarrel in *Vǫlsunga saga* from *Þiðreks saga,* but see Finch, "Brunhild and Siegfried," pp. 237–40. I shall argue below that *Meiri* had a hall quarrel, which the author of *Vǫlsunga saga* accounted for as a retrospective dialogue between Gudrun and Brynhild (70.19–72.15) in an effort not to duplicate the river quarrel of *Forna*. Cf. Mohr in *Dichtung und Volkstum,* p. 106.

[30]The disingenuousness of this inquiry so soon after the stunning revelation of Brynhild's deception at the conclusion of the river quarrel has been duly noted, e.g., Neckel, "Zu den Eddaliedern der Lücke," p. 311, and Ussing, p. 102. The explanation is that the inquiry preceded the hall quarrel in the version of the story provided by *Meiri*; it is awkward in *Vǫlsunga saga* because the saga author inserted the river quarrel from *Forna* ahead of the inquiry.

wealth and power. Sigurd's slaying of Fáfnir is worth more than all of King Gunnarr's power, Brynhild replies. A stanza spoken by Brynhild is included at this point in the prose paraphrase and proclaims that Sigurd's feat will live forever and that Gunnarr did not dare to cross the flame wall. Gudrun argues that Grani balked at the flames and that there is no reason to question Gunnarr's courage. Brynhild now alters course and says that she will make no secret of her ill feelings toward Grimhild. Gudrun replies that there is no cause to reproach her since she treats Brynhild like a daughter. Brynhild persists and attributes the whole catastrophe to Grimhild because she gave Sigurd the potion of forgetfulness. Gudrun calls this a great lie. Brynhild then turns her anger on Gudrun and accuses her of taking Sigurd while pretending not to have betrayed her; it is wrong that she and Sigurd should reign together and she should suffer the consequences. Gudrun retorts that she intends to enjoy the possession of Sigurd to spite Brynhild and that no one has suspected *them* of sharing an improper intimacy. Brynhild says that she will live to regret such ill words, but that they should quarrel no more. Gudrun reproaches her for initiating the quarrel and pretending to be conciliatory though she has wicked intentions. Brynhild again bids them desist. She claims that she has concealed her grief for a long time, but that she loves only Gunnarr. Gudrun replies that Brynhild's mind looks far into the future.

Brynhild takes her grief with her to bed. Gunnarr learns that she is ill and asks what grieves her, but she makes no reply and lies as if dead. When he inquires more closely, she asks what he did with the ring Buðli gave her at their last parting when Gjúki came and threatened to harry or burn unless she were given to Gunnarr. Buðli had taken her aside and asked whom she wanted of those who had come. She offered instead to defend the land and command a third of the army. She was then confronted with two options, to marry the man Buðli chose, or to lose her wealth and his affection. She considered whether she should do his will or wage war, but she felt unequal to the contest and promised to marry the man who rode Grani with Fáfnir's treasure, crossed the flame wall, and killed the men she specified. Only Sigurd had the courage to make the ride. He killed the serpent and Reginn and five kings, not Gunnarr, who paled like a corpse and who is no champion. But Brynhild had vowed at home that she would love only the most outstanding man. That man is Sigurd and she has now broken her oath since she does not have him. For that reason she will bring about Gunnarr's death. She has Grimhild to thank for her plight, the worst of all women. Gunnarr replies by taking up Grimhild's defense, maintaining ironically that she at least did not love her husband as Brynhild does, nor did she torment dead men or murder anyone (obscure references to Brynhild's early career as a shield maiden). Brynhild claims to have had no clandestine affair and to have done no misdeeds, such not being her nature, but she would eagerly kill Gunnarr. She is about to carry out her threat, but Hǫgni puts her in fetters. Gunnarr protests the fetters and she brushes the protests aside, saying that he will never see her happy again in his hall, drinking or gaming or conversing or weaving with gold or advising. Her greatest grief, she says, is that she is not married to Sigurd. The scene concludes as she weaves so hard that she rends the work asunder and asks that the door be opened to allow her grief to be heard far off. A great outburst of sorrow is audible everywhere in the residence.[31]

A brief connecting piece of narrative mixed with discourse follows before the next major dialogue scene. Gudrun asks her maidens why they are so cheerless and what panic has gotten into them. One lady-in-waiting (Svafrlǫð) answers that it is an evil day and that the hall is full of grief. Gudrun tells her to get up and awaken Brynhild so that they can go to their weaving and be of good cheer. She refuses, saying that Brynhild has not drunk mead or wine for many days and suffers the wrath of the gods. Gudrun bids Gunnarr seek her out and say that they cannot endure her grief. Gunnarr says that he is forbidden to meet her or share her wealth, but he goes nonetheless and questions her repeatedly without eliciting an answer. He withdraws and sends Hǫgni in his place. Hǫgni agrees reluctantly, but he too is unable to draw Brynhild out. They then apply to Sigurd, who vouchsafes no reply, and so matters stand in the evening. The next day when Sigurd comes home from the hunt, he meets Gudrun and tells her that he foresees that Brynhild's illness will have great consequences and that she will die. Gudrun replies that she is in a wondrous state and has slept for seven days without anyone's daring to awaken her. Sigurd surmises that she is not sleeping, but pondering deep designs against them. Gudrun replies in tears that it is a great grief to know of Sigurd's death; he should rather meet with her, to see whether her excesses will subside, and give her gold to allay her wrath.

The dialogue section concludes with a protracted conversation

---

[31]Neckel, "Zu den Eddaliedern der Lücke," pp. 303–5, argued that this dialogue between Brynhild and Gunnarr is a free recasting of *Skamma* 35–41, but Panzer, II, 222, agreed with Heusler in attributing it to *Meiri*. Schneider, "Verlorene Sigurddichtung," pp. 2–3, also derived it from *Meiri*, which in turn harmonized *Forna* (the flame wall) and *Skamma* (the family pressure on Brynhild to wed).

between Brynhild and Sigurd.[32] He finds her room open, removes her bedclothes, and bids her put aside her grief. She asks how he dares to visit her since no one was more guilty of betrayal than he. Sigurd inquires into her silence and sorrow and she declares that she will recount her wrath. Sigurd says she is bewitched if she believes him to be hostile to her—she has married the man she chose. She denies that Gunnarr crossed the fire and paid her a bridal fee of men slain in battle. She had wondered about the man who came into her hall and thought she could recognize Sigurd's eyes, but she could not distinguish clearly because of the mist that lay over her destiny. Sigurd protests that he is no greater than the sons of Gjúki, who killed the king of the Danes and King Buðli's brother. Brynhild says that she harbors many grievances against them and asks not to be reminded of her sorrow; it was Sigurd who slew the serpent and crossed the flames, deeds not performed by the sons of Gjúki. Sigurd replies that they are not man and wife, but she was wed to a great king. Brynhild recalls that her heart did not laugh in her breast at the sight of Gunnarr and she insists that she is hostile to him though she hides it from others. Sigurd objects that it is monstrous not to love such a king and asks what it is that grieves her most; he thinks that Gunnarr's love is better than gold. She replies that her greatest grief is that she cannot redden a sword in Sigurd's blood. Sigurd tells her to be patient—she will not have long to wait for the fulfillment of her wish, though it will turn against her since she is not destined to outlive him by much. Brynhild charges him with malice because he has deprived her of all joy and she cares nothing for life. Sigurd now proposes a solution: she should go on living and love both Gunnarr and himself. He offers her all his gold if only she will agree to live. Brynhild replies that he does not understand her; he is superior to all men, but no woman is more hostile toward him than she. Sigurd finally declares that he has loved her more than himself, but was a victim of treachery. When his vision cleared, it grieved him that she had not become his wife, but he bore it as best he could. What has been prophesied must come to pass and he will not complain. Brynhild replies that he has spoken too late and that there is no remedy. Sigurd professes that he would be glad if they shared one bed and became man and wife, but Brynhild declares that she will die rather than betray Gunnarr. She reminds him of the time they swore oaths on the mountain, but says that all this is void and that

[32]It is generally agreed that this dialogue belongs to *Meiri*. However, Felix Scheidweiler, "Zu den Eddaliedern der Lücke," *ZDP*, 44 (1912), 320–29, considered it to be a separate "Situationslied."

she has no wish to live. Sigurd replies that he did not remember her name or recognize her until she was married and that this grieves him greatly. Brynhild declares that she swore an oath to marry the man who crossed the flame wall; her wish is to marry that man or die.[33] Sigurd moves a step further by stating that he would rather marry her and leave Gudrun than that she should die, and his sides swell so that the byrnie bursts. Brynhild replies that she wants neither him nor any other man, and Sigurd departs.

A stanza (25) describing the bursting of the byrnie is quoted from "Sigurðarkviða" (the most tangible evidence that there was a third "Sigurðarkviða" distinct from *Forna* and *Skamma*).

The remainder of the story in *Vǫlsunga saga* depends largely on *Skamma*. The outlines of *Meiri* therefore become sketchier. First in order is a passage based on *Brot* 2 in which Gunnarr inquires anew into Brynhild's grief and she denounces Sigurd for deceiving them both when he entered her bed and then revealing all to Gudrun (77.26–78.5). Next comes a duplicate of this scene from *Skamma* 11–12. Gunnarr visits Brynhild again and she threatens to leave him and return to her family unless he kills Sigurd and Sigurd's son (78.10–13). The saga author then records a passage from *Skamma* 17–20 in which Gunnarr consults Hǫgni on the killing of Sigurd, and Hǫgni warns against breaking their oaths and eliminating a pillar of strength on the deceitful advice of Brynhild (78.20–79.6). Gunnarr persists and counters Hǫgni's objection by proposing that they incite their younger brother Gotþormr, who is not bound by oath, to do the deed (79.6–9). Hǫgni continues to protest, but Gunnarr declares that either he or Sigurd will die (79.9–13—unclear from what poetic source if any). The following passage (79.13–80.17) does not correspond exactly to either *Forna* or *Skamma* and probably represents the slightly fuller account of *Meiri*.

Gunnarr bids Brynhild arise and be of good cheer. She does so, but vows not to share her bed with Gunnarr until the deed is done. Gunnarr confers once more with his brothers and declares that the taking of Brynhild's virginity is a mortal offense.[34] He suggests once more that they incite Gotþormr and they instill the requisite fierce-

---

[33]If the whole dialogue belongs to *Meiri,* this passage (*Vǫlsunga saga* 77.7–9) comes closest to guaranteeing the flame wall for that poem.

[34]As Schneider, "Verlorene Sigurddichtung," pp. 7–8, pointed out, this charge proves Brynhild's slander of Sigurd for *Meiri*. The slander presumably occurred in conjunction with her threat not to share Gunnarr's bed unless Sigurd is killed. The saga author was obliged to suppress the slander because he had already recorded it from *Forna* (77.29–78.1) and did not wish to repeat it.

ness in him with the aid of a magic wolf stew.[35] Sigurd is all unsuspecting and abandoned to his fate. Gotþormr invades his bedchamber, but retreats twice at the sight of his piercing eyes. The
third time Sigurd has dozed off and Gotþormr plunges his sword into
him. The aftermath is told according to *Skamma,* but a statement by
Hǫgni that Brynhild's prophecy has been fulfilled and Gudrun's prediction that her brothers will miss Sigurd in battle may belong to
Meiri (82.4–11). With the possible exception of a few words reporting Brynhild's self-immolation (85.6–8), *Vǫlsunga saga* sheds no
light on the conclusion of *Meiri.* As Heusler ("Lieder der Lücke,"
p. 274) pointed out, Brynhild's mounting of the pyre and last-minute
gifts to her ladies-in-waiting deviate from *Skamma* and may reflect
Meiri.

This is the raw material for our reconstruction of *Meiri,* which
must be established by subtracting those passages that *Vǫlsunga
saga* derives from *Forna* (both the lost and extant sections) and
Skamma, as well as the saga author's own additions and har-
monizations. What remains is *Meiri.* A further guide to the contents of *Meiri* is the testimony of the prophetic poem *Grípisspá,*
which clearly differs in narrative details from *Forna* and *Skamma*
and must depend on the alternative version provided by *Meiri.*

Despite the complications of the procedure, there is considerable agreement in the various reconstructions undertaken by
Heusler, Neckel, and Schneider. Heusler ("Lieder der Lücke,"
pp. 266–75) arrived at the following outline. *Meiri,* like *Forna* and
Skamma, began with Sigurd's arrival at Gjúki's court, but in this
version he is Brynhild's betrothed. Accordingly, he must drink
the potion of forgetfulness concocted by Grimhild before he is
married to Gudrun. The wooing of Brynhild follows and is made
possible by an exchange of shapes executed on Grimhild's instructions (*Grípisspá* 37–39). But the precise details of the wooing
are unclear, and Heusler inclined to the view that there was no
flame wall in *Meiri* because the *Grípisspá* poet omitted this feature. The interview with Buðli was mentioned briefly, but Heimir
was not referred to in *Meiri* and was inserted by the saga au-

[35]That this passage derives from *Meiri* is demonstrated by stanza 26 in *Vǫlsunga saga,* which differs from the corresponding fourth stanza of *Brot.* This is
the best evidence that *Meiri* was a conscious reworking of the earlier Sigurd
poems.

thor.[36] Brynhild's parting conversation with Heimir (*Vǫlsunga saga* 68.27–69.4) is consequently also the saga author's invention; in *Meiri* the conversation was with Buðli. On their return from the wooing expedition the group is welcomed by Grimhild; Sigurd remembers his old oaths to Brynhild, but remains silent (*Grípisspá* 45). Heusler remains in doubt about the presence of the quarrel in *Meiri*. On the one hand, it is omitted in *Skamma* and *Grípisspá*. On the other, Snorri may have made use of a quarrel variant from *Meiri* (see Chapter 5 on *Snorra Edda*). The long sequence of dialogues (*Vǫlsunga saga* 70.7–77.26) Heusler attributed in its entirety to *Meiri*. After the confrontation between Brynhild and Sigurd, Gunnarr goes to his wife and bids her get up. She incites him to kill Sigurd on pain of withholding sex, at the same time accusing Sigurd of breaking his oath and sleeping with her. Gunnarr transmits the accusation to his brothers and plots Sigurd's murder. Hǫgni resists and Gunnarr counters by proposing to use the unsworn brother Gotþormr for the deed. The wolf stew is administered to him and he kills the unsuspecting hero in his bed. Hǫgni comments that the prophecy is fulfilled and Gudrun predicts that Sigurd will be missed in battle. Whether or not *Vǫlsunga saga*'s concluding words on Brynhild's mounting of the pyre derive from *Meiri*, Heusler believed that this poem must have culminated with her suicide.

Gustav Neckel summarized the contents of *Meiri* under ten points:[37]

1. Sigurd arrives at Gjúki's court and his godlike appearance is described by one of the courtiers (*Vǫlsunga saga* 64.5–10). Neckel associates the description with the teichoscopy (view from a wall) of the *Nibelungenlied* (stanzas 71–73, 79, 85) and supposes that a German lay served as model for *Meiri*.

2. Sigurd is given the potion of forgetfulness. He then swears blood brotherhood with Gunnarr and Hǫgni and is offered Gudrun's hand. Neckel assumes that the wedding is not celebrated immediately, but that Gunnarr makes a pact with Sigurd to give him his sister's hand in return for his help on the wooing expedition.

---

[36]Léon Polak, *Untersuchungen über die Sigfridsagen*, Diss. Berlin 1910 (Berlin: Universitäts-Buchdruckerei, 1910), pp. 121–25, and Panzer, II, 191 (note), disagreed and attributed the mention of Heimir to *Forna*, but Lehmgrübner, p. 19, returned to Heusler's view. See also Wieselgren, p. 267.

[37]"Zu den Eddaliedern der Lücke," pp. 322–29.

3. The details of the wooing cannot be determined.

4. The two weddings are celebrated simultaneously as in *Grípisspá* 43 and the *Nibelungenlied*. Gudrun notices Brynhild's dejection and questions Sigurd about her state. Sigurd has intimations of woe and is evasive.

5. Instead of staging the traditional quarrel, the *Meiri* poet allows the realization of what has happened to ripen in silence. This realization is followed by a dialogue between Brynhild and Gudrun (*Vǫlsunga saga* 70.19–72.13) in which the pattern of the quarrel is reversed to the extent that each woman praises the other's husband instead of maintaining the superiority of her own.

6. The next section (omitting *Vǫlsunga saga* 72.16–74.5, which Neckel regarded as the saga author's elaboration of *Skamma*) consisted of a discussion of Brynhild's state involving Gudrun, Gunnarr, Hǫgni, Sigurd, and a lady-in-waiting (74.11–75.5).

7. Sigurd converses at length with Brynhild.

8. Sigurd's suggestion of adultery gives Brynhild the idea for the slander with which she incites Gunnarr.

9. Sigurd is murdered.

10. That *Meiri* ended with Brynhild's suicide is suggested by her declared wish to die (76.13, 77.3–4, 77.8–9) and the agreement of later sources (*Skamma, Helreið Brynhildar,* and *Oddrúnargrátr* 19).

Hermann Schneider went over the same ground again.[38] According to his reconstruction, Sigurd comes to Gjúki's court, is given the potion of forgetfulness, swears blood brotherhood with Gunnarr and Hǫgni, and marries Gudrun. He goes on plundering raids and performs great feats with his blood brothers. Gudrun gives birth to a son Sigmund. In evaluating the wooing sequence, Schneider disagreed with Neckel's interpretation of *Vǫlsunga saga* 29.5–48 as an elaboration of *Skamma*. Considered as a reflection of *Meiri,* the passage gives us to understand that the Gjukungs threaten Buðli with war unless he surrenders Brynhild. She considers doing battle, but attempts to elude the pressure by swearing to marry only the man who crosses the flame wall. That man is of course Sigurd, to whom she is already betrothed. The deception is effected as in *Forna* with Sigurd's crossing of the flame wall. Unlike Heusler, Schneider assigned Brynhild's parting visit with Heimir to *Meiri.* He then deviated from Neckel in

[38]"Verlorene Sigurddichtung," pp. 1–8 and *Germanische Heldensage,* I, 136–39.

supposing that *Meiri* had a somewhat fuller version of the quarrel than *Forna,* ending in the river. The author of *Vǫlsunga saga* used the fuller details of the encounter in *Meiri* (70.19–72.13), then canceled the variant abruptly when it progressed to the river stage and duplicated *Forna* too closely (72.13–15). There followed the dialogue between Gunnarr and Brynhild (*Vǫlsunga saga* 29.5–48) and the core dialogue between Brynhild and Sigurd. Brynhild then incites Gunnarr against Sigurd with the false charge of faithlessness, Hǫgni demurs, Gunnarr persists, and Gotþormr is enlisted to murder Sigurd. Schneider agreed with Heusler and Neckel that *Meiri* ended with Brynhild's suicide. In a concluding discussion (pp. 8–10) Schneider speculated that *Meiri* may have begun with a scene depicting the prior betrothal, a scene that served as a model for the "Falkenlied" and Sigurd's forcible entry into Brynhild's fortress in *Oddrúnargrátr* 18.

Per Wieselgren's reconstruction of *Meiri* in his *Quellenstudien zur Vǫlsungasaga* lies somewhat apart from the main line established by Heusler, Neckel, and Schneider. The chief differences are that *Meiri* included the whole of Sigurd's prehistory (p. 293), combined the awakening of Sigrdrífa with the wooing of Brynhild (p. 311), and included an elaborate version of the wooing (p. 340). The quarrel of the queens in Wieselgren's *Meiri* is most faithfully reflected by the version in *Snorra Edda* (pp. 272–75, 333–38). In addition, Wieselgren separated the hall dialogue between Brynhild and Gudrun from the dialogue sequence in *Meiri* and attributed it to an independent "Brynhildarkviða," which he reconstructed in German verse (pp. 280–88).

A fair degree of concurrence clearly exists about the general outline of *Meiri,* at least among Heusler, Neckel, and Schneider, but details are open to debate. Was the prior betrothal scenically realized? Was there a flame wall? Was there a quarrel scene? How much of the dialogue sequence in *Vǫlsunga saga* belonged to *Meiri?* These matters require further analysis.

We will proceed on the assumption that the *Meiri* poet knew both *Forna* and *Skamma. Forna* betrays no knowledge of a prior betrothal while *Skamma* is ambiguous and can be interpreted either way. *Meiri,* however, is perfectly precise. At the conclusion of her momentous dialogue with Sigurd in *Vǫlsunga saga,* an undisputed derivative from *Meiri,* Brynhild refers specifically to

their betrothal oaths (77.1–3: "And she reminds him now of the
time they met on the mountain and swore oaths").[39] Once the
betrothal oaths are established for *Meiri*, we must determine their
source. A number of possibilities exist. The *Meiri* poet may have
extrapolated the prior betrothal from the hints of Brynhild's
jealousy in *Forna* and *Skamma*. Or he may have taken the idea
from *Skamma* if he understood that poem to imply the betrothal.
Or he may have taken the idea from the same tradition that is less
clearly implied in *Skamma*. Finally, he may have borrowed the
prior betrothal from a foreign source. Evidence will be compiled
later in the argument suggesting that *Meiri* absorbed material
from a German version of the story. In the matter of the prior
betrothal the German versions are not transparent; both the
Nibelungenlied and *Þiðreks saga* are about as ambiguous as
Skamma. Nonetheless, a case will be made for believing that they
both imply the prior betrothal. If the idea is rooted in Germany,
perhaps *Skamma* and in any case *Meiri* probably derived it from

---

[39]The location on the mountain may suggest that the betrothal refers to the
identification of Sigrdrifa as Brynhild (Lehmgrübner, pp. 25–26), but Brynhild is
also specifically placed on a mountain in *Vǫlsunga saga* 61.26–27: "Su holl
[Brynhild's hall] var buinn med gulle ok stod a einu berge" ("That hall was
decorated with gold and stood on a mountain"). In her parting conversation with
Heimir she similarly refers to her oaths on the mountain (68.32–69.1: "er ek vann
eida a fiallenu"—"when I swore oaths on the mountain"). Heusler (p. 270) argued
wrongly on the basis of this passage that *Meiri* connected the prior betrothal with
the *Erweckungssage* rather than the falcon story; if Brynhild's residence was on a
mountain in the dream episode, it was presumably on the same mountain in the
falcon episode. There is also a reference to the oaths in Brynhild's conversation
with Gudrun (71.1–2: "Ecke haufum ver launmęle haft, ok þo haufum vid eida
svarit . . ."—"We had no secret trysts, but we swore oaths"). This remark seems
most likely to be inherited from the quarrel scene as refashioned in *Meiri*. All
these references must be to the betrothal oaths sworn by Sigurd and Brynhild in
her tower, although this scene is never explicitly alluded to in the saga passages
attributable to *Meiri*. This lack of explicitness in fact is one argument for believing
that Heusler's "Falkenlied" must have been part of *Meiri*. If *Meiri* included the
scene of the prior betrothal, it is comprehensible that the remainder of the text was
so vague on the subject—the reader could be assumed to know the situation. If
Meiri had made no mention of the betrothal scene, a more exact reference would
have been necessary in retrospect. As things stand, Brynhild's three mentions of
the sworn oaths refer directly to the phrasing that Heusler attributed to the "Falkenlied" and that I attribute to the beginning of *Meiri* (60.14–16: "ok þess sver ek
vid gudinn, at ek skal þik eigha eda eingha konu ella" ("and I swear by the gods
that I will marry you and no other woman"), and 60.17–18: "ok svaurdu nu eida af
nyiu" ("and they swore oaths anew").

a German source, the first in tentative form and the latter more decisively.[40]

The form of the prior betrothal in *Vǫlsunga saga* is determined by the falcon motif. As mentioned above (n. 26), the closest analogue to this motif is to be found in Giambattista Basile's *Pentamerone* from the early seventeenth century. It appears therefore that the betrothal scene was modeled on a folktale, just as Sigurd's birth was remodeled according to the Constance tale in the version preserved in *Þiðreks saga* (see Chapter 4). Schneider ("Verlorene Sigurddichtung," pp. 8–10) speculated that *Meiri* and *Oddrúnargrátr* 18 (in which Sigurd enters Brynhild's fortress forcibly) derived the scene from a common source and that the "Falkenlied" subsequently took the scene from *Meiri*. Because I believe that "Falkenlied" and *Meiri* were identical, I propose to revise this theory and assume that *Meiri* and *Oddrúnargrátr* 18 derived the scene from a common source. We will observe below (Chapter 4, n. 22) that the forcible entry of *Oddrúnargrátr* 18 corresponds unmistakably to the much-disputed chapter 168 of *Þiðreks saga*. This motif is therefore of German origin and the original form of the prior betrothal included the forcible entry of chapter 168 and *Oddrúnargrátr* 18. At some point in the transmission of the tale from Germany to Iceland this original form was altered according to a folktale with hunting scenery and escaped hawk. In this new form it appears in *Meiri*. Whether the change represents a German variant, an innovation in the Icelandic prototype, or the *Meiri* poet's innovation cannot be determined.[41]

The second section of *Meiri*, the interpretation of Gudrun's

---

[40]On German influence in *Skamma* see Wolfgang Mohr, "Wortschatz und Motive der jüngeren Eddalieder mit südgermanischem Stoff," *ZDA*, 76 (1939), 204, and Schneider, *Die deutschen Lieder*, pp. 28–30. On German influence in *Meiri* see Boer, *Untersuchungen*, I, 55; II, 7–8; III, 109 (n. 2); Neckel, "Zu den Eddaliedern der Lücke," pp. 322–25; Panzer, II, 225; Helmut de Boor, *Die färöischen Lieder des Nibelungenzyklus*, Germanische Bibliothek, Untersuchungen und Texte, 12 (Heidelberg: Winter, 1918), pp. 119–21. The influence was denied by Schneider, *Germanische Heldensage*, I, 183.

[41]In attaching the falcon story to *Meiri*, I revert to the position of Boer, *Untersuchungen*, I, 87. The connection was rejected by Polak, p. 92; Ussing, pp. 98–99; and Lehmgrübner, pp. 31–32. Wieselgren, p. 241, rejected the falcon poem altogether. He believed that the prior betrothal was invented by the *Meiri* poet (p. 292).

dreams (Heusler's "Traumlied") also has a German prehistory.[42] It corresponds to the *Nibelungenlied* (stanzas 13–14), a passage in which Kriemhilt dreams of a falcon rent by two eagles. Her mother Uote interprets the falcon as her future husband. The sanguinary conclusion of the falcon dream is omitted in *Meiri* and a stag dream is added, but clearly the motif is identical in the two texts. The easiest explanation is that the *Meiri* poet added the monitory dream or dreams from a German source. Whether Gudrun's mother (Uote in the *Nibelungenlied* and Grimhild in *Meiri*) originally acted as interpreter is hard to say. It is a difficult role for Grimhild because she would be in the position of prophesying her own perfidy (the drugged mead). On the other hand, the meeting between Gudrun and Brynhild at this early juncture in the story is somewhat strange. Perhaps the lady-in-waiting Svafrlǫð, who interprets the hawk dream in *Meiri*, held the role in the original. The poet of *Meiri* then developed a companion scene to show off Brynhild's well-known prophetic gifts (and keep his heroine on center stage), while the *Nibelungenlied* poet reassigned the sooth-saying to Uote in line with his recasting of the scene on the model of Heinrich von Veldeke's *Eneide*. The discussion of distinguished kings with Brynhild may be taken to foreshadow the concern with status in the later quarrel of the queens.

Sigurd's arrival at the court of Gjúki does not differ in substance from *Forna* and *Skamma* although Neckel, seconded by Helmut de Boor, attributed some of the details to a German

[42]The idea that the "Traumlied" was a prefatory section of *Meiri* goes back to Golther, pp. 196–97. Heusler, "Lieder der Lücke," p. 253, argued against the connection on the ground that no Eddic Sigurd poem places Gudrun in the foreground and that *Skamma* and *Meiri* are at pains to emphasize Brynhild's preeminence. The "Traumlied" was also considered a separate entity by Boer, *Untersuchungen*, I, 87–88; Ussing, pp. 99–100; and Lehmgrübner, p. 35. Wieselgren, p. 244, did not consider it to be a lost poem, but "a *þáttr* from oral tradition." Friedrich Panzer, "Nibelungische Ketzereien: 3. Thidrekssaga und Nibelungenlied, Irrungen und Wirrungen. 4. Das Traumlied in der Völsungasaga," *BGDSL*, 75 (1953), 255–72, argued that it was derived from the *Nibelungenlied*. Gerhard Eis, "Das eddische 'Traumlied'," *ANF*, 71 (1956), 177–86, argued that the *haukr* in the dream of *Vǫlsunga saga* could not be derived from the *falke* of the *Nibelungenlied* and proposed a common source with a hawk, which the *Nibelungenlied* poet changed into a falcon on the basis of a Romance poem or Der Kürenberger. On the background of the dream see also Emil Ploss, "Byzantinische Traumsymbolik und Kriemhilds Falkentraum," *GRM*, 39 (1958), 218–26.

model.[43] The potion of forgetfulness has no counterpart outside of *Meiri*. Heusler ("Lieder der Lücke," p. 268) was uncertain whether it was traditional or an invention of the *Meiri* poet. If it had any traditional status in Germany, it would have been dropped in both the *Nibelungenlied* and *Þiðreks saga* because the prior betrothal, which it was intended to erase in Sigurd's memory, was suppressed in these texts. The oaths of blood brotherhood in *Meiri* must have had their counterpart in *Forna* judging from the reference to them in *Brot* 17; they were also mentioned in the first stanza of *Skamma*. *Vǫlsunga saga* 65.29–30 tells us that Sigurd marries Gudrun at this point, but the evidence is contradicted by *Grípisspá* 43, according to which Sigurd and Gudrun marry later in a double ceremony together with Gunnarr and Brynhild. Since *Grípisspá* depends on *Meiri*, it is a reliable index to the sequence of events in this poem. The easiest solution is to assume that *Vǫlsunga saga* opted for the chronology of *Forna* (perhaps to make room for the birth of Gudrun's son Sigmund mentioned in *Skamma* 12), while *Grípisspá* adopted the chronology of *Meiri*. Since the double wedding of *Meiri*/*Grípisspá* corresponds to Adventure 10 in the *Nibelungenlied*, German influence has been invoked to account for the change.[44]

Peculiar to *Meiri* also is the idea that Sigurd accompanies his new sworn brothers on warlike campaigns abroad. The primary passage is *Vǫlsunga saga* 65.32–66.2: "They traveled far and wide and performed many great deeds and killed many princes

[43]Neckel, "Zu den Eddaliedern der Lücke," pp. 322–23, and de Boor, p. 119.

[44]To my knowledge, Wolfgang Golther was the first to explain the double wedding in *Grípisspá* 43 from German influence: "Studien zur germanischen Sagengeschichte: I Der Valkyrjenmythus, II Über das Verhältnis der nordischen und deutschen Form der Nibelungensage," *Abhandlungen der Königlich Bayerischen Akademie der Wissenschaften*, First class, vol. 18, 2d section (Munich, 1888), 486–87. Heusler, "Lieder der Lücke," p. 267 (n. 65), agreed that the feature in *Grípisspá* was German, but did not attribute it to *Meiri*. Neckel, "Zu den Eddaliedern der Lücke," p. 324, considered that the double wedding in *Grípisspá* derived from *Meiri* and ultimately from German influence. Scheidweiler, p. 322, and de Boor, pp. 119–20, concurred. Schneider, "Verlorene Sigurddichtung," p. 12, opposed Neckel's view that *Meiri* had the double wedding. Wieselgren, p. 330, assumed the double wedding for *Meiri*, but did not consider that German influence was necessary. Dietrich von Kralik, *Die Sigfridtrilogie im Nibelungenlied und in der Thidrekssaga*, I (Halle: Niemeyer, 1941), 413, believed that the double weddings in *Grípisspá* 43 and the *Nibelungenlied* were separate developments.

and no one accomplished such feats as they did. Then they returned home with much booty.'' Sigurd presumably referred to
these feats in his final conversation with Brynhild when he dis-
claims any superiority over the Gjukungs (75.22–23): "They
killed the king of the Danes and a great chieftain in the person of
Buðli's brother." This campaign is verified by chapter 7 of
Norna-Gests þáttr.[45] Norna-Gestr recalls his days with Sigurd
(p. 322): "Then Sigurd married Gudrun the daughter of Gjúki. He
then stayed for some time with the Gjukungs, his kinsmen. I was
with Sigurd north in Denmark. I was also with Sigurd when King
Sigurðr hringr sent the sons of Gandálfr, his kinsmen, against the
Gjukungs, Gunnarr and Hǫgni, and demanded that they pay him
tribute or endure warfare, but they wished to defend their land.
Then the sons of Gandálfr challenge the Gjukungs to a pitched
battle at the frontier and return. But the Gjukungs ask Sigurd the
Dragonslayer to go to battle with them." There follows a description of the campaign and Sigurd's contribution (he puts Starkaðr
to flight with a blow of his sword hilt in the teeth). The campaign
concludes as in *Vǫlsunga saga*: "We took great booty and the
kings went home and remained there for some time." The Danish
scene, the booty-laden return, and the timing in conjunction with
Sigurd's marriage to Gudrun accord well with *Vǫlsunga saga*.
That this campaign has its origin in a German tale is suggested by
Sigurd's encounter with Dietrich and his followers in *Þiðreks
saga* I.322–II.37, at the conclusion of which Sigurd and Gudrun
marry. The situation is not the same, but we may surmise that
Sigurd's Danish campaign was displaced by a campaign intended
to integrate him into the Dietrich cycle, which is the organizing
principle of *Þiðreks saga*. The Danish campaign is further
documented as a traditional part of the German story by the
Dano-Saxon war of Adventure 4 in the *Nibelungenlied.*[46] Prior

[45]Guðni Jónsson, ed., *Fornaldar sögur Norðurlanda,* I (n.p.: Íslendingasagnaútgáfan, 1954), 322–24.

[46]The legendary background of the Dano-Saxon war was first dealt with by Karl
Müllenhoff, "Ueber Siegfrieds Sachsen- und Dänenkriege," *Nordalbingische
Studien: Neues Archiv der Schleswig-Holstein-Lauenburgischen Gesellschaft für
vaterländische Geschichte,* 1 (1858), 191–207. Karl Droege, "Zur Thidrekssaga,"
ZDA, 66 (1929), 36–37, suggested more directly that Siegfried's adventures in
Bertangaland could be a substitution for the Saxon war in the *Nibelungenlied* and
pointed out motival similarities. See also Gregor Sarrazin, "Der Ursprung der

betrothal, monitory dream, double wedding, and Danish campaign in *Meiri* appear then to have a uniform German etiology.

Grimhild now proposes that Gunnarr should woo Brynhild and
instructs Gunnarr and Sigurd in the art of shape shifting. Both
items are peculiar to *Meiri*. In *Forna* it is not clear where the
initiative for the wooing originates and *Skamma* passes over the
matter in silence. In *Þiðreks saga* it is Sigurd who proposes the
suit (II.38.6–14) and in the *Nibelungenlied* (stanza 325) it is
Gunther's spontaneous idea. Given the evidence, it is not possible to penetrate to the original form, but it is clear that the *Meiri*
poet was the first to activate the figure of Grimhild. Grimhild
drugs Sigurd into oblivion, proposes the wooing of Brynhild, provides the means of deception (the shape shifting), and therefore
becomes the special target of Brynhild's wrath in *Vǫlsunga saga*.
The poet created a witch. If we inquire into the meaning of such
an innovation, the answer might be an effort to exculpate Sigurd.
Having given the prior betrothal firm contours, the *Meiri* poet
found himself with Sigurd, greatest hero of the North, cast as a
bounder. In order to counteract this impression, he drew
Grimhild and her potion forth from the wings to answer for the
crime.[47] Sigurd becomes the sad instrument of her perfidy.

The extent to which the consultation of the wooers with Buðli
and Heimir is the work of the *Meiri* poet or the author of *Vǫl-*

Siegfried-Sage," *ZVL*, 11 (1897), 113–24; Karl Droege, "Die Vorstufe unseres
Nibelungenliedes," *ZDA*, 51 (1909), 178–81; Carl Wesle, "Brünhildlied oder Sigfridepos?" *ZDP*, 51 (1926), 40–41; Wieselgren, p. 331; and von Kralik, pp. 114,
297–98, 353–56. Schneider, *Germanische Heldensage*, I, 184, contended that the
Danish war was of Scandinavian origin and passed from *Meiri* to the German
"Brünhildenlied," not vice versa. Friedrich Panzer, "Zur Erzählung von Nor-
nagest," *Vom Werden des deutschen Geistes: Festgabe Gustav Ehrismann zum
8. Oktober 1925, dargebracht von Freunden und Schülern*, ed. Paul Merker and
Wolfgang Stammler (Berlin and Leipzig: de Gruyter, 1925), pp. 27–34, found a
model for Norna-Gestr in the story of one of Charlemagne's soldiers who lived
more than 300 years. The larger context of the tale (including *Widsith*) is dealt
with by Margaret Schlauch, "Wīdsīth, Vīthförull, and Some Other Analogues,"
PMLA, 46 (1931), 969–87. Joseph Harris illuminated the German background of
Norna-Gestr's tales in "*Guðrúnarbrǫgð* and the Saxon Lay of Grimhild's Perfidy," *Mediaeval Scandinavia*, 9 (1976), 173–80.

[47]Wolfgang Mohr in *Dichtung und Volkstum*, p. 109: "Auch der Dichter des
langen Sigurdliedes, der die Vorverlobung in seine Liedhandlung aufnahm, wurde
bald gewahr, dass er da ein Kuckucksei ausbrütete, und schaffte die Sache durch
den Vergessenheitstrank schnell wieder aus der Welt."

sunga saga is uncertain. The sources assign Brynhild's family three differing roles: (1) Buðli and Heimir acquiesce (*Vǫlsunga saga* 66.12–21), (2) Atli forces Brynhild to marry Gunnarr against her will (*Skamma*), and (3) Buðli forces her to choose one of the suitors (*Vǫlsunga saga* 72.25–26). Since there are three versions and three poems among which to distribute them, the solution would appear to be straightforward. Acquiescent father and foster father are mentioned in the context of a passage that Heusler assigned with good reason to *Forna* and must belong to that poem. Atli's injunction to wed Gunnarr demonstrably belongs to *Skamma*. Therefore Buðli's pressure on his daughter to choose a suitor must belong to *Meiri*. Hermann Schneider came closest to resolving the problem ("Verlorene Sigurddichtung," p. 3). He assumed that the *Meiri* poet harmonized *Forna* and *Skamma* by combining Brynhild's autonomy in the former with the family pressure in the latter. When she sees that marriage is unavoidable (*Skamma*), she agrees to marry the man who crosses the flame wall (*Forna*), knowing that the feat can be accomplished only by her betrothed Sigurd. The only difficulty remaining in Schneider's explanation is that it presupposes the flame wall for *Meiri*. Since the flame wall is not mentioned in *Grípisspá,* the attribution of it to *Meiri* has always been in doubt.[48] The decisive passage, which seems to have eluded all the critics but Wieselgren (p. 332), is *Vǫlsunga saga* 77.6–9: "Then Brynhild said: 'I swore an oath to marry the man who crossed my flame wall and I wish to honor that oath or die.'" This passage, which is part of the dialogue between Brynhild and Sigurd and indisputable testimony of *Meiri,* guarantees not only the flame wall, but also the nature of the oath with which she placates Buðli according to Schneider's solution. The situation in *Meiri* is therefore that the suitors visit Buðli and oblige him by force of arms to give Brynhild in marriage. She seeks to turn the situation to her advantage by stipulating that she will marry the man who crosses the flame wall, but she is tricked when Sigurd appears in Gunnarr's shape and forces

[48]Heusler, "Lieder der Lücke," p. 268, was inclined to believe that there was no flame wall. Neckel, "Zu den Eddaliedern der Lücke," p. 324, ventured nothing on the details of the wooing. Schneider, "Verlorene Sigurddichtung," pp. 3–4, assumed the flame wall without argument and Wieselgren, p. 332, also assigned it to *Meiri.*

her to make good her promise. Presumably the couple goes through the sham nuptials separated by a sword before parting (*Grípisspá* 41). In other words, the wooing sequence in *Meiri* is very similar to what we must suppose for *Forna*, and it is difficult to decide what details in the description of *Vǫlsunga saga* 67.27–68.24 belong to which poem.

Two puzzles remain. Why did the *Meiri* poet alter *Skamma* by transferring Atli's autocratic role to Buðli? Perhaps this was a consequence of harmonization. Confronted with the approval of Brynhild's father in *Forna* and the autocracy of her brother in *Skamma*, the *Meiri* poet resolved the contradiction by taking the father from *Forna* and the autocracy from *Skamma*, thus settling on an autocratic father. The second puzzle concerns the nature of this autocracy. Why does Brynhild's family force her marriage? Perhaps the question should rather be phrased: Why must the Gjukungs force the family to pressure Brynhild? No such necessity existed in *Forna*, but in *Meiri* and perhaps in *Skamma* the prior betrothal to Sigurd precluded a new betrothal. The prior betrothal thus explains the force brought to bear by the Gjukungs on a reluctant family and the transmission of this pressure from Atli or Buðli to Brynhild.[49] Particularly interesting in this section of *Meiri* is the evidence that the poet was exactly familiar with both *Forna* and *Skamma* and that an important part of his strategy was to reconcile these two accounts.

After the return of the wooing expedition to Gjúki's court, the next key scene is the quarrel of the queens and the revelation of Brynhild's deception. Because *Vǫlsunga saga* took the quarrel scene from *Forna* and since *Meiri*'s delegate *Grípisspá* omits it altogether, it is difficult to establish the nature of the scene in *Meiri*. Heusler ("Lieder der Lücke," p. 271) was in doubt; Nekkel (*ZDP*, 39 [1907], 325) excluded it from *Meiri,* but Schneider ("Verlorene Sigurddichtung," p. 5) and Wieselgren (*Quellenstudien,* pp. 334–35) restored it. In the quarrel scene in *Vǫlsunga saga* (69.13–70.7 = *Forna*) Brynhild offends Gudrun by wading further out into the stream. When Gudrun protests, Brynhild boasts that her father is more powerful and that her husband

---

[49]This construction may of course be used as (tenuous) evidence that *Skamma* presupposes the prior betrothal.

performed many bold deeds and crossed the flame wall while Sigurd was Hjálprekr's thrall. Gudrun retorts angrily that Sigurd is the foremost of men, that he was Brynhild's first lover after he crossed the flame wall, and that he took the ring Andvaranautr from her. Brynhild pales and departs.

The only verbal exchange between Gudrun and Brynhild directly attributable to *Meiri* is one of the retrospective dialogues which follow the revelation (70.19–72.13). The dialogue is a continuation of the previous quarrel, to which it refers directly. Gudrun asks (70.20): "Does our (previous) conversation grieve you?" This question is posed the following morning in the women's *skemma* ("chamber"), where they are seated together. At the conclusion of the dialogue, Brynhild goes to bed and the remaining dialogues take place in her bedchamber. A curious feature of the dialogue is the setting in the *skemma*. If Brynhild is going to be confined to her bed by grief, we might expect this state immediately after the painful revelation in the river. But *Vǫlsunga saga* allows her to go to bed, then rise in the morning apparently for the sole purpose of conversing with Gudrun before retreating once more to her bedchamber, this time permanently. The dialogue between Gudrun and Brynhild is therefore somewhat inorganic in the context of the bedside dialogues aimed at retrieving Brynhild from her grief. The explanation may be that it was not originally one of the retrospective dialogues, but *Meiri*'s version of the quarrel.

The dialogue is summarized above. We shall see in the subsequent discussion (Chapter 5 between notes 42 and 43) that it corresponds to two scenes in the *Nibelungenlied* and is in fact a conflation of two original scenes that were peculiar to the version with the prior betrothal. In the first of these scenes (equivalent to *Vǫlsunga saga* 70.19–71.3) Gudrun inquires into Brynhild's grief, and Brynhild replies that her rival will suffer the consequences of having Sigurd and that she begrudges her the possession of both him and his treasure. Gudrun protests that she knew nothing of the betrothal, but Brynhild maintains that Gudrun and her family knew perfectly well of the oaths and she vows vengeance. This exchange is equivalent to the scene in the *Nibelungenlied* (stanzas 618–24) in which Brynhild weeps at the sight of Kriemhilt and Siegfried and presses Gunther for an explanation of Kriemhilt's marriage to a vassal. The equivalence is shown by the framing of both scenes in the same way; they begin with an inquiry into Brynhild's grief and end with her threat of reprisals. This new scene originates in the altered circumstances of the version with the prior betrothal. Since Brynhild has been by preference betrothed to Sigurd, she cannot very well initiate a quarrel with Gudrun by claiming in all innocence that Gunnarr is the superior man.[50] In order to avoid this potential illogicality, the version with the prior betrothal anticipates the quarrel with a confrontation between the queens in which Brynhild vows vengeance for the disaffection of her betrothed.

The actual quarrel in *Meiri* (*Vǫlsunga saga* 71.7–72.13) rehearses the traditional issues, the debate over the relative distinction of the husbands (71.6–9) and Sigurd's feats in killing Fáfnir and crossing the flame wall (71.10–20). These are issues debated in *Forna* (*Vǫlsunga saga* 69.18–70.1 and *Snorra Edda,* ed. Finnur Jónsson, p. 131.3–8), but they are managed differently in *Meiri.*[52] Here Gudrun tries to reconcile Brynhild to her marriage instead of contesting her marital advantage. The *Meiri* poet has borrowed the quarrel motifs from *Forna* (or the equivalent tradition) and converted them into conciliatory terms, that is, he uses the quarrel material in line with the later efforts to placate Brynhild. Thus Gudrun finds herself lauding Gunnarr, while Brynhild praises Sigurd.[52]

---

[50]Wieselgren, p. 334, read Neckel, "Zu den Eddaliedern der Lücke," p. 325, in this sense.

[51]Cf. Neckel, ibid.

[52]The key to this shift is stanza 24 in *Vǫlsunga saga* (p. 71): "Sigurdr vaa at orme, / enn þat siþan mun / engum fyrnazt, / medan aulld lifir. / Enn hlyre þinn / hvarke þordi / elld at rida / nę yfir stigha." ("Sigurd slew the serpent and that will never perish while the world lives. But your brother neither dared to ride the fire nor surmount it.") This stanza is echoed in *Snorra Edda,* ed. Finnur Jónsson, p. 131.2–7: "Þa geck Gvðrvn a ana eptir henni ok sagþi, at hon matti firir þvi þva ofaʀ siN hadd í ǫni, at hon atti þaN maN, er eigi G(vnnarr) ok engi aNaʀ iveroldv var iafnfrækn, þviat *hann vá Fafni* ok Regin ok toc arf eptir baþa þa. Þa svarar Brynhildr: 'meira var þat vert, er Gvnaʀ reið vaforlogann, en *Sigvrþr þorþi eigi.*'" ("Then Gudrun went into the river after her and said that she might wash her hair higher up in the river because she was married to a man who was unequaled in bravery by Gunnarr or any other man because *he slew Fafnir* and Regin and took their inheritances. Then Brynhild answers: 'It was worth more that Gunnarr crossed the magic flames, but *Sigurd did not dare.*'") In *Snorra Edda* the content of the first half-stanza is attributed to Gudrun and the content of the second to

Because the quarrel scene in *Meiri* could not conclude on a conciliatory note, the interview between Gudrun and Brynhild continues with the latter's excoriation of Grimhild (71.23–29), whom she perceives as the mastermind of the deception. This is a familiar preoccupation of the *Meiri* poet. The conversation then shifts back to Brynhild's resentment of Gudrun's marriage (71.30–72.4). Gudrun retorts that she has every intention of enjoying her possession of Sigurd and that no one suspects *them* of having been too familiar. In other words, this is an oblique form of the accusation that Brynhild has been Sigurd's lover, the final stage in the traditional quarrel as we find it in the other texts, *Forna, Þiðreks saga,* and the *Nibelungenlied.* In some form it must also have been the culmination of the quarrel in *Meiri,* but in *Vǫlsunga saga* it is weakened to an innuendo because the revelation has already emerged from the river quarrel, which the saga author took from *Forna* and which cannot be repeated here. The earlier charge of sexual familiarity is therefore merely an allusion in the later passage and the conversation then tapers off for the same reason; the violent denouement has already been expended in the river scene and does not bear repetition.

Brynhild's subsequent dialogue with Gunnarr (72.18–74.1) is divided into two sections: (1) a review of the compulsion under which she married Gunnarr, thus breaking her oath to love only the most outstanding man, and (2) her attack on Grimhild, followed by Gunnarr's defense. There are no new themes here. As we have seen above, the account of Brynhild's marriage is the *Meiri* poet's harmonization of *Skamma* and *Forna,* and the incrimination of Grimhild reinforces a theme already brought out in the confrontation between Brynhild and Gudrun. The scene con-

---

Brynhild. In *Vǫlsunga saga* both half-stanzas are attributed to Brynhild. De Boor, pp. 94–95, believed that the stanza was spoken originally by Gudrun in the quarrel context, but to justify the conjecture he was obliged to mistranslate *hlyre* as "Gemahl" (husband) rather than "Bruder" (brother). The error was corrected by von See, "Freierprobe und Königinnenzank," p. 172. There are two possibilities. Either the stanza belongs to Gudrun in the *Forna* river quarrel and "hlyre þinn" ("your brother") was originally "hlyre minn" ("my brother"), i.e., Gunnarr (changed to "hlyre þinn" by the saga author when he reassigned the stanza to Brynhild), or it belongs to Brynhild and is a *Meiri* duplicate of a *Forna* stanza underlying Snorri's account just as stanza 26 of *Vǫlsunga saga* is a *Meiri* duplicate of *Brot* 4. If it is a *Meiri* stanza, we may observe how mechanically the *Meiri* poet went about converting the quarrel scene in *Forna* into conciliatory terms.

cludes with an attempt on Gunnarr's life thwarted by Hǫgni and a
great outburst of grief audible throughout the hall and perhaps
modeled on Gudrun's outburst in *Skamma* 29–30. The following
connecting piece in *Vǫlsunga saga* 74.5–75.5 must also derive
from *Meiri*. It describes Brynhild's catatonic state of grief and
various attempts to rouse her from it. The concept may well be
connected with *Guðrúnarkviða* I and the attempts to resuscitate
Gudrun described in that poem (see Chapter 3).

The highlight of the dialogue sequence in *Meiri* is the final
conversation between Brynhild and Sigurd (*Vǫlsunga saga*
75.5–77.13). Here the poet did not simply fit and join old timbers
from *Forna* and *Skamma,* but conceived a new idea, the analysis
of Brynhild's and Sigurd's emotions in direct confrontation. In
previous versions the reader or listener was given only an oblique
look at these psychological interiors. Brynhild was resentful because she was cheated of her oath and cheated emotionally, but
the feeling emerges only in her spasmodic expression of pain and
her cold-blooded revenge. Sigurd was never probed at all. Now
they stand opposite one another and debate the issue. The scene
was inspired by questions in the poet's mind. What was the emotional mechanism of Brynhild's revenge? What were the feelings
of the physically overt and emotionally opaque Sigurd? If they
were really so clearly intended for one another, what stood in
their way? Were the impediments insurmountable or could they
be leveled by open discussion? The task the poet set himself was
to press the issue, to measure the impasse, to study the ways in
which the protagonists might have extricated themselves and
averted the calamity. The dialogue invites an examination of
whether the tragedy is really ordained by the circumstances or
whether it is an artificial plot construct that collapses on closer
inspection. The answer to these questions is that the impasse was
indeed profound. The harder one looks, the more insoluble the
dilemma becomes. *Meiri* tests the strength of the dilemma and
forces the underlying issues into the open. Neither *Forna* nor
Skamma reveals what their poets thought of the story, but the
Meiri poet speculated openly for us. His thoughtfulness is concentrated almost entirely in the dialogue between Brynhild and
Sigurd.

Sigurd begins with the weak protest that Brynhild got the man she chose, a notion which she easily confutes with a reference to Gunnarr's failure. Here the poet formulates his first question, the rationalistic question attached to all stories of sexual imposture: how could Brynhild fail to recognize her earlier suitor Sigurd? The answer is that she could sense something was wrong, but a blindness imposed by fate hindered her full realization. Reverting to Gunnarr's inadequacy, Sigurd argues that he recognizes the Gjukungs as his equals and makes reference to their exploits. Brynhild brushes these matters aside as not comparable with Sigurd's slaying of Fáfnir and crossing of the flame wall. Sigurd counters with an inevitable appeal to the status quo—Brynhild is married not to him but to Gunnarr and should, by implication, make the best of it. Brynhild's reply is as indefeasible as Sigurd's appeal is hollow: her heart did not leap to meet Gunnarr and, not loving the man she lives with, she must perforce hate him. Sigurd shies away from this logic and makes a shallow exhortation in the name of decency, maintaining that it is monstrous not to love a king such as Gunnarr. His remonstrance gets short shrift, and Brynhild confesses that she would dearly love to redden a sword in Sigurd's blood. This marks a turning point in the discussion. Thus far Sigurd has presented a series of half-hearted arguments in an attempt to reconcile Brynhild to her fate, and she has riddled them with candor and scorn. It has been an uneven contest of false representations, which do not touch the issue, and forthright confessions. Brynhild's domination of the story as a whole is attributable in no small measure to the bold strokes with which she projects her personality in this scene. Sigurd must finally capitulate before her emotional firmness and put aside his own formulaic rectitude. To her desire to see his blood he can only oppose the intimation that neither of them has long to live.

The subterfuges are now laid aside and Sigurd is prepared to talk. Brynhild blames him very simply for her joylessness. He then puts forward the first in a series of realistic solutions: she should continue to live in the possession of Gunnarr and himself. Brynhild must explain to him that a little domestic engineering will not alter the fact that she loves and hates him more than any man. Under the pressure of such frankness Sigurd yields and confesses that he too loved Brynhild, but was himself a victim of treachery. Too late, is Brynhild's answer. Sigurd returns to the possibility of a marital compromise, but Brynhild rejects any notion of a double life and lapses into a mournful revery on their broken oaths. As Brynhild seems to subside into resignation, Sigurd swells with new feeling. He now offers to abandon Gudrun and his byrnie splits from uncontainable grief.[53] But Brynhild has become an emotional void, and the conversation closes.

What has the *Meiri* poet achieved with this dialogue? Above all, he has sharpened the psychological focus. Sigurd did not deceive Brynhild because of some unrevealed flaw in his nature; they were both deceived. This is the most elegant solution to be found anywhere in the literature of the legend. There are no villains, only victims. Brynhild acquires stature because of her clarity and her refusal to toy for an instant with any form of short-range accommodation. Sigurd acquires stature because he is raised from an emotional cipher to an equal participant in the passion.[54] There are versions of the story (*Þiðreks saga* and *Nibelungenlied*) in which Sigurd's death betokens simply the incontinence of fate while Brynhild remains somehow missing in the action. In *Meiri* they are so hopelessly constricted in their plight that their deaths acquire a poetic logic.

In elaborating *Forna*, the poet of *Skamma* introduced misproportions; he skipped breathlessly over the early action, tacitly requiring the reader to refer to the older poem, then weighted the end with long-winded postmortems. The *Meiri* poet was more judicious. Instead of an allusive treatment of the early phases, he

---

[53]This passage gives us a terminus ante quem for *Meiri* if we believe it was borrowed by *Egils saga*, chap. 78. See *Egils saga Skalla-Grímssonar*, Íslenzk fornrit, 2, ed. Sigurður Nordal (Reykjavik: Hið Íslenzka Fornritafélag, 1933), p. 244. Andreas Heusler assumed imitation in *Nibelungensage und Nibelungenlied: Die Stoffgeschichte des deutschen Heldenepos*, 6th ed. (Dortmund: Ruhfus, 1965), p. 15. On the most recent dating of *Egils saga* to around 1240 rather than 1220 see Jónas Kristjánsson, "Egilssaga og konungasögur," *Sjötíu ritgerðir helgaðar Jakobi Benediktssyni*, II (Reykjavik: Stofnun Árna Magnússonar, 1977), 449–72 (esp. 470–72).

[54]I cite two of Heusler's lapidary formulations: "Sigurd, der bei den zwei Vorgängern überhaupt nur eine Rolle, keinen Charakter hat, ist ungemein weich, wehmütig, milde gezeichnet…" ("Lieder der Lücke," p. 286); "So ist nun der Konflikt auch in die Seele Sigurds getragen worden, der nach älterer Anschauung, selbst noch in der Sig. sk.—genau wie im NL—, mit der Kindesunschuld des lichten Helden durch eigenen und fremden Trug hindurch in den Tod geht" (p. 287). Jan de Vries, "Het Korte Sigurdlied," pp. 51–52, also ruminated on the curious lack of psychological profile in most poetic treatments of Sigurd.

provided a full preface by including an account of the prior betrothal and Gudrun's monitory dreams. Lest this prefatory weight
overbalance the whole, he then expanded the central section with
a sequence of dialogues. Unfortunately, we are less certain of the
conclusion (the inciting of Gunnarr, the murder council, the slaying of Sigurd, and the fate of Brynhild) because the author of
Vǫlsunga saga chose to follow the relevant narrative in *Skamma*.
The implication may be that *Meiri* was briefer than *Skamma*, but
that is not saying a great deal since *Skamma* devotes sixty-three
of seventy-one stanzas to this phase of the action. *Meiri* could
have used fifty stanzas and still have been shorter. Given the
silence of *Vǫlsunga saga*, we cannot go beyond a probable outline. Heusler ("Lieder der Lücke," p. 272) and Schneider ("Verlorene Sigurddichtung," pp. 7–8, and *Germanische Heldensage*,
I, 138) agreed that Brynhild accused Sigurd of sleeping with her
and threatened to withhold her favors unless Gunnarr avenged
the affront. They agreed further ("Lieder der Lücke," p. 272;
"Verlorene Sigurddichtung," p. 7) that Gunnarr took counsel
with his brothers and incited Gotþormr despite Hǫgni's re-
monstrances. Heusler (p. 273), Neckel (*ZDP*, 39 [1907], 327), and
Schneider (p. 8) all agreed that Gotþormr murdered Sigurd in his
bedchamber after twice retreating before his piercing gaze. All
three (Heusler, p. 274; Neckel, p. 329; Schneider, p. 8) agreed
that the poem ended with Brynhild's suicide. This last detail is the
most problematical, but Neckel's argument that Brynhild repeatedly expresses her wish to die and that the suicide is
documented in *Helreið Brynhildar* 14 and *Oddrúnargrátr* 19 is
solid. The evidence, as far as it goes, thus suggests that *Meiri* was
full on every point, but did not overload the finale in the manner
of *Skamma*.

"Brynhildar táttur"

We have dealt thus far with the reconstruction of *Meiri* on the
basis of *Vǫlsunga saga* and *Grípisspá*. A further possibility was
offered by Helmut de Boor in his dissertation *Die färöischen
Lieder des Nibelungenzyklus* (1918). De Boor analyzed the legendary forms of the Faroese Sigurd ballads and was led to believe
that *Meiri* served as a model for the ballad titled "Brynhildar

táttur."⁵⁵ The book was reviewed in a brief and unsatisfactory
way, and de Boor's view of *Meiri* has never gained currency.⁵⁶
This fate probably was a matter of timing. De Boor's book ap-
peared just as the great surge of Nibelung interest had crested and
Heusler's views had already been established. The learned com-
munity was not open to a radical revision or ready to rethink the
problem. Even at this late date de Boor deserves a hearing. We
may begin by reviewing the content of "Brynhildar táttur."

> King Buðli is introduced with his daughter Brynhild. Buðli visits
> her in her chamber and asks if anyone will arrive that day on whom
> her heart is set. Her reply is negative. Buðli asks how long she will
> reject all suitors and she responds that only Sigurd the son of Sig-
> mund would seem to her an honorable match. Buðli is surprised that
> she should love a man she has never seen, and she explains that her
> destiny was shaped by the Norns. Buðli asks why Sigurd is greater
> than other men, and Brynhild replies that he fells a hundred hea-
> thens at a time, that his harness sparkles with gold, and that he slew
> a serpent and took away twelve chests of gold. Buðli now asks how
> to attract this man, and Brynhild proposes to dwell in a hall in the
> wilderness surrounded by a flame wall that only Sigurd can cross.
> Buðli builds the hall and two dwarves conjure up the necessary
> flames.
>   One day Gunnarr and his men come to Buðli's hall and sue for
> Brynhild's hand. He urges her to accept, but she withdraws in si-
> lence to her flame-circled retreat and remains inaccessible. Sigurd
> now learns from the conversation of birds that she is asleep on a
> mountain and sets out in quest of her. Grimhild stops him on the
> way, offering him her daughter, but he declines to interrupt his
> journey. Arriving at the mountain, he clears the flames, cleaves the
> gate with his sword, and finds Brynhild asleep in bed clad in a

---

⁵⁵De Boor was obliged to consult the ballads in manuscript in the Royal Library
in Copenhagen. "Brynhildar táttur" has since been published in *Føroya kvæði
(Corpus Carminum Færoensium)*, ed. Christian Matras, I, pts. 1–2 (Copenhagen:
Munksgaard, 1951–54).
⁵⁶The reviews I am aware of are Wolfgang Golther in *Literaturblatt für germanische und romanische Philologie*, 41 (1920), 371–74; Gustav Neckel in *Anzeiger für deutsches Altertum*, 39 (1920), 19–21; Walther Heinrich Vogt,
Literarisches Zentralblatt für Deutschland, 71 (1920), 979–80. Wieselgren, p. 255,
indicated that de Boor later recanted in a review of Hempel's *Nibelungenstudien*
in *ZDP*, 52 (1927), 475, but de Boor's words do not amount to a disavowal. See
also Schneider, *Germanische Heldensage*, I, 156–57.

byrnie. He splits the byrnie with his sword and she awakens. She asks how he learned of her, and he credits the birds. She advises him to seek Buðli's approval, but he refuses. They then consummate their ordained love and Brynhild conceives Sigurd's daughter Áslaug. He swears an unspecified oath and gives her twelve rings.

Gudrun now casts a spell drawing Sigurd to Gjúki's court. Brynhild gives him a ring and warns him not to visit Grimhild, who is full of deceit. He departs and passes Buðli on the way. Buðli predicts his marriage to Gudrun and the magic potion (brewed by Gudrun in this version), adding his own warning against Grimhild. Nevertheless Sigurd is arrested on his path by Grimhild's magic. Gudrun adds her voice to the wooing, then retires to mix her potion. It has its effect and Sigurd forgets everything but the thought of marrying Gudrun. Brynhild learns what has happened and is pierced to the heart. She and Gudrun meet in the bath (an inexplicable scene in this context and made possible only by the lightning synapses of ballad style); Gudrun refuses to share Brynhild's water with an arrogance prompted by her possession of Sigurd. She asks Brynhild who gave her the ring she sees on her finger. Sigurd, is the reply. Gudrun now asks why Gunnarr should not wed her, and Brynhild echoes the tradition by stating that she will not have two kings in one hall. Gudrun reminds her that Sigurd took her virginity, and Brynhild vows that he will die for these words. She appeals to Gunnarr (we must assume that they are married despite the ballad's failure to note the fact) and threatens to withhold her favors as long as she must endure the sight of Sigurd. She withdraws to her bed, where Sigurd, hearing of her design, visits her. He meets her charge of faithlessness by protesting that his mind was turned (by the potion). At the sight of Sigurd she gives birth to their daughter Áslaug and orders her exposed on the river. She now ponders Sigurd's death. Hǫgni (Gunnarr in versions B, C, and D) comes home from the hunt and volunteers to kill the man who has caused her woe. She designates Sigurd. Hǫgni points out that they are sworn brothers, but she urges him on notwithstanding and continues to override his protests. Hǫgni finally acquiesces and asks Brynhild to devise a scheme. She advises giving the victim salted food and nothing to drink. Sigurd and Brynhild meet once more and he vows to wed her on his return from the forest. She refuses. In a second interview Buðli tries to dissuade his daughter from her intention, but without success.

The Gjukungs and Sigurd now ride out while Brynhild remains behind and weeps. Sigurd's food is salted and when his thirst compels him to drink at a fountain, Hǫgni and Gunnarr attack him from behind with swords. He manages to strike Gunnarr down with his fist before expiring. Brynhild learns of his death, swoons, and retires to bed. In the meantime Gunnarr and Hǫgni return with the corpse (Grani having refused to bear any burden other than Sigurd) and deposit it first in Brynhild's bed, then in Gudrun's. (The poet reviews Brynhild's deeds and Gudrun's vengeance for Sigurd, adding such literary parallels as the plotting of Kjartan's death by Guðrún Ósvífrsdóttir [*Laxdæla saga*] and Delilah's overcoming of Samson.) Gudrun awakens in her husband's blood and vows vengeance. Brynhild bursts with grief. Grimhild and her sons seek to console Gudrun with the prospect of marriage to Atli, but she once more vows vengeance.

The view prevalent before de Boor's book was that the Faroese ballad drew primarily on *Vǫlsunga saga*, but in the concluding portions alternated material from *Vǫlsunga saga* and *Þiðreks saga*. De Boor's analysis of the correspondences to *Þiðreks saga* showed that the source of the ballad must have been in some respects closer to German tradition than *Þiðreks saga*, that is, a source dependent on German tradition, but not *Þiðreks saga* itself. This source de Boor identified as *Meiri*, all the more readily because the Faroese ballad can be shown to contradict *Forna* and *Skamma* on a number of points, whereas it shows special affinities to *Meiri*. These affinities are summarized under ten headings (pp. 83–109):

1. Both ballad and *Meiri* are based on the prior betrothal.
2. Consequently both emphasize the importance of Grimhild and the potion of forgetfulness.
3. According to both ballad and (as de Boor surmises on the basis of *Grípisspá*) *Meiri*, the potion is administered to Sigurd immediately after his arrival with no interval of military campaigning as in *Vǫlsunga saga*.
4. Both place Brynhild under the tutelage of her father Buðli, whereas she is independent in *Forna* and under Atli's aegis in *Skamma*.
5. The ballad omits and *Meiri* deemphasizes the crossing of the flame wall.
6. The ballad's version of the quarrel diverges from *Vǫlsunga saga* and is closer to *Snorra Edda*, which Heusler tentatively derived from *Meiri*.
7. The exchange of rings differs from the account in *Vǫlsunga saga* and must therefore be closer to an anterior source.
8. Brynhild's refusal to share Gunnarr's bed is a feature shared by *Meiri* and the ballad.

9. The dialogue between Sigurd and Brynhild is in both ballad and *Meiri*. (Under 9a. de Boor argues that Áslaug is not an invention of *Vǫlsunga saga* for the purpose of harmonizing the account with the genealogy of *Ragnars saga loðbrókar*, but is taken from a prior tradition. Her appearance in the ballad therefore does not prove its dependence on *Vǫlsunga saga*.)

10. The statement that Sigurd did not suspect foul play is shared by the ballad and a passage in *Vǫlsunga saga* that Heusler ("Lieder der Lücke," p. 273) attributed to *Meiri*. This is also the last we hear of *Meiri* in *Vǫlsunga saga* and significantly enough the last correspondence between ballad and *Vǫlsunga saga*.

Having argued thus far that the first part of the ballad was based on *Meiri*, de Boor then proceeded to derive the second part of the ballad, normally explained as a combination of *Vǫlsunga saga* and *Þiðreks saga*, from the same source. He began by detaching stanza 26 in *Vǫlsunga saga* (the steeling of Gotþormr with a magic stew) from *Meiri* since it implies the murder of Sigurd in his bedchamber contrary to the forest death of German tradition. Instead, he attributes the reference to Sigurd's forest death in "Frá dauða Sigurðar" (Neckel-Kuhn, p. 201: "But the Germans say that they killed him outside in the forest.") to *Meiri*, considering it to be a German version only indirectly. De Boor then reviews the German influences in *Meiri* (pp. 119–21) and argues that there is no reason to suppose that the conclusion of the poem did not adhere to the German account of Sigurd's forest murder.

A number of the points made by de Boor are problematical. I reduce them to seven fundamentals, stating in each case de Boor's contention and my own objections.

1. "Brynhildar táttur" and *Meiri* are based on the prior betrothal and therefore emphasize Grimhild's role and the potion of forgetfulness. Objection: The ballad may just as well have taken these features from *Vǫlsunga saga* as from *Meiri*.

2. In "Brynhildar táttur" and *Meiri* the potion of forgetfulness is administered to Sigurd immediately after his arrival at Gjúki's court; there is no interlude of military campaigning as in *Vǫlsunga saga*. Objection: There is no basis for supposing that the military campaigning is an "arbitrary expansion" (p. 84) in *Vǫlsunga saga*. It corresponds to the campaign against the sons of Gandálfr in *Norna-Gests þáttr*, Sigurd's encounter with Dietrich and his retainers in *Þiðreks saga*, and the Dano-Saxon war in the *Nibelungenlied*. It is therefore likely to be one of the German influences that entered Norse tradition

through *Meiri*. If so, *Meiri* and "Brynhildar táttur" differ in this respect.

3. "Brynhildar táttur" and *Meiri* place Brynhild under the tutelage of her father Buðli, whereas she is independent in *Forna* and dependent on her brother Atli in *Skamma*. Objection: If my reconstruction of *Forna* is correct, it included Buðli in an acquiescent role. "Brynhildar táttur" is therefore no closer to *Meiri* than to *Forna*, rather the contrary, since the Buðli of our ballad is a thoroughly acquiescent figure.

4. "Brynhildar táttur" omits and *Meiri* deemphasizes the crossing of the flame wall in the wooing of Brynhild. Objection: *Vǫlsunga saga* 77.6–9 makes it certain that *Meiri* did include the crossing of the flame wall. The ballad therefore deviates from *Meiri*.

5. The quarrel of the queens in "Brynhildar táttur" is closer to *Meiri* (as mediated by *Snorra Edda*) than to *Forna* (as mediated by *Vǫlsunga saga*). Objection: De Boor misread *Snorra Edda* to mean that Gudrun initiates the quarrel as in the ballad (p. 87: "Guðrún watet wie in SE. weiter in den Strom hinaus"—"Gudrun wades out into the river as in *Snorra Edda*"). In fact, *Snorra Edda* says that Brynhild started the quarrel by wading farther out (ed. Finnur Jónsson, p. 130: "Then Brynhild waded out into the river from the shore"). Snorri thus agrees with *Vǫlsunga saga* (and presumably *Forna*). Furthermore, if my reconstruction of *Meiri* is correct, it contained no river quarrel, only the hall quarrel.

6. Brynhild's refusal in "Brynhildar táttur" to share Gunnarr's bed until Sigurd is slain corresponds to the same refusal in *Meiri*. Objection: This item in the ballad may just as well have been taken from *Vǫlsunga saga* as from *Meiri*.

7. Only *Meiri* and "Brynhildar táttur" include the dialogue between Brynhild and Sigurd. Objection: This item too may just as well have been taken from *Vǫlsunga saga* as from *Meiri*.

Clearly no single exhibit in de Boor's evidence is valid beyond doubt, that is, there is no case in which "Brynhildar táttur" and *Meiri* agree to the exclusion of all other sources. The derivation of the ballad from *Meiri* has no advantages over a derivation from *Vǫlsunga saga*. When, therefore, de Boor takes the next step and proposes that the end of *Meiri* can be deduced from "Brynhildar táttur" because the beginning of the ballad can be so deduced, the claim has not been proven and the analogy has no basis. The latter part of the argument must stand on its own and not rest on unsubstantiated appeals to cumulative evidence.

The derivation of *Meiri*'s conclusion from the ballad is difficult because it requires us to assume that the *Meiri* poet took over the German variant of Sigurd's death in the forest instead of the Norse variant, which located the murder in his bedchamber. Since Gotþormr is specifically associated with this latter version and is incited to carry out the murder in a stanza (*Vǫlsunga saga* 26) normally assigned to *Meiri* because it manifestly belongs to neither *Forna* nor *Skamma,* de Boor is obliged to rid himself of this evidence that *Meiri* placed the murder in the bedchamber. He does so by detaching stanza 26 from *Meiri* and considering it a separate skaldic stanza. This is a far-fetched proposal. The only thing that is skaldic about the stanza is one kenning, and no skaldic stanzas are quoted elsewhere in *Vǫlsunga saga.* De Boor must also assume that the murder scene in *Vǫlsunga saga,* with Gotþormr's repeated shrinking before Sigurd's piercing gaze, derives not from *Meiri,* but is rather an elaborated version of *Forna.* Independent elaborations in *Vǫlsunga saga* are, however, not the rule and should not be invoked to salvage special arguments. Finally, if it were true that both *Forna* and *Meiri* had the forest death, it would be peculiar that the author of *Vǫlsunga saga* opted for the minority view in *Skamma.*

The demonstrable German influences in *Meiri* make the hypothesis of a German conclusion theoretically possible, but all immediate evidence in *Vǫlsunga saga* points in the opposite direction. We must therefore conclude that de Boor's reconstruction of Sigurd's death in *Meiri* is not persuasive and fits the available evidence less well than Heusler's. A rejection of de Boor's hypothesis does not of course alter the general probability that *Meiri* was composed in such a way as to integrate a number of features from the competing German version of the story. The prior betrothal (suppressed but detectable in *Þiðreks saga* and the *Nibelungenlied*), the penetration into Brynhild's stronghold (*Þiðreks saga,* chap. 168), the falcon dream (*Nibelungenlied*), Sigurd's military campaign with the Gjukungs (*Nibelungenlied* and by implication *Þiðreks saga*), the double wedding (*Nibelungenlied*), and the hall quarrel (*Þiðreks saga*) all look like concessions to German tradition. In this respect *Meiri* is analogous to *Atlamál,* which, as I have argued elsewhere, consciously recast *Atlakviða* in order to bring it into line with the story as it was told in Germany.[57] Both poems appear to belong to a late Eddic school bent on revising the indigenous lays in accord with foreign models by expansion and harmonization. The poet of *Atlamál* fell artistically short of the example established in *Atlakviða*, but the poet of *Meiri* invested *Forna* with new psychological depths.

Summary

The reconstruction of *Meiri* is an arduous exercise. In order to clarify the outline and the sources of information, I therefore append a summary in tabular form with references to the texts that underlie the reconstruction.

Sigurd goes hunting, comes to Brynhild's tower, enters, and exchanges oaths with her.	*Grípisspá* 27–31 *Vǫlsunga saga* 58.8–60.19 *Oddrúnargrátr* 18 *Þiðreks saga* I.315.9–317.10
Gudrun's hawk and stag dreams, the latter interpreted by Brynhild	*Vǫlsunga saga* 61.6–63.25 *Nibelungenlied* 13–14
Sigurd comes to Gjúki's court.	*Vǫlsunga saga* 64.3–19
Sigurd swears blood brotherhood with the Gjukungs.	*Grípisspá* 37 *Vǫlsunga saga* 65.27–28
Sigurd performs great deeds with his blood brothers.	*Vǫlsunga saga* 64.19–22, 65.32–66.2, 75.22–23 *Norna-Gests þáttr* chap. 7 *Nibelungenlied* Adventure 4
Grimhild administers the potion of forgetfulness.	*Grípisspá* 31–33, 35.1–2, 45.1–2 (all by implication) *Vǫlsunga saga* 65.2–8
Grimhild proposes the wooing of Brynhild.	*Grípisspá* 35 *Vǫlsunga saga* 66.4–9
Grimhild instructs Sigurd and Gunnarr to exchange shapes.	*Grípisspá* 37–39 *Vǫlsunga saga* 67.1–2, 75.17–20
Sigurd woos Brynhild in Gunnarr's shape after crossing the flame wall.	*Grípisspá* 36, 39 *Vǫlsunga saga* 67.30–68.18 (interwoven with *Forna*), 72.25–26, 77.6–9

[57]"Did the Poet of *Atlamál* Know *Atlakviða?*" (forthcoming).

Sigurd spends three nights with Brynhild, his sword separating them.	*Grípisspá* 41 *Vǫlsunga saga* 68.18–24
Return to Gjúki's court	*Vǫlsunga saga* 69.4–9
Double wedding	*Grípisspá* 43 *Nibelungenlied* Adventure 10
Sigurd remembers all his oaths but says nothing.	*Grípisspá* 45 *Vǫlsunga saga* 69.9–11
Gudrun inquires into Brynhild's grief.	*Grípisspá* 45.5–6 *Vǫlsunga saga* 70.19–23 *Nibelungenlied* 618–24
The queens quarrel in the hall.	*Vǫlsunga saga* 70.19–72.13 *Þiðreks saga* II.259.10–261.18
Gunnarr interviews Brynhild (she reviews the circumstances of her marriage and attacks Grimhild).	*Vǫlsunga saga* 72.18–73.32
Discussion of Brynhild's state	*Vǫlsunga saga* 74.5–75.5
Sigurd interviews Brynhild (he urges Gunnarr on her, but finally confesses his love).	*Vǫlsunga saga* 75.5–77.13
Brynhild incites Gunnarr by accusing Sigurd of sleeping with her and threatening to withhold her favors.	*Grípisspá* 47, 50.1–2 *Vǫlsunga saga* 77.28–78.5, 79.14–16
The murder council (Hǫgni's reluctance)	*Grípisspá* 51.3–4 *Vǫlsunga saga* 78.20–79.13, 79.16–21
The brothers concoct a wolf stew to steel Gotþormr for the task.	*Vǫlsunga saga* 79.21–80.5
Gotþormr murders Sigurd in his bed.	*Vǫlsunga saga* 80.9–17
Brynhild's suicide	*Vǫlsunga saga* 85.6–10 *Helreið Brynhildar* 14 *Oddrúnargrátr* 19

Comparison of the Sigurd Poems

The issues in the preceding discussion are sufficiently complex to warrant a review of the argument up to this point. Our material comprises three Sigurd poems, the partially extant *Sigurðarkviða in forna,* the fully preserved *Sigurðarkviða in skamma,* and the lost *Sigurðarkviða in meiri,* which must be reconstructed from the prose of *Vǫlsunga saga* with the aid of *Grípisspá* and indications in other sources. The evidence suggests that *Forna* was the oldest and briefest of these pieces and was known to the poets of *Skamma* and *Meiri*. *Skamma* was second in line. It hurried over the portions of the tale covered by *Forna* and concentrated on the elegiac moments following Sigurd's death. *Meiri* was the latest and longest of the three. On some points it harmonizes *Forna* and *Skamma*, but it also adjusts the story to include a number of elements from the German tradition of Siegfried. In particular it emphasizes Sigurd's prior betrothal to Brynhild and her fatal jealousy, a feature only adumbrated in *Forna* and at most latent in *Skamma*.[58]

Forna begins with Sigurd's arrival at the court of the Gjukungs and gives no account of his youthful adventures or his first encounter with Brynhild. He marries Gudrun, then seconds Gunnarr in his wooing of Brynhild, who has vowed to have only the most distinguished man. When Sigurd crosses the flame barrier in Gunnarr's stead and goes through the motions of wedding her, he therefore participates in her deception and contravenes her will. The deception is subsequently revealed in the quarrel of the queens and Brynhild avenges herself by claiming that Sigurd slept with her and must die. The murder is carried out by the three brothers Gunnarr, Hǫgni, and Gotþormr in the forest. Brynhild laments what she herself demanded, either because the man she was bound by oath to possess is now dead or because the oath was understood to imply an erotic attachment. She reproaches the brothers for breaking the bonds of blood brotherhood and reveals that Sigurd had placed a sword between them during the proxy nuptials.

The strength of this poem lies in the compressed passion intimated by the poet but not fully divulged. Sigurd cheats Brynhild of her oath and betrays the secret to Gudrun. Gudrun, in a moment of competitive pride, flings the revelation in Brynhild's face. Brynhild goes deathly pale and silent, then inflames Gunnarr with the charge that the destroyer of her oath, Sigurd, also broke his own oath to Gunnarr. Gunnarr retaliates blindly by in turn break-

---

[58]The clearest picture of the erotic evolution in the three poems is given by Gustav Neckel, "Aus der nordischen Nibelungendichtung," *GRM*, 1 (1909), 349–56.

ing his oath of blood brotherhood and killing Sigurd.[59] The poem
concludes with Brynhild's bursting revelation of her own deprav-
ity and the depth of her misery. If there is an objective problem, it
is the conflict between contracts and emotions. Brynhild's overriding oath to herself severs a web of personal bonds and tears the
social fabric painstakingly woven from a multiplicity of commitments. Her strength, apparent in her unnegotiable insistence on
the best man, becomes the source of her weakness. Her needs
prescribe his death and her own undoing. *Forna* may be viewed
as a comment on the limitations of the oath when personal re-
quirements impose more immediate demands. In this version
Sigurd counts for very little. The poem does not turn on his commitment to Brynhild or the extent of the deception he practices on
her. It turns rather on Brynhild's commitments to herself and her
failure to satisfy them. The poet's power lies in his ability to make
us feel the magnitude of her failure.

Skamma is not so conceptually unified. Much of Brynhild's
resonance and some scenes in which she is emotionally on trial
are omitted—notably the proxy nuptials and the quarrel of the
queens. *Skamma* therefore fails to refocus some important
moments in her passion and does not recapture the vivid sequence of dramatic crests which characterizes *Forna*. Instead,
the poet uses the retrospection of the Eddic elegies and projects
Brynhild largely in terms of her parting words. Since the retrospection is partial, the emotional background remains unclear.
Brynhild has in some way promised herself to Sigurd (stanza 39),
but the exact nature of the commitment is not explained. She is
then tricked by Sigurd, since she refers to the sword that separated them (stanza 68), but this motif is clouded by her report that
she was forced to accept Gunnarr on pain of having her property
confiscated by her brother Atli. Atli is therefore as much impli-
cated in her misfortune as Sigurd, who, paradoxically, must have
won her for Gunnarr only after Atli had forced the issue. Nor is
there any reference to Brynhild's vow to have only the greatest of
men. The reasons which compel her to plot Sigurd's death con-

[59]Heusler, "Die Lieder der Lücke," p. 277: "Die Eide sind das Beherrschende,
nicht die Sympathien." On the theme of broken oaths in *Forna* see Mohr in
Dichtung und Volkstum, pp. 105–6, and Hans Kuhn, p. 192; rpt. *Kleine Schriften*,
II, 81.

sequently are obscure; only the lines ''I loved one and not several'' (stanza 40.1–2) suggest her passionate attachment and disappointment. The lines of Brynhild's personality that are so clear in *Forna* are thus effaced.

What the *Skamma* poet gives us in return for the blurring of Brynhild are a rationalistic rewriting on the one hand and more overt theatricality on the other. It is rational, for example, that the oaths of blood brotherhood are not ignored in the heat of revenge, as they are in *Forna*. Instead, the poet hits on a scheme to salvage the oaths by shifting the murder to the unsworn brother Gotþormr. The resulting preservation of oaths is ingenious, but it cancels the pattern of broken oaths in *Forna*, in which Gunnarr appropriately breaks his oath in retaliation for the breach of which Sigurd stands accused. The larger social logic of broken oaths that underlies the symmetry of *Forna* is discarded in *Skamma*.

On the theatrical side, the murder appears in a garish new light. It is no longer acted out behind the scene as in *Forna*. Sigurd is stabbed in his bed and Gudrun awakens in her husband's gore. The effect of the older version was to maintain Brynhild in sole possession of the limelight. *Skamma* gives Gudrun and Sigurd a larger share of center stage and diffuses the exclusive focus on Brynhild. There is now room for Sigurd's dying words to his wife and her expression of grief (stanzas 25–29), matters that had no relevance in *Forna*. When Brynhild returns to the spotlight, her parting words also raise questions of relevance. The rehearsal of her marriage is curiously factual compared to the stricken outbursts of *Forna*, and the following step-by-step forecast of what lies ahead for her survivors (stanzas 53–64), though it builds on her monitory dream of Gunnarr's death in *Brot* 16, also seems otiose in such detail. The dream in *Brot* casts a dark shadow over the future at the darkest moment of the poem, thereby intensifying the mood. The forecast in *Skamma*, on the other hand, sheds a far too explicit light over coming events and is an oddly impassive epilogue to a stirring catastrophe. The final theatrical stroke is Brynhild's Didoesque suicide with its public panoply. The Brynhild of *Forna* subsided into isolated grief; the Brynhild of *Skamma* dies with fanfare and grand display that obscure our view of her private sorrow. Compared to *Forna*, *Skamma* is a secondary rumination on the tragedy of Brynhild, without the force or unity of the original.

If *Forna* is a study of Brynhild's personality and *Skamma* a loose reflection on her fate, *Meiri* is a firmly restrung drama of jealousy.[60] The story is no longer of Brynhild's thwarted will, but of her blighted love and Sigurd's faithlessness. Whatever suggestions of emotional attraction were to be found in *Forna* and *Skamma* are resolutely filled in. The new unifying idea is that Brynhild was first betrothed to Sigurd and was therefore cheated of her sexual destiny. The prior betrothal dominates the structure of the poem. A preface is added to visualize the moment at which it occurs in Brynhild's lonely tower. Her later resentment is predicated not on a feeling that she was tricked into being false to herself, but on the knowledge that she lost the man she wanted. The long central dialogues probe the loss. They go beyond the question of deception to analyze the reasons why she cannot after all have Sigurd, either alone or in tandem with Gunnarr. In the course of the debate her pride becomes eroticized and she finally seeks revenge not to reassert her power and personality, but to slake her jealousy. The sexual nature of her motivation emerges from her threat not to share Gunnarr's bed until Sigurd is dead.

Sigurd too changes personality. In *Forna* he was hardly more than an instrument of Brynhild's downfall. In *Skamma* his role is confined to an extraneous dying conversation with his wife Gudrun; he never addresses a word to Brynhild. In *Meiri* he is admitted to the drama. His melancholy on first seeing Brynhild and his stubborn wooing make it clear that strong feelings are at stake. They surface again in his last dialogue with Brynhild when he declares that he loved her more than himself and was no less deceived than she. The gesture to underscore his passion is the splitting of his byrnie. He becomes an equal partner in the emotional crisis. At the same time, he has contracted a surplus of guilt. He does not function merely as Gunnarr's thoughtless lieutenant in the wooing of Brynhild and as an accomplice in her deception. He loves and is faithless. To account for this paradox

---

[60]Heusler, "Lieder der Lücke," p. 288: "In dem Dichter der Sig. sk. haben wir den elegischen, in dem der Sig. m. den dramatischen Psychologen der Werbungssage."

the poet has recourse to Grimhild and her magic potion. The invention of a potion to induce a guiltless hero may strike us as an artificial device. A guilty hero is at least as interesting as a guilt-less one, and a story of love and abandonment does nothing to strain credulity. The modern reader may wish to consider the story without Grimhild's brew, just as he might prefer to read the story of Tristan and Isolde without resort to the magic potion that excuses the betrayal of Mark. What is significant in *Meiri* is the conversion of Sigurd from a dull paradigm of strength to a feeling hero. The tale of Brynhild thus becomes a two-sided story. The risk involved in this alteration lies in the compromising of Brynhild's central position, but Sigurd's inclusion in a reciprocal relationship only sharpens our perception of Brynhild's plight. The more compelling are the reasons for her fulfillment, the keener is her loss. Beyond this, the poet goes to some lengths to maintain Brynhild's domination. The long dialogues that make up the bulk of what is preserved for us in *Vǫlsunga saga* are Brynhild's dialogues. She is the constant factor, while the remain-ing characters circle nervously around her in vain efforts at con-solation. Sigurd is only the last and most important in a series of would-be exorcists.

The striking achievement of this our latest Brynhild poet was to create from heroic tradition a full-fledged love story. The *Meiri* poet participates in the transition from epic to romance and is the only Norse poet to interpret native narrative in such a way.[61] Elsewhere romance in Iceland sprang from foreign seed. *Meiri* is thus comparable with the contemporary German *Nibelungenlied,* which also transformed native tradition in romance terms. But the Icelander made a more challenging choice of heroine. Instead of weaving his romance from the emotional wisps of Gudrun, as the *Nibelungenlied* poet did, he capitalized on Brynhild's demon-strated capacity for passion and recolored her personality to

---

[61]There are of course affinities to the school of saga writing represented by *Bjarnar saga hítdælakappa, Laxdæla saga, Kormáks saga,* and *Gunnlaugs saga.* The romantic strains in these sagas are often considered to be traceable to foreign influences, but the role of *Meiri* may be no less important. Cf. Paul Schach, "Some Observations on the Influence of *Tristrams saga ok Ísöndar* on Old Icelandic Literature" in *Old Norse Literature and Mythology: A Symposium,* ed. Edgar C. Polomé (Austin: University of Texas Press, 1969), pp. 105 and 125–26.

blend with the new erotic fashions. The Brynhild of *Meiri* is surely the most successful composite of uncompromising action in the heroic mold with the erotic melancholy of later romance.

But lest a poem that exists only by the grace of surmise appear in all too hypnotic a light, it should be pointed out that there are flaws in the composition as well as remarkable successes. These are to be explained for the most part as products of narrative acquisitiveness, the tendency of medieval poets to include everything from earlier versions and to reconcile disparate accounts rather than to sacrifice a known variant. In this case the poet was building not only on the sinewy outlines of *Forna,* but also on the looser design of *Skamma,* which he was reluctant to ignore. The most obvious concession to *Skamma* is the family meddling in Brynhild's marriage. But, whereas the *Skamma* poet leaves it unclear how the family compulsion relates to Sigurd's deception of Brynhild by impersonation, the *Meiri* poet harmonizes these two conflicting motifs with some degree of plausibility. Brynhild negotiates a compromise with her father which makes her choice of suitor contingent on his crossing the flame wall. This solution allows for the family infringement reported in *Skamma* while leaving reasonable latitude for the impersonation to which Brynhild falls victim. What it does not solve is the dramatic irrelevance of Buðli's interference.

A second obvious concession to *Skamma* is the web of prophecy that subtends *Meiri.* To be sure, the prophetic tones are as old as *Forna;* both the raven in the forest (*Brot* 5) and Brynhild's dream (*Brot* 16) anticipate the Burgundian extinction at the hands of Atli. But only *Skamma* spins out the prophetic threads. Sigurd's dying words look into the fate of his son and Brynhild previews in detail the sequel to her death. *Meiri* borrows Brynhild's sybilline gifts from this latter passage. She foresees Sigurd's marriage to Gudrun already in their first interview and her foresight is exploited in detail when she interprets Gudrun's dream. By and large, however, the poet avoids the pitfall of disturbing dramatic moments with a prosaic account of coming events in the style of *Skamma.* Most of Brynhild's prophetic utterances are brief, enough to create the requisite atmosphere of doom without becoming digressive.

A third possible concession to *Skamma* is the matter of ornamental display. In *Skamma* 39 Brynhild commits herself to Sigurd "who sat with gold on Grani's back." In *Meiri* the picture is detailed. When Sigurd arrives at Heimir's residence, we are told (*Vǫlsunga saga* 57.17–21): "Four men unloaded the gold from his horse, the fifth took charge of his horse. There you could see many rare and excellent treasures; they amused themselves by looking at the byrnies and helmets and great rings and a wondrously great golden goblet and all manner of arms." When he arrives at Gjúki's hall, one of the king's men comments (*Vǫlsunga saga* 64.6–9): "I think one of the gods is riding here; this man is all dressed in gold; his horse is much larger than other horses and his arms are fair beyond measure." These gold-laden passages from *Meiri* are no doubt responsible for suggesting to the author of *Vǫlsunga saga* that he interpolate an even more ornate description of Sigurd's appearance from *Þiðreks saga* (*Vǫlsunga saga*, chap. 23 [22]). The most egregious glitter belongs to the dream preface: Gudrun arrives at Brynhild's hall with golden wagons while Brynhild's hall itself is trimmed with gold and silver (*Vǫlsunga saga* 61.26–62.4). This opulence may originate in the mention of Brynhild's gold treasures in *Skamma* 47 and 49.

But despite the prophetic and ornamental overlay in *Meiri*, there is a clearly shaped idea that informs the whole. Sigurd belongs to Brynhild and betrays her. In bitterness of heart she renounces Gunnarr's bed until Sigurd has been slain in the bed of her rival. The drama of individual claims has become a sexual drama and the symmetry of oaths in *Forna* has given way to a symmetry of beds. Whether the drama burns itself out on the double pyre of *Skamma* 66–67—the facsimile of the single bed (68.6: "beð einn") they occupied but failed to share in their first meeting—is not certain, but only in *Meiri* is such a conclusion fully motivated. It is this belated union that places Sigurd and Brynhild in the tradition of Tristan's and Isolde's honeysuckle embrace and the common tomb of Romeo and Juliet.[62]

[62]Cf. Virginia C. Gildersleeve, "Brynhild in Legend and Literature," *MP*, 6 (1909), 343.

CHAPTER 2

Sigurd's Youth

We have begun with an analysis of the three so-called Sigurd poems in the *Edda*, but what becomes especially clear from this survey is that the poems are about Brynhild, not Sigurd. The paradox has not gone unnoticed. Guðbrandur Vigfússon designated the relevant group of Eddic poems as the "Brunhild-Lays" or "Brunhild Group" and wrote of *Skamma:* "The first in order and importance of the Brunhild Group is the *Long Lay of Brunhild,* headed 'Kvida Sigurdar' in R simply from the first line having Sigurd's name in it; it is *par excellence* the *Brunhild Lay.*"[1] Heusler regularly referred to the story as the *Brünhildsage.* K. C. King's advocacy was more explicit: "I have for years been of the opinion that we should not call this story a Siegfried story at all. Heusler saw the point when he called the reconstructed original lay the *Brünhildlied,* but still scholars persist in talking as if Siegfried were the principal character." And again: "The hero of the *Eckenlied* is not Ecke but Dietrich, and so we may keep the title 'Siegfriedlied' if we like, but we must

---

[1]*Corpus Poeticum Boreale,* ed. Gudbrand Vigfusson and F. York Powell, I (Oxford: Clarendon, 1883), 293. The objection is echoed by Chr. Aug. Mayer, "Brünhilde: Eine Untersuchung zur deutschen Heldensage," *ZVL,* 16 (1905), 132; Virginia C. Gildersleeve, "Brynhild in Legend and Literature," *MP,* 6 (1909), 347; Friedrich Panzer, *Studien zur germanischen Sagengeschichte,* II: *Sigfrid* (Munich: Beck, 1912), 216; Finnur Jónsson, "Sagnformen i heltedigtene i Codex Regius," *Aarbøger for nordisk oldkyndighed og historie* (1921), p. 65; Wilhelm Lehmgrübner, *Die Erweckung der Walküre,* Hermaea 32 (Halle: Niemeyer, 1936), p. 20; and Jan de Vries, "Het Korte Sigurdlied," *Mededeelingen der Koninklijke Nederlandsche Akademie van Wetenschappen,* Afd. Letterkunde. N.R., 2 (1939), no. 11, 49, and *Altnordische Literaturgeschichte,* II (Berlin: de Gruyter, 1942), 155; 2d ed., II, 148.

remember that Siegfried is not the hero: Brünhild is the heroine."[2]

Why then do we not refer more regularly to the "Brynhild legend"? Part of the answer lies in the titles assigned to the pertinent poems by Codex Regius. Another part lies in the dwindling of Brynhild's role in the later German sources (*Þiðreks saga* and *Nibelungenlied*) and the inappropriateness of classifying these texts as Brynhild stories. A further explanation may be that Sigurd stands alone in a series of adventures which precede his betrothal to Brynhild and his marriage to Gudrun. If the cluster of stories is considered together, Sigurd has a palpably larger role. There is an enigma in this situation. If Sigurd was the dominant figure in the cycle, why was he displaced by Brynhild in the central poems? Or conversely, if Brynhild was originally the dominant figure, why was Sigurd later credited with a series of youthful exploits and not Brynhild?

As a preamble to the answer, we may review briefly the fullest and most skillfully argued reconstruction of the preliterary development published by the Dutch scholar Léon Polak.[3] As the title of his book suggests, Polak placed Sigurd at the center. He theorized that at the outset there was a Legend A according to which Sigurd acquired the Nibelung treasure by killing a dragon. To this Legend A was added a Legend B, according to which the Burgundian brothers Gunnarr and Hǫgni coveted Sigurd's treasure and slew him in order to win possession of it. At the same time, a separate legend existed about the Burgundians which Polak designated C. In the earliest form of this legend (C I) the Burgundians possessed a treasure, which Atli coveted and attempted to win by deceitfully arranging for their murder. Legend C I developed into Legend C II when this Burgundian treasure was identified with Sigurd's Nibelung treasure. Then Legend C II developed into C III when the Burgundians, now in possession of the Nibelung treasure, became known as the Nibelungs (the stage represented by the Eddic poem *Atlakviða*). At this point Legend B was prefixed to Legend C III and the story

[2] K. C. King, *Das Lied vom Hürnen Seyfrid* (Manchester: Manchester University Press, 1958), pp. 44–45.

[3] Léon Polak, *Untersuchungen über die Sigfridsagen,* Diss. Berlin, 1910 (Berlin: Universitäts-Buchdruckerei, 1910).

of Sigurd's murder was joined with the story of how Atli destroyed the Burgundians. The final stage was the amalgamation of Legend A with the remainder (B and C III) so that Sigurd's acquisition of the treasure, his murder by the Burgundian brothers, and the murder of the Burgundians by Atli became a single narrative sequence.

One must not disparage the stout-hearted precision of Polak's results. His argument is a model of clarity and logic. Nonetheless, an obvious illusion exists in the development of the legend as he pictured it; he allowed large scope for the lifeless treasure and none whatever for the passionate and dominating figure of Brynhild. We must suppose that she was grafted onto the story of covetousness at some stage, but how a personality of such magnitude grew from the roots of avarice is impossible to imagine. Since she is the core of the three most impressive poems of the cycle, she must be considered also the substance of the legend. She must have dominated from the outset, and Sigurd must always have been in her shadow. Rather than trying to imagine Brynhild as a late accretion to the Sigurd legend, we may more easily imagine that Sigurd's adventures were expanded because of a flattering association with such a powerful heroine. (It is of course possible that Brynhild's betrothed was originally someone else ultimately displaced by Sigurd because of the latter's importance in other stories.) But why was the lesser figure, Sigurd, celebrated in a series of pendant stories while the greater figure, Brynhild, remained fixed in her original context? The answer seems to lie in social and literary psychology. In medieval literature (with the exception of *Hervarar saga*) women are not assigned youthful exploits, while the development of semiindependent *enfances* for male heroes is a regular feature. The *Nibelungenlied* illustrates the point: Siegfried's youth would not be complete without some reference to military and erotic adventures, whereas Kriemhilt's youthful pursuits are limited to a conversation with her mother. It is therefore easy to understand how Sigurd's role might be expanded while Brynhild's remained static despite the intriguing references to the exploits of her shield-maiden years.

The growth of Sigurd stories prefatory to his meeting with Brynhild is abundant. They include the following episodes:

1. The story of his father Sigmund
2. The circumstances of his birth and fostering
3. His interview with his uncle Grípir
4. His vengeance for his father
5. His slaying of the dragon
6. His interview with the warrior maiden Sigrdrífa

Rather than proceeding chronologically, thus placing the reader at six removes from the action of the three "Sigurd" poems discussed above, I propose to go backward, treating one episode at a time.

The interview with Sigrdrífa is included in the Eddic poem *Sigrdrífumál,* the first part of which (through the first long line of stanza 29) is preserved in Codex Regius and the end of which is lost in the lacuna. The prose preface in Regius sets the scene in the following terms:

> Sigurd rode up to Hindarfjall and was heading south to Frankland. On the mountain he saw a great light, as if a fire were burning, and the gleam reached the heavens. And when he approached, he found a circle of shields and a banner flying above. Sigurd entered the shield circle and saw a person lying there asleep fully armed. First he took the helmet off. Then he saw that it was a woman. The byrnie was as tight as if it had grown to the skin. Then he split the byrnie from the neck downward with Gramr, and similarly both sleeves. Then he took the byrnie off her. She awakened, sat up, saw Sigurd...

A conversation follows in which Sigurd names himself and the woman identifies herself as the valkyrie Sigrdrífa. She explains that in a battle between two kings, Hjálm-Gunnarr and Agnarr, she had killed Odin's favorite (Hjálm-Gunnarr). In retaliation he stuck her with a "sleep thorn," decreeing that she should never be victorious in battle again and condemning her to a wedded life. But she swore in response never to wed a man who knew fear. Sigurd asks her to instruct him in wisdom and there follows a long sequence of runic charms (stanzas 5–19) and general gnomic precepts (stanzas 22–29.1).

This account in Regius is covered by chapters 21 (20) and 22 (21) in *Vǫlsunga saga.* The opening exchange is fuller in the saga than in Regius and reveals that the woman recognizes her visitor

as Sigurd the slayer of Fáfnir. But the most important deviation
from Regius is that the saga identifies the woman as Brynhild. In
this new guise she rehearses stanzas 5–6, 10, 12, 7–9, 11, 13,
15–20 of *Sigrdrífumál* in that order. Chapter 22 in the saga gives a
prose paraphrase of some further gnomes and concludes with a
betrothal between Brynhild and Sigurd: "Sigurd said: 'There is
no one wiser than you and I swear that I will marry you and you
suit my nature.' She replies: 'You would be my first choice even
if I could choose among all men.' And they settled this with oaths
between them." The central issue is whether *Vǫlsunga saga*'s
identification of Sigrdrífa as Brynhild is correct. But before turning to this question, we must resolve a second problem. Did the
meeting with Sigrdrífa conclude with a betrothal? Heusler judged
that the betrothal must already have been present in the source of
Vǫlsunga saga because the saga author had no reason to invent it.
Since it constituted an unnecessary (and awkward) duplication of
the prior betrothal to Brynhild in her tower, it must have been
imposed on the saga author by his source. He would not have
burdened himself with a meaningless duplication voluntarily.[4]

Heusler assumed that *Sigrdrífumál* contains the detritus of an
old narrative poem which told the story of Sigurd's betrothal to
Sigrdrífa and which he called the "Erweckungslied."[5] The remnants of the "Erweckungslied" (*Sigrdrífumál* 20–21, 37.4–6) do
not reveal the identity of the warrior maiden. *Grípisspá* (15 and
27) clearly distinguishes between the warrior maiden and
Brynhild. The prose inserts attached to *Sigrdrífumál* in Regius
make the same distinction. Snorri's version in "Skáldskaparmál"
states that her name was Hildr, also called Brynhildr, indicating
some uncertainty about the identification.[6] *Vǫlsunga saga* 48.16

---

[4]Heusler, "Die Lieder der Lücke im Codex Regius der Edda," *Kleine Schriften*, II, ed. Stefan Sonderegger (Berlin: de Gruyter, 1969), 225. See also B. Symons, "Untersuchungen ueber die sogenannte Völsunga saga," *BGDSL*, 3
(1876), 256. R. C. Boer, "Sigrdrifumál und Helreið," *ZDP*, 35 (1903), 302–3, and
Lehmgrübner, pp. 11–12, concurred with Heusler, but Polak, p. 93, Henrik Us-
sing, *Om det indbyrdes forhold mellem heltekvadene i ældre Edda* (Copenhagen:
Gad, 1910), and Per Wieselgren, *Quellenstudien zur Vǫlsungasaga* (Tartu: K.
Mattiesens Buchdruckerei, 1935), pp. 249–50, disagreed. Finnur Jónsson,
"Sagnformen," p. 51, believed that the betrothal was added by the author of
Vǫlsunga saga in imitation of the Helgi legend.

[5]Heusler, "Lieder der Lücke," p. 228. Cf. Boer, pp. 291–302.

[6]*Edda Snorra Sturlusonar*, ed. Finnur Jónsson (Copenhagen: Gyldendal, 1931),
p. 130.13–14.

and *Norna-Gests þáttr,* Chapter 6, make the identification with certainty. In the course of a complex argument Heusler made what appears to me the decisive point that this confusion in the sources could not have arisen had it been clear from the outset that Sigrdrífa was identical with Brynhild.[7] On the other hand, it would be comprehensible, given Sigrdrífa's mysterious status, if this shadowy figure were secondarily identified with Brynhild. The identification would have been facilitated by the description of both Sigrdrífa and Brynhild as warrior maidens and wise women (Sigrdrífa in runic and gnomic lore and Brynhild in prophecy). There was an additional similarity between their remote situations on mountains (Sigrdrífa on Hindarfjall in the prose before *Sigrdrífumál* and Brynhild in her tower in *Vǫlsunga saga* 61.26–27, 77.1–3), one deep in her magic sleep and the other inaccessible in her enchanted flame wall.[8]

The betrothals to Sigrdrífa and Brynhild appear then to be originally independent episodes. The question is why Sigurd was credited with so many broken engagements. Youthful amours seem to have been a standard feature of his legend. Even the *Nibelungenlied* (26.3–4) retains the motif:

> er begunde mit sinnen   werben sœniu wîp:
> die trûten wol mit êren   des küenen Sivrides lîp.

(He began with prudence to woo beautiful women; bold Siegfried was indeed a worthy object of their affections.)

---

[7]Heusler, "Lieder der Lücke," p. 238. Boer, p. 323, believed that there originally was no betrothal between Sigurd and Brynhild, but that there was also no betrothal between Sigurd and the valkyrie Sigrdrífa, only a love encounter. See also Jónsson, "Sagnformen," p. 51. For a review of the older opinions on the identity of Sigrdrífa and Brynhild, see B. Sijmons, "Sigfrid und Brunhild: Ein Beitrag zur Geschichte der Nibelungensage," *ZDP,* 24 (1892), 11–12.

[8]The location of Brynhild on a mountain in *Vǫlsunga saga* may of course be attributable to the author's identification of Sigrdrífa with Brynhild, but it should be noted that *Snorra Edda* (ed. Finnur Jónsson, p. 130.11 and 24), with its uncertain identification of the two, also places both on a mountain. We need not assume with Heusler ("Lieder der Lücke," p. 234) that *Snorra Edda* combined sources. *Vǫlsunga saga* 61.26–27 and 77.1–3 both derive from *Meiri.* See T. M. Andersson, "The Lays in the Lacuna of Codex Regius" in *Speculum Norrœnum: Norse Studies in Memory of Gabriel Turville-Petre,* ed. Ursula Dronke, Guðrún P. Helgadóttir, Gerd Wolfgang Weber, and Hans Bekker-Nielsen (Odense: Odense University Press, forthcoming). See also Lehmgrübner, pp. 25–26.

Whether this is some vague reference to Sigurd's early wooing or just a courtly flourish is impossible to say, but a reminiscence of the prior betrothal is not impossible. Perhaps Sigurd was considered to have a record of broken pledges, and it was an easy matter to compound his faithlessness to Brynhild with a new faithlessness to Sigrdrífa. Polak (*Untersuchungen,* pp. 91–92) speculated that the Sigrdrífa episode was added simply to convey wisdom to the young hero. It thus serves as a gnomic counterpart to Grípir's prophecy, another phase in Sigurd's instruction. Given Sigurd's history of youthful involvements, the elaboration of the simple gnomic interview with Sigrdrífa into a romantic interlude was then possible.[9]

We turn now to the heroic adventures of Sigurd's youth, his vengeance for his father and his slaying of the dragon Fáfnir. This portion of the story is told in the two Eddic poems called *Reginsmál* and *Fáfnismál* in modern editions. *Reginsmál* is prefaced by the following prose paragraph in Regius:

> Sigurd went to Hjálprekr's stud and chose a horse which was henceforth called Grani. At that time Reginn, the son of Hreiðmarr, had come to Hjálprekr. He was the most skilled of men and a dwarf in stature; he was wise, of a fierce disposition, and a sorcerer. Reginn fostered Sigurd, instructed him, and loved him dearly. He told Sigurd about his ancestry and about the time Odin, Hœnir, and Loki had come to Andvari's Falls; in that waterfall (or rushing river?) there was an abundance of fish. Andvari was the name of a dwarf who had long been in the falls in the likeness of a pike and who got his food there. "Our brother was named Otr," said Reginn, "and he often went into the falls in the likeness of an otter. He had caught a salmon and sat on the riverbank eating as he dozed. Loki killed him with the cast of a stone. The Æsir thought that was a lucky stroke and flayed the pelt from the otter. That same evening they sought lodging with Hreiðmarr and showed off their catch. Then we seized them and required them to ransom their lives by filling the otter's pelt with gold and covering the outside with red gold. They sent Loki

---

[9]We shall see below that Hermann Schneider, "Verlorene Sigurddichtung," *ANF,* 45 (1929), 15–34 (summary p. 27), and *Germanische Heldensage,* I (Berlin and Leipzig: de Gruyter, 1928; rpt. 1962), 144–47, did not believe that *Sigrdrífumál* referred to an incident in Sigurd's early adventures.

to raise the gold. He visited Rán and got her net and then went to Andvari's Falls and cast the net in front of the pike. It swam into the net."

The poem itself comprises twenty-six stanzas, seventeen in *ljóðaháttr* 'song meter' (1–4, 6–10, 12, 19–22, 24–25) and nine in *fornyrðislag* 'epic meter' (5, 11, 13–18, 23, 26). In addition there are nine short pieces of prose interspersed among the stanzas. The narrative content, as distinct from gnomic, explanatory, and conversational stanzas, is as follows:

Stanzas 1–4	Loki demands Andvari's gold.
Prose 1	Andvari holds back one ring, which Loki promptly seizes.
Stanza 5	Andvari curses the gold (presumably the ring in particular), saying that it will be the death of two brothers and the source of contention for eight princes.
Prose 2	When the Æsir covered the otter's pelt, Hreiðmarr noticed one uncovered hair and Odin was obliged to produce the ring Andvaranautr to cover it.
Stanzas 6–9	Loki prophesies that the gold will cause the death of Hreiðmarr and his son (Fáfnir).
Prose 3	Fáfnir and Reginn demand a share of the head ransom, but Hreiðmarr refuses. Fáfnir stabs his father to death as he sleeps.
Stanzas 10–11	Hreiðmarr calls out to his daughters Lyngheiðr and Lofnheiðr. Lyngheiðr replies that there is little prospect that a sister will avenge a father by killing a brother. Hreiðmarr recommends bearing a daughter, whose son will avenge her grief.
Prose 4	Hreiðmarr died and Fáfnir took the gold. Reginn asked for his share of the inheritance and was refused. He sought counsel from his sister Lyngheiðr.
Stanza 12	Lyngheiðr recommends a friendly request rather than an attack with a sword.
Prose 5	All of this Reginn told Sigurd. One day Sigurd came to Reginn's house and was welcomed in the following terms.
Stanzas 13–14	Reginn praises the "son of Sigmund" and "descendant of Yngvi" and promises to foster him.
Prose 6	Reginn tells Sigurd that Fáfnir is brooding on the treasure in the shape of a dragon on Gnitaheiðr. He forges a sword for him that is so sharp that it splits a lock of

	wool floating in the Rhine.[10] With it Sigurd cleaves Reginn's anvil. Then Reginn urges him to kill Fáfnir.
Stanza 15	Sigurd objects that the sons of Hundingr (his father's killers) will laugh aloud if he seeks gold before getting vengeance for his father.
Prose 7	Hjálprekr supplies Sigurd with a fleet to carry out his vengeance. They are overtaken by a storm and head for a promontory. A man stood on the promontory and spoke to them.
Stanzas 16–18	He asks them to identify themselves and Reginn does so. The man in turn identifies himself as Hnicarr (Odin).
Prose 8	They land, Odin comes aboard, and the storm slackens.
Stanzas 19–25	Odin advises Sigurd on battle auguries and strategies.
Prose 9	Sigurd slew Hundingr's sons, Lyngvi and three brothers, in a great battle.
Stanza 26	Reginn proclaims that an eagle is now carved on the back of Sigmund's killer and praises Sigurd.

The poem *Fáfnismál* continues the story. It too is prefaced with a prose paragraph.

Sigurd went home to Hjálprekr's residence. Then Reginn incited Sigurd to kill Fáfnir. Sigurd and Reginn went up to Gnitaheiðr and found Fáfnir's trail when he slithered to the water. There Sigurd dug a large trench on the track and went into it. And when Fáfnir slithered off the gold, he spewed poison, but that passed over Sigurd's head. But when Fáfnir slithered over the trench, Sigurd pierced him to the heart with his sword. Fáfnir shook himself and thrashed with head and tail. Sigurd leapt out of the trench and then each saw the other.

As in *Reginsmál,* there follows a sequence of stanzas (forty-four) with interspersed prose and a mixture of meters. Stanzas 1–31, 34, 37–39 are in *ljóðaháttr,* stanzas 32–33, 35–36, 40–44 in *fornyrðislag.* The contents are outlined as follows:

Stanza 1	Fáfnir inquires into Sigurd's identity.
Prose 1	Sigurd hides his name because according to an ancient

[10]This curious motif is paralleled in the Irish *Togail Bruidne Dá Derga:* Anni Heiermeier, "Zwei irisch-isländische Parallelen," *Zeitschrift für keltische Philologie und Volksforschung,* 22 (1941), 61.

superstition it was a great peril to be cursed by a dying man.

Stanzas 2–22   Sigurd at first conceals his name with a riddle,[11] then identifies himself as Sigurd the son of Sigmund. Fáfnir asks who incited him and Sigurd credits his own boldness. Fáfnir accuses him of being a captive and Sigurd counters that he has just demonstrated his free status. Fáfnir informs him of the curse on the gold, but Sigurd philosophizes that everyone must die. Fáfnir reaffirms the judgment of the Norns. Sigurd questions him on the Norns and the island Óscópnir and is given some mythological lore without apparent relevance. Fáfnir recalls his "helmet of terror" and his poison and Sigurd points out that they did him no good. Fáfnir advises him to ride home and abandon the gold, but Sigurd has no such intention. Fáfnir's last words are that Reginn contrived his death and will do the same to Sigurd.

Prose 2   Reginn, absent during the encounter, returned as Sigurd was wiping the blood off his sword.

Stanzas 23–26   Reginn hails Sigurd and gives himself some of the credit as well.

Prose 3   Reginn cuts the heart out of Fáfnir with a sword named Riðill and drinks the blood from the wound.

Stanzas 27–31   Reginn instructs Sigurd to roast the heart while he naps. Sigurd chides him for being absent while the fight was under way. Reginn retorts that Sigurd would have been helpless without his sword. Sigurd replies that courage is better than a sword.

Prose 4   Sigurd roasts the heart and tests it with his finger. He burns the finger and puts it in his mouth. As soon as he tastes the dragon's blood, he understands the language of birds and hears some *igður* chirping in the brush.[12]

---

[11]Sigurd refers to himself as "gǫfuct dýr" ("noble beast"). On the interpretation of the riddle, see Panzer, II, 85; Jónsson, "Sagnformen," pp. 42–43; Albert Kjær, "Zu Fáfnismál Str. 2" in *Festschrift Eugen Mogk zum 70. Geburtstag 19. Juli 1924* (Halle: Niemeyer, 1924), pp. 54–60; and Magnus Olsen, "Gǫfugt dýr (Fáfnismál 2)," *ANF*, 67 (1952), 30–34. Ólafur M. Ólafsson, "Sigurður duldi nafns síns," *Andvari*, N.F. 12 (1970), 182–89, is not available to me.

[12]On the acquisition of knowledge by placing a finger in the mouth, see Robert D. Scott, *The Thumb of Knowledge in Legends of Finn, Sigurd, and Taliesin* (New York: Publications of the Institute of French Studies, 1930). On the identification of the *igður*, which appear only in the context of this story, see the intrigu-

Stanzas 32–39   One *igða* remarks that Reginn is contemplating re-
                 venge and that Sigurd should kill him and make off
                 with the treasure himself. Sigurd proclaims his inten-
                 tion to do so.
Prose 5   Sigurd cuts off Reginn's head, eats Fáfnir's heart, and
                 drinks the blood of both Reginn and Fáfnir. The *igður*
                 speak up once more.
Stanzas 40–44   They direct Sigurd to Gjúki, where he will marry the
                 king's daughter. Then they describe a hall on Hin-
                 darfjall surrounded by fire and occupied by Sigrdrífa,
                 who was put to sleep by Odin and cannot awaken be-
                 cause of the sentence of the Norns.
Prose 6   Sigurd goes to Fáfnir's lair, which is constructed with
                 iron, takes two chests of gold, the "helmet of terror," a
                 golden byrnie, the sword Hrotti, and many valuables.
                 He loads them on Grani, but Grani refuses to move
                 until Sigurd mounts him as well.

A first observation is that these poems cover two incidents: (1)
Sigurd's slaying of the dragon Fáfnir and winning of the treasure
and (2) his vengeance against the sons of Hundingr, the slayers of
his father. The dragon adventure, including the prehistory of the
treasure, is recounted in *Reginsmál* 1–12 (with four prose inserts)
and *Fáfnismál* 1–39 (with four prose inserts). The tale of Sigurd's
vengeance is told in *Reginsmál* 13–26 (with four prose inserts). A
second observation is that both *Reginsmál* and *Fáfnismál* are a
jumble of stanzas in two meters. The dragon adventure is covered
by ten *ljóðaháttr* stanzas and two *fornyrðislag* stanzas in *Reginsmál* and thirty-five *ljóðaháttr* stanzas in *Fáfnismál*. The tale of
vengeance is covered by eight *fornyrðislag* stanzas and six
ljóðaháttr stanzas in *Reginsmál* (the latter group comprises
Sigurd's exchange with Odin in *Reginsmál* 19–22 and 24–25). In
other words, the dragon adventure appears to be told almost exclusively in *ljóðaháttr,* while the vengeance story (minus the
gnomic dialogue with Odin) is told in *fornyrðislag.* This distribution led Heusler to postulate that *Reginsmál* and *Fáfnismál* are a
conflation of two anterior poems, a *ljóðaháttr* poem about Fáf-

---

ing ornithological excursus in F. L. Grundtvig, *Løsningsstenen: Et sagnhistorisk
studie* (Copenhagen: Karl Schønbergs Boghandel, 1878), pp. 119–21. Grundtvig
identified the *igða* as *parus palustris.*

nir's treasure, which Heusler called the "Hortlied," and a *forn-yrðislag* poem about Sigurd's vengeance, which he called the "Vaterrachelied."[13]

These anterior poems are difficult to grasp from a selective perusal of the amalgam *Reginsmál-Fáfnismál*, but they may be read as Heusler imagined them in Felix Genzmer's Thule translation, where they are entitled "Das Lied vom Drachenhort" and "Sigurds Vaterrache."[14] "Das Lied vom Drachenhort" comprises *Reginsmál* 1–12, *Fáfnismál* 1–25, 28–30, a hypothetical stanza provided by the translator (41), 26–27, 34, and 37–39. "Sigurds Vaterrache" comprises 7 hypothetical stanzas constructed from the prose of *Vǫlsunga saga* and *Reginsmál* 13–18, 23, 26, 19–22, and 24. The "Hortlied," as we shall refer to the former, tells of the gods' acquisition of Andvari's treasure, the curse laid on it by Andvari, the surrender of the treasure including the cursed ring Andvaranautr to Hreiðmarr, Fáfnir's killing of Hreiðmarr (at this point there is a considerable narrative gap filled in by prose), Fáfnir's dying words to Sigurd, Reginn's congratulations and instructions to roast Fáfnir's heart, and the birds' counsel advising Sigurd to kill Reginn. The "Vaterrachelied," as we shall refer to the second poem, recounts Sigmund's dying words to his wife Hjǫrdís advising her to preserve the fragments of his sword (this much reconstructed from the prose of *Vǫlsunga saga*), Reginn's welcoming of Sigurd and his urging to kill Fáfnir, Sigurd's insistence on carrying out his vengeance first, his sea voyage and interview with Odin, and his slaying of the sons of

[13]Andreas Heusler, "Altnordische Dichtung und Prosa von Jung Sigurd," *Sitzungsberichte der Preussischen Akademie der Wissenschaften*, phil.-hist. class (1919), pp. 164–65; rpt. in his *Kleine Schriften*, I, 28–29. Jónsson, "Sagnformen," p. 47, proposed complete variants in *ljóðaháttr* and *fornyrðislag* covering both the dragon adventure and the vengeance story. Heinrich Hempel, "Sigurds Ausritt zur Vaterrache," *Beiträge zur Runenkunde und nordischen Sprachwissenschaft* (*Festschrift Gustav Neckel*), ed. Kurt Helmut Schlottig (Leipzig: Harrassowitz, 1938), pp. 166–67; rpt. in his *Kleine Schriften*, ed. Heinrich Matthias Heinrichs (Heidelberg: Winter, 1966), pp. 192–93; followed the lead of R. C. Boer, *Die Edda mit historisch-kritischem Commentar*, II: *Commentar* (Haarlem: H. D. Tjeenk Willink & Zoon, 1922), 179, and rejected Heusler's construction, believing that the vengeance episode is merely a *fornyrðislag* insert in the *ljóðaháttr* "Drachenkampflied." Schneider, I, 143–44, concurred with Heusler.

[14]Felix Genzmer, trans., *Edda*, I: *Heldendichtung*, 2d ed. (Düsseldorf and Cologne: Eugen Diederichs Verlag, 1963), 115–29 and 133–38.

Hundingr. (Odin's *ljóðaháttr* gnomes in *Reginsmál* 19–22 and 24 are appended separately in Genzmer's translation.)

Not everything works in this solution. There are two *fornyrðislag* stanzas from *Reginsmál* (5 and 11) which must be included in the *ljóðaháttr* "Hortlied." Heusler did not account for them and referred to Polak. Polak labeled them interpolations and referred to Boer. Boer discredited stanza 5 because of the content:[15]

> The gold   that Gustr had
> Will be the bane   of brothers two
> And eke strife   for eight kings;
> My property   no profit brings.

Boer argued that Gustr has no place in the story since the treasure belongs to Andvari, that no one had been able to figure out who the eight kings were,[16] and that it would be illogical for Andvari to curse Fáfnir and Reginn (if these are the two brothers meant) while addressing Loki. Similarly, he rejected stanza 11 (p. 97) because it does not answer stanza 10 with unimpeachable logic. This sort of argumentation is clearly too demanding and the stanzas in question would presumably never have been challenged had they been in *ljóðaháttr*. Stanzas 5 and 11 remain an unresolved puzzle.

The same sort of puzzle is created by Odin's *ljóðaháttr* gnomes in the *fornyrðislag* context of the "Vaterrachelied." Heusler (p. 29) again referred to Polak, who disposed of them as interpolations (p. 23), as had Boer before him (III, 96). Genzmer's solution was to print them separately at the end of "Sigurds Vaterrache." Heusler also sidestepped the issue of the *fornyrðislag* stanzas *Fáfnismál* 32–33 and 35–36, in which the birds warn Sigurd against Reginn's vengeance and which must belong to the *ljóðaháttr* "Hortlied." Metrically they are at one with the concluding stanzas of *Fáfnismál* (40–44), in which the birds direct Sigurd to Gjúki's residence and describe Sigrdrífa asleep on Hindarfjall. These latter stanzas Heusler considered to be a group of

---

[15]Heusler, "Jung Sigurd," *Kleine Schriften,* I, 29; Polak, p. 25; R. C. Boer, *Untersuchungen über den Ursprung und die Entwicklung der Nibelungensage,* III (Halle: Verlag der Buchhandlung des Waisenhauses, 1909), 96.

[16]See Wieselgren, p. 296.

lausavísur (detached stanzas) designed to provide a transition to the next section of the narrative.[17] Genzmer printed all nine stanzas as a separate "Vogelweissagung" or "Bird Prophecy" (pp. 130–32), but as Polak (p. 21) had already pointed out, the first four are a *hvǫt* ("incitation" of Sigurd to kill Reginn) and only the last five are a prophecy. The *fornyrðislag* stanzas *Fáfnismál* 32–33, 35–36, and 40–44 therefore are a riddle. Their meter sets them apart from Heusler's "Hortlied" and they are furthermore not integral in this poem. Stanzas 32–33 and 35–36 duplicate the *ljóðaháttr* stanzas 34 and 37–39 with which they are combined, and stanzas 40–44 are an unnecessary epilogue to the killing of Reginn. The duplication together with the metrical misfit suggest that these stanzas are not part of the "Hortlied," but belong to an alternative poem in *fornyrðislag*. We may conceive of this poem as a variant version of the "Hortlied," just as *Atlamál* is a variant of *Atlakviða* and *Skamma* and *Meiri* are variants of *Forna*. The editor responsible for the complex *Reginsmál-Fáfnismál* would thus have had at his disposal not two but three poems, Heusler's "Hortlied" and "Vaterrachelied" plus a variant version of the "Hortlied" in *fornyrðislag*.

In the light of this hypothesis let us look once again at *Reginsmál* 5 and 11, the two other *fornyrðislag* intruders in the *ljóðaháttr* mass of the "Hortlied." *Reginsmál* 5 clearly is a duplicate also:

> The gold   that Gustr had
> Will be the bane   of brothers two
> And eke strife   for eight kings;
> My property   no profit brings.

The gist of the stanza is that the gold will be the death of two kinsmen. The following stanza 6 in *ljóðaháttr* says the same thing in slightly different form:

> The gold is paid up (said Loki),   and you have
>   ample ransom for my head;
> For your son   it will bring no luck,
>   it will be the bane of you both.

---

[17]Heusler, "Jung Sigurd," pp. 51–53. Cf. Lehmgrübner, pp. 14–17.

In the first stanza the words are addressed by Andvari to Loki, in the second by Loki to Hreiðmarr. In the first, the gold will cause the death of two brothers (presumably Fáfnir and Reginn), in the second the death of father and son (presumably Hreiðmarr and Fáfnir). I suggest that they are duplicate curse stanzas (also echoed in *Fáfnismál* 9) from slightly different contexts. The first is a general prophecy not aimed at the immediate listener (Loki), while the second partakes of some baleful hostility toward the listener (Hreiðmarr). The latter (stanza 6) belongs to the "Hortlied" in *ljóðaháttr* and the former (stanza 5) to the postulated third poem in the conflation, the variant "Hortlied" in *fornyrðislag*. They were similar enough in wording and sentiment so that the compiler thought of them together, but different enough in context so that they were not mutually exclusive and could be placed in sequence, one to summarize Andvari's message to Loki and the other to summarize Loki's message to Hreiðmarr.

The same thinking may be applied to *Reginsmál* 11, which to some extent duplicates the *ljóðaháttr* stanza *Reginsmál* 10. In the latter the dying Hreiðmarr addresses his daughters and one of them, Lyngheiðr, replies that a daughter cannot very well avenge her father against her brother. That is in itself a terminal point beyond which there cannot be much debate. But stanza 11 continues with Hreiðmarr's admonition to his daughter (presumably Lyngheiðr) to bear a daughter if she cannot bear a son so that the daughter's son may avenge her grief. Boer complained of the disjunction between these two stanzas because there had been no talk of bearing a son in the first one. The disjunction is comprehensible if the stanzas come from different poems. In the *ljóðaháttr* poem Hreiðmarr announced his death and Lyngheiðr bewailed her inability to take revenge. In the *fornyrðislag* poem Lyngheiðr perhaps wished for a son to help her in her need, and Hreiðmarr replied that a grandson would do as well. The discrepancy however was slight enough so that there was no problem in juxtaposing the stanzas. Indeed, the discrepancies in both sets of duplicate stanzas are so slight as to suggest that one poem is a rather superficial reworking of the other.

My hypothesis then is that the compiler of *Reginsmál-Fáfnismál* used a "Hortlied A" in *ljóðaháttr* and a "Hortlied B" in *fornyrðislag*. If we speculate on the reasons for a revision in *fornyrðislag,* we may think in terms of metrical functions. The story of the ''Hortlied'' is on the dividing line between mythology, to which *ljóðaháttr* is appropriate, and heroic legend, to which *fornyrðislag* is appropriate. It begins in the world of the Æsir when the gods Odin, Hœnir, and Loki seize Andvari's treasure, but it continues in the world of Sigurd's heroic deeds. The mythological preface—and perhaps the world of dragons, shape-shifters, and speaking birds as well—determined the choice of *ljóðaháttr* in ''Hortlied A.'' But a later poet wished to refocus the poem on Sigurd's secular adventures and chose the form of *fornyrðislag* in accord with the other Sigurd poems familiar to him. Since we have only eleven stanzas of this latter poem, we cannot say much about the narrative. It must have retreated to the mythological prehistory of the treasure because it records Andvari's curse on the gold as he surrendered it to Loki. It included accounts of Hreiðmarr's death and his dying words to his daughter and of Reginn's death (counseled by the birds), as well as the birds' prophecy concerning Gjúki and Sigrdrífa. One clear differentiation in ''Hortlied B'' is the expanded role of the birds; nine of the eleven extant stanzas involve these loquacious creatures. Heusler (p. 52) interpreted their prophecy as a group of *lausavísur* designed as a transition to the Brynhild story. This is surely a correct analysis of their function, but rather than being *lausavísur,* they are more likely to be a prophetic appendage to ''Hortlied B'' in the style of Brynhild's preview of the Burgundian disaster, which affords a similar transition to that story, at the end of *Skamma.* That ''Hortlied B'' was a very late poem, even later than *Meiri,* is suggested by the inclusion of Sigrdrífa in the prophecy of Sigurd's fate and her apparent equation with Brynhild (*Fáfnismál* 42 places Brynhild's flame wall on Sigrdrífa's Hindarfjall). The recent date of the poem may account for the fact that the compiler of the amalgam subordinated it to ''Hortlied A'' and mined it for only eleven stanzas.

To increase the number of hypothetical poems from two to three may strike the reader as less than thrifty, but the proposed solution offers the following advantages: (1) It liberates us from the assumption of *lausavísur* in a narrative context; (2) it allows us to postulate a ''Hortlied A'' in pure *ljóðaháttr* with no *fornyrðislag* intrusions; (3) it may help to explain the unusual amount of prose used in Regius to fill out the verse—the compiler had too much repetitive verse to include and resorted to brief paraphrases.

We must return now to the "Vaterrachelied." The remnants in *Reginsmál* 13–18, 23, and 26 indicate that it contained at least Reginn's welcoming of Sigurd and incitation against Fáfnir, Sigurd's insistence on carrying out the vengeance for his father before undertaking other adventures, his sea voyage and encounter with Odin, and his slaying of Hundingr's sons. It presumably also included the gnomic exchange between Sigurd and Odin in *ljóðaháttr* (*Reginsmál* 19–22 and 24–25).[18] This can of course be only a fraction of the original poem. Heusler ("Jung Sigurd," pp. 35–36) assumed that it was designed to connect Sigurd with his father. The connection was made by leaving the fragments of Sigmund's sword in the possession of his wife Hjǫrdís so that she could transmit them to Sigurd. Sigurd in turn gave them to his foster father Reginn, who forged them into a new sword to serve as an instrument of vengeance. But that Sigurd procured a sword, was incited by Reginn, given a fleet by Hjálprekr and counsel by Odin, then slew the sons of Hundingr—this seemed to Heusler too slight a matter for a full lay. He therefore speculated that the "Vaterrachelied" also included an account of Sigmund's death.

This part of the story can be read only in the prose pages of *Vǫlsunga saga*. Chapter 11 tells how Sigmund and Hundingr's son Lyngvi wooed the same woman, Hjǫrdís the daughter of King Eylimi. Hjǫrdís chose Sigmund despite his advanced age because he was the greater king. In reprisal Lyngvi gathered a great army and attacked Sigmund. When the battle had raged for a time, a one-eyed man in a broad hat and a blue, hooded cloak (Odin) confronted Sigmund with a spear. Sigmund struck at the spear

---

[18]This excrescence may not be as difficult to explain as the metrical jumble in the "Hortlied" because it constitutes a special dialogue with a god dealing primarily with the magical matter of auspices. Formally it could be modeled on the *ljóðaháttr* insert "Hrímgerðarmál" found in the *fornyrðislag* poem *Helgakviða Hjǫrvarðssonar*, all the more so because the situations are similar and the hero in each case has gone to sea to avenge a kinsman. See Jónsson, "Sagnformen," p. 40. Jónsson went on in this passage to posit two poems, a *Reginsmál* A in *ljóðaháttr* and a *Reginsmál* B in *fornyrðislag*. See also his *Den oldnorske og oldislandske litteraturs historie*, I (Copenhagen: Gad, 1920), 269–70; and Ussing, pp. 64–85.

and his sword broke in two. At that point the tide of battle turned
against him and he fell together with his father-in-law Eylimi.
Chapter 12 continues with an account of how Lyngvi seeks for
Sigmund's wife and treasure without success because she has
taken refuge with a maidservant in the forest. She subsequently
visits Sigmund on the battlefield. He declines to be healed since
Odin has withdrawn his support, but he informs her that she will
give birth to a son to whom she should pass on the fragments of
his sword. From them will be forged another sword named Gramr
and destined to do great deeds. Vikings now appear offshore
under the command of Álfr, son of King Hjálprekr of Denmark.
Hjǫrdís exchanges clothes with her maid to conceal her identity,
and they are brought to the Danish court. Here her beauty
arouses suspicions and her real identity is revealed by a trick
question, which elicits the fact that she is accustomed to wealth.[19]
Henceforward she is maintained at Hjálprekr's court in great
honor.

Chapter 13 tells of the posthumous birth of Sigurd, Hjǫrdís'
marriage to Álfr, and Reginn's fostering of Sigurd. The fullest
incident recounts how Sigurd chose a horse from Hjálprekr's stud
with the advice of an old man with a full beard (Odin). They drive
all the horses into the river Busiltjǫrn, and all make for shore
except one. Odin relates that this horse is a descendant of his own
horse Sleipnir and Sigurd names him Grani. Chapter 14 tells how
the gods acquired Andvari's treasure and surrendered it to
Hreiðmarr as an indemnity for Otr. Chapter 15 tells the story of
Sigurd's sword Gramr. He tests Reginn's first manufacture by
striking it against his anvil, on which it splits. Reginn forges a
second sword with the same result. Sigurd now goes to his mother
and requests the fragments of his father's sword. With these
fragments Reginn forges a third sword so strong that it cleaves the
anvil to the ground and so sharp that it severs a strand of wool in
the river.

Not all of this narrative can be assigned to the "Vaterrachelied," but Heusler singled out Odin's desertion of Sigmund
in battle (based on the tale of Harald Battletooth) and Hjǫrdís'
custodianship of the sword fragments as probable components.

---

[19]On the folktale background of this motif see Panzer, II, 81–82.

The latter motif presupposes the threefold testing of Reginn's steel, which must therefore also have belonged to the "Vaterrachelied." Heusler ("Jung Sigurd," pp. 45–46) assumed that this motif was an elaboration of Sigurd's smashing of the anvil in the "Hortlied"; in the "Vaterrachelied" the demonstration of overpowering strength became a test of the sword.[20] Similarly, the wool test in the river is borrowed from the "Hortlied," but because of the Danish locale the river is not equated with the Rhine of the sixth prose insert in *Reginsmál* and remains unidentified.

The gist of the "Vaterrachelied" is that Sigurd avenges the death of his father by killing the sons of Hundingr, but this role as avenger creates a problem inasmuch as it belongs to Helgi Hundingsbani in the Eddic cycle of Helgi poems. Heusler therefore proposed that Helgi was the original killer of Hundingr (as the name Helgi Hundingsbani would seem to guarantee), but that one Helgi poet made his hero the son of Sigmund in order to magnify his status. As a result, the killing of Hundingr was reinterpreted as an act of revenge for Helgi's father Sigmund. Because of the new genealogy Helgi and Sigurd became brothers and the poet of the "Vaterrachelied" discovered that the vengeance for Sigmund had been preempted by Helgi, to the detriment of Sigurd. To salvage the honor of his hero, he speculated that Hundingr had already been slain during Sigmund's lifetime (by Helgi), a version of the events accepted by the later *Helgakviða Hundingsbana* I. Such a surmise left the way open for Sigurd to take revenge by killing the sons of Hundingr.

This is admittedly a complicated calculation, which goes in part beyond the confines of our legend. What it amounts to is that the poet of the "Vaterrachelied" modeled Sigurd's vengeance for his father on the role of Helgi in the Helgi cycle. Heusler arrived at the following chronology of the legendary accounts ("Jung Sigurd," p. 48):

1. The "Hortlied," in which Sigurd was named the son of Sigmund
2. The account in some Helgi poem that Helgi avenged his father by killing Hundingr
3. *Vǫlsungakviða in forna* (so named and quoted in *Helgakviða Hun-*

[20]The smashed anvil recurs in *Þiðreks saga*, I.307.13–308.1, and *Das Lied vom Hürnen Seyfrid*, stanza 5.

dingsbana II, Neckel-Kuhn, p. 153), in which Helgi is identified as the son of Sigmund in order to confer additional status on him

4. A poem about Harald Battletooth in which Harald is deserted at the last moment by his protector Odin, the model for Sigmund's abandonment in his last battle[21]

5. The "Vaterrachelied," in which Sigmund remains alive at the time of Hundingr's death at the hands of Helgi so that the later vengeance for Sigmund can be ascribed to Sigurd

6. *Helgakviða Hundingsbana* I, in which Sigurd's role as avenger of his father is accepted and Helgi's killing of Hundingr is no longer conceived of as an act of vengeance.

The discussion has once again carried us far afield and it may be useful to summarize Heusler's reconstruction of the "Vaterrachelied" one final time. It began with Sigmund's death in battle when he found himself abandoned by Odin at the crucial moment. There was presumably a scene on the battlefield in which Sigmund turned over his broken sword to Hjǫrdís for safekeeping, then some mention, perhaps hardly more than tacit, of Hjǫrdís' removal to Denmark and Sigurd's posthumous birth.[22] There followed the threefold forging and testing of the sword Gramr, Reginn's egging of Sigurd against Fáfnir, and Sigurd's insistence on his vengeance priority. The vengeance was mounted, and Odin reappeared to counsel Sigurd and reestablish his protection of the Volsung dynasty. In the ensuing battle the sons of Hundingr, Lyngvi and three brothers, fell. The final stanza (*Reginsmál* 26) recorded the carving of the blood eagle on the back of "Sigmund's bane" and a concluding eulogy of Sigurd.

Guided largely by Heusler, we have thus far been able to disengage from the complex transmissions of the *Poetic Edda* and *Vǫlsunga saga* a "Vaterrachelied" in *fornyrðislag* describing Sigurd's vengeance for Sigmund, a "Hortlied A" in *ljóðaháttr* relating his slaying of Fáfnir and acquisition of the treasure, a

---

21. See the accounts of Harald Battletooth in Saxo Grammaticus, *Saxonis Gesta Danorum,* ed. C. Knabe, P. Herrmann, J. Olrik, and H. Ræder, I (Copenhagen: Munksgaard, 1931), 218–20, and *Sögubrot af fornkonungum* in *Fornaldar sögur Norðurlanda,* I, ed. Guðni Jónsson (n.p.: Íslendingasagnaútgáfan, 1959), 360–61.

22On the relocation of Sigurd's youth in Denmark, see Wolfgang Mohr, "Entstehungsgeschichte und Heimat der jüngeren Eddalieder südgermanischen Stoffes," *ZDA,* 75 (1938), 228.

variant version of this poem in *fornyrðislag* which we called
"Hortlied B," an "Erweckungslied" in which Sigurd roused
Sigrdrífa from her magic sleep and plighted his troth to her, and
three "Sigurd" poems (*Forna, Skamma,* and *Meiri*) dealing with
his fatal involvement with Brynhild and the Gjukungs. Of all these
poems, we have only one in its original form (*Skamma*). The
others are wholly or partially lost in the lacuna of Regius or splin-
tered in the transmission.

   How did this trying disarray come about? It cannot be attributed to the Eddic compiler. The loss of the fifth gathering in
Codex Regius occurred after his work was complete, and he had
no reason to create the odd conflation in *Reginsmál-Fáfnismál.*
Heusler's solution ("Jung Sigurd," p. 49) was to posit an earlier
collection of Sigurd poems which included "Hortlied," "Vaterrachelied," "Erweckungslied," "Falkenlied," "Traumlied,"
and *Meiri,* and which he called the "Sigurdliederheft." This collection served to provide a simple biography of Sigurd in poetic
form with prose connectors wherever necessary. For the latter
part of the story no problem arose because *Meiri* observed a
biographical sequence, but the chronology was disrupted by
"Hortlied" and "Vaterrachelied." The prehistory of the treasure
and Sigurd's fostering by Reginn (as told in the "Hortlied") precede his vengeance, while the killing of Fáfnir and the winning of
the treasure (also told in the "Hortlied") come after the vengeance. Thus the "Vaterrachelied" interrupts the chronology of
the "Hortlied." To maintain the biographical order, the compiler
of the "Sigurdliederheft" therefore inserted parts of the "Vaterrachelied" in the middle of the "Hortlied," thus producing the
conflation which the Eddic compiler inherited. We cannot plausi-
bly attribute the conflation to the Eddic compiler himself because
his purpose appears to have been the preservation of whole
poems, variant versions set side by side when he had more than
one in hand, not the dismemberment of poems to fit a biographical scheme. This latter strategy must belong to some predecessor
and Heusler's "Sigurdliederheft" fills the necessary slot.[23]

---

[23]It should be noted that Hans Kuhn, "Das Eddastück von Sigurds Jugend,"
Miscellanea Academica Berolinensia, II, no. 1 (Berlin, 1950), 30–46; rpt. in his
Kleine Schriften, ed. Dietrich Hofmann, II (Berlin: de Gruyter, 1971), 88–101,
broke with Heusler's derivation of Sigurd's early adventures from poetic sources

Aside from the biographical order, there is a further anomaly in the transmission of the Sigurd legend in Codex Regius. In addition to a number of poems, the early sections up to Sigurd's departure for the court of Gjúki include a large amount of prose. These prose inserts were studied systematically by Finnur Jónsson.[24] He determined that they differed substantially from prose inserts elsewhere in the collection and do not derive from the poems themselves, but presuppose additional information from some other source. Furthermore, they are fuller and more numerous than the prose pieces in the rest of the collection. This observation led Jónsson to conjecture that there was a prose "Sigurðar saga" used by the compiler of Regius to supplement his Eddic poems. Such a "Sigurðar saga" is referred to by the author of *Norna-Gests þáttr* (at the end of chapter 6) and by Snorri in his *Prose Edda* (the commentary to "Háttatal" 35). Jónsson observed further that the prose of Regius and Snorri's "Skáldskaparmál" (ed. Finnur Jónsson, pp. 126.19–130.10) tell the same story and concluded that they derived from the same written "Sigurðar saga." Snorri abbreviated the text in his extract, as did the Eddic compiler, while the author of *Volsunga saga* expanded it in places. Jónsson's view of the relationships was thus:

by proposing that they existed chiefly as a prose narrative, into which individual stanzas and stanza groups were intercalated at a late date. The "Sigurdliederheft" was rejected by Wieselgren, p. 248, as a groundless assumption.

[24]Finnur Jónsson, "Sigurðarsaga og de prosaiske stykker i Codex Regius," *Aarbøger* (1917), pp. 16–36. The idea of a "Sigurðar saga" had already been in the air for half a century. See Sophus Bugge, ed., *Norrœn fornkvæði* (Christiania: P. T. Mallings Forlagsboghandel, 1867), p. xliii; A. Edzardi, "Kleine Beiträge zur Geschichte und Erklärung der Eddalieder," *Germania,* 23 (1878), 186–87 (note), and review of E. Wilken, *Die prosaische Edda* in *Germania,* 24 (1879), 356 and 360–63; B. Symons, review of this book and the same author's *Untersuchungen zur Snorra Edda* in *ZDP,* 12 (1881), 110–12, and again in *Die Lieder der Edda* (Halle: Verlag der Buchhandlung des Waisenhauses, 1906), pp. lxxii–lxxiv.

Heusler ("Jung Sigurd," pp. 55–56) saw the relationships some-what differently. He took *Vǫlsunga saga* to be the best represen-tative of "Sigurðar saga." Whenever *Snorra Edda* is closer to the Eddic prose than to *Vǫlsunga saga*, we must suppose that *Snorra Edda* made use of the Eddic collection.

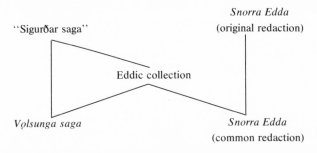

Heusler saw no need to assume that Snorri or his redactor made use of "Sigurðar saga."

In calculating the extent of "Sigurðar saga," Finnur Jónsson conjectured that it covered the whole of Sigurd's prehistory and was the source of Chapters 1–8 in *Vǫlsunga saga*. It concluded with Sigurd's death. Heusler disagreed on this point as well, sup-posing that "Sigurðar saga" began only with the story of Signý and Sigmund (*Vǫlsunga saga* 5.14) and that the prefatory matter connecting the Volsungs with Odin (Odin—Sigi—Rerir—Volsung) was added by the author of *Vǫlsunga saga*, who was also responsible for making the story of Sigurd into a genealogical preface to *Ragnars saga loðbrókar*. "Sigurðar saga" thus con-tained the narrative of *Vǫlsunga saga* 5.14–20.8, chapters 10–12, portions of chapter 13, and chapter 15 (that is, the tale of Signý, the tale of Sinfjǫtli's death, and the story of Sigurd's revenge for his father). The Helgi material in chapter 9, Sigurd's selection of a horse with Odin's aid in chapter 13, and Reginn's account of the treasure in chapter 14 may be attributed to the author of *Vǫl-sunga saga*. Since "Sigurðar saga" is only one element among several in Codex Regius and *Vǫlsunga saga*, it cannot be evaluated in much detail, but judging from the pertinent sections in *Vǫlsunga saga*, Heusler considered it to be a story in vivid saga style. Whatever poems it may have been based on (only two lines survive from a Signý poem, *Vǫlsunga saga*, p. 19) were more thoroughly dissolved than the poetic sources in *Vǫlsunga saga*. The author of "Sigurðar saga" seems therefore to have been less indentured to his poetic sources and to have taken a freer hand in converting poetic lay into saga prose.

The existence of a "Sigurðar saga" has not been disputed, but both Hermann Schneider and Per Wieselgren made further efforts to reconstruct its contents. Schneider concentrated on the Sigrdrífa episode recorded in *Vǫlsunga saga*, chapters 21 (20) and 22 (21), and Codex Regius (Neckel-Kuhn, pp. 189–97) and attributed it to "Sigurðar saga" as a form of the prior betrothal.[25] He assumed that the author of "Sigurðar saga" knew the prior betrothal from *Meiri* and knew *Helreið Brynhildar* as well (on *Helreið* see below Chapter 3). He interpreted the encounter between Brynhild and Sigurd in *Helreið* as their first meeting (not the proxy wooing for Gunnarr) and identified her as Sigrdrífa, thus producing the combination of Sigrdrífa's Hindarfjall with Brynhild's flame wall that we find in the bird prophecy (*Fáfnismál* 40–44) previously identified by Heusler as a verse insert in "Sigurðar saga." From the conflation of *Meiri* and *Helreið* arose the version of Sigurd's prior betrothal with Sigrdrífa-Brynhild in "Sigurðar saga." Schneider believed that this adventure was not the subject of the "Erweckungslied." He attributed only the second stanza of *Sigrdrífumál* to this poem and believed that it was not about Sigurd at all. Most of the verse that we find in Regius associated with *Sigrdrífumál* was gathered by the Eddic compiler himself, whereas the prose in Regius and *Vǫlsunga saga* derives from "Sigurðar saga." Finally, he explained the mysterious meeting between Brynhild and Sigurd in *Þiðreks saga*, chapter 168 (below Chapter 4), as a combination of a German source with "Sigurðar saga." The point of this meeting, Brynhild's betrothal with Sigurd, was however lost or forgotten (Schneider, "Verlorene Sigurddichtung," p. 33).

Wieselgren's reconstruction was more ambitious.[26] Whereas Heusler equated the early chapters of *Vǫlsunga saga* only selectively with "Sigurðar saga" and refrained from any attempt to retrieve the outlines after Sigurd's vengeance for his father,

---

[25]"Verlorene Sigurddichtung," *ANF*, 45 (1929), 15–34.
[26]*Quellenstudien zur Vǫlsungasaga*, pp. 246–63.

Wieselgren derived most of the early sections of *Vǫlsunga saga* from "Sigurðar saga" (*Vǫlsunga saga* 1.1–20.9, 24.25–37.27, 38.14–42.12 and all the stanzas of *Sigrdrífumál* as they stand in *Vǫlsunga saga*) and tried in addition to establish the remainder of the text.[27] He argued that it contained the hawk dream of *Vǫlsunga saga* chapter 26 (25), Sigurd's betrothal to Brynhild in the "Falkenlied" form with a stipulation that he should later cross the flame wall, his arrival at Gjúki's court in some form analogous to *Vǫlsunga saga* chapter 28 (26), the wooing and quarrel sequences in a form modeled on *Forna,* the consultation on Brynhild's state just prior to her climactic interview with Sigurd (*Vǫlsunga saga* 74.4–75.5), Sigurd's murder in the forest, the death of the Burgundians, and Gudrun's revenge. A detailed analysis of Wieselgren's arguments would carry us too far beyond our topic, and any precise restoration of such a spectral quantity as "Sigurðar saga," especially in the latter phases, would probably not command general agreement.

The discussion has now generated two new entities, the "Sigurdliederheft" and "Sigurðar saga." The "Sigurdliederheft" appears to be a necessary assumption to account for the chronological splicing of the "Hortlied" (or "Hortlieder" A and B) with the "Vaterrachelied" bequeathed to the compiler of the Eddic collection. "Sigurðar saga" is a necessary assumption to account for the large body of supplementary prose in the Eddic collection and the full account of Sigurd's ancestry in the early chapters of *Vǫlsunga saga.*

The next piece that requires our attention is the Eddic poem *Grípisspá* (*The Prophecy of Grípir*). It is the first poem in the Sigurd group, coming just after the Helgi poems and just before *Reginsmál.* In a very brief prose preface we are told that Sigurd came to the hall of Grípir, his maternal uncle. He requests a meeting with Grípir and is cordially received (stanzas 1–5). To a general inquiry about his future Grípir gives a glowing response (6–7). The remainder of the poem is given over to alternating questions and answers anticipating the following events:

1. Sigurd's vengeance against the sons of Hundingr (9)
2. The killing of Fáfnir and Reginn (11)

---

[27]Unlike Schneider, Wieselgren did not believe that "Sigurðar saga" equated Sigrdrífa with Brynhild (p. 249).

3. Sigurd's seizure of the gold and ride to Gjúki (13)
4. Sigurd's release of Sigrdrífa, who is not named in the poem (15)
5. Sigrdrífa's instruction of Sigurd (17)
6. Sigurd's arrival at Heimir's residence (19)
7. (After some intervening reluctance on Grípir's part to prophesy further) Brynhild Buðladóttir's presence in Heimir's hall (27)
8. Sigurd's lovesickness at the sight of Brynhild (29)
9. Sigurd's swearing of oaths with Brynhild and subsequent oblivion (31)
10. Grimhild's deception of Sigurd (33)
11. Grimhild's proposal that Gunnarr woo Brynhild (35)
12. The oaths of blood brotherhood and Sigurd's exchange of shapes with Gunnarr (37)
13. Sigurd's proxy betrothal to Brynhild (39)
14. The chaste nuptials (41)
15. The double wedding (43)
16. Sigurd's recollection of his prior oaths and silence (45)
17. Brynhild's charge that Sigurd broke his oaths (47)
18. Grípir's reassurance that the charge is false (49)
19. Gudrun's pain when her brothers kill Sigurd (51)

There has never been any doubt that *Grípisspá* is a secondary piece.[28] The sources are palpable: stanza 9 shows knowledge of the "Vaterrachelied" (the killing of Hundingr's sons), stanzas 11 and 13 indicate knowledge of the "Hortlied" or "Hortlieder" (the killing of Fáfnir and Reginn and the acquisition of the gold), and stanzas 15 and 17 show knowledge of the "Erweckungslied" (the encounter with the sleeping princess and her communication of runic lore). For the later part of the story *Grípisspá* is clearly dependent on *Meiri*. So much is suggested most obviously by Sigurd's prior betrothal to Brynhild (stanza 31) and Grimhild's conspicuous role in deceiving Sigurd (33) and instigating Gunnarr's wooing of Brynhild (35). The dependence on *Meiri* is verified by verbal correspondences between *Grípisspá* and prose passages in *Vǫlsunga saga* that must derive from *Meiri*. Stanza 29 is clearly connected with *Vǫlsunga saga* 58.14–16. Grípir's welcoming of Sigurd seems to be modeled on Sigurd's reception

---

[28]For example, A. Edzardi, "Beiträge zur Geschichte und Erklärung der Eddalieder," *Germania,* 23 (1878), 325–33; Ussing, pp. 124–26; Lehmgrübner, pp. 33–35; Siegfried Gutenbrunner, "Eddalieder aus der Schreibstube," *ZDP,* 74 (1955), 250–53.

at Heimir's hall (*Vǫlsunga saga* 57.13–18) and later at Gjúki's court (*Vǫlsunga saga* 64.11–17). The third echo links stanza 45 (Sigurd's recollection of his earlier oaths) with *Vǫlsunga saga* 69.9–11, a passage that must derive from *Meiri* inasmuch as there were no such prior oaths in any other version.

It is of course possible that these passages in *Vǫlsunga saga* take their wording from *Grípisspá,* but it seems unlikely that the elaborate receptions given Sigurd by Alsviðr and Gjúki should have been modeled on two lines of *Grípisspá.* A dependence on *Grípisspá* seems all the more unlikely because the author of *Vǫlsunga saga* manifests an obvious lack of interest in this poem. He disposes of Sigurd's encounter with his uncle in a miniature chapter of thirteen lines and treats the total prophecy in a single sentence (38.5–7). This short shrift might suggest that the author knew full well that *Grípisspá* was a secondary product and for the most part a recapitulation of *Meiri.*

Two special matters should be noted in connection with *Grípisspá.* Clearly it adheres closely to the account of *Meiri* and nothing in it need be referred to *Forna* or *Skamma.* When, therefore, stanza 43 records the double wedding that pairs off Gunnarr with Brynhild and Sigurd with Gudrun, it seems strongly indicated that this item belonged to *Meiri* despite the different order in *Vǫlsunga saga.* This inference is easily justified when we take into account that the order in *Vǫlsunga saga* corresponds to what must have stood in *Forna.* The second important item is the failure of *Grípisspá* to identify the maiden on the mountain (Sigrdrífa) with Brynhild. Since the dependence on *Meiri* is so thoroughgoing, it is difficult to believe that this identification was made in *Meiri* and then canceled in *Grípisspá.* Heusler must therefore have been wrong in assuming that the equation between Brynhild and Sigrdrífa was already present in *Meiri.*[29] This last step in the legendary development was taken only by the author of *Vǫlsunga saga.*

When was *Grípisspá* composed? It antedates the Eddic collection, but it postdates *Meiri,* on which it depends for its version of the story. It does not belong in the sphere of "Sigurðar saga," a prose narrative and not the occasion for the composition of a new

---

[29]Heusler, "Lieder der Lücke," p. 270, and "Jung Sigurd," p. 58.

poem. It therefore belongs somewhere between *Meiri* and the Eddic collection represented by Regius. Heusler conjectured that it was composed as a preface or a sort of table of contents to the "Sigurdliederheft" used by the compiler of the Eddic collection ("Jung Sigurd," p. 49). This proposal makes good sense because the "Vaterrachelied" and "Hortlied," for the understanding of which the "Sigurdliederheft" is the necessary instrument, are both clearly referred to in *Grípisspá*. The argument of course is circular: *Meiri* is judged to be a part of the "Sigurdliederheft" because *Grípisspá* refers to it and *Grípisspá* is judged to be the program for the "Sigurdliederheft" because it summarizes *Meiri*. Nonetheless, the pieces fit and no better solution offers itself.

We may go a step beyond the relative dating of *Grípisspá* and suggest an absolute terminus post quem. Richard L. Harris reminds us of Vigfússon's observation in *Corpus Poeticum Boreale* (II, 372) that Gunnlaugr Leifsson's *Merlínusspá* shows a knowledge of *Grípisspá*.[30] Vigfússon noted three sets of verbal correspondences, two of which may be significant enough to suggest borrowing.[31]

Hon mun ríkiom þér   rúnar kenna,
allar, þær er aldir   eignaz vildo,
oc á mannz tungo   mæla hveria,
lif með lækning;   lifðu heill, konungr!

(She will, mighty one,   teach you runes,
All that men should   wish to acquire,
And to speak in   every tongue of man,
Life [health?] with healing;   good fortune, oh king!) [*Grípisspá* 17]

Þa man vakna viðr en danski *ok* manz roddv mæla sialfri.

(Then the Danish wood will awake and speak with the very speech of man.) [*Hauksbók* 273.7–8]

---

[30]Richard L. Harris, "A Study of *Grípisspá*," *Scandinavian Studies*, 43 (1971), 344. Jakob Benediktsson also notes influence from *Grípisspá* and other Eddic poems in his article "Merlínusspá," *Kulturhistorisk leksikon for nordisk middelalder*, 11 (1966), 557.

[31]*Merlínusspá* is quoted from *Hauksbók*, ed. E. Jónsson and F. Jónsson (Copenhagen: Thiele, 1892–1896).

sérðu Sigurðar   snǫr brǫgð fyrir,
þau er hæst fara   und himinscautom?

(Do you foresee   Sigurd's bold deeds
That will fare highest   under heaven's ends?) [*Grípisspá* 10.5–8]

Han mvnv tigna tvngvr lyða sa mvn gramr vera gvmnvm tiðaztr ey mvn vppi oðlings frame ok hans hroðr fara með hímínskavtvm.

(The tongues of men will honor him. He will be the most beloved prince to men. The prince's deeds will live forever and his fame fare to the ends of heaven.) [*Hauksbók* 278.32–34]

Despite the theory of Eddic influence on *Merlínusspá,* it seems more likely that the poet of *Grípisspá* borrowed from Gunnlaugr's poem rather than vice versa. The phrases in question are taken over by Gunnlaugr from Geoffrey's Latin and need not be sought out in Eddic models. The Latin originals are:[32]

Excitabitur Daneium nemus et in humanam vocem erumpens clamabit...

(The Danish wood will be aroused and bursting into human voice will cry out...) [p. 97.22–23]

In ore populorum celebrabitur: et actus ejus cibus erit narrantibus.

(He will be praised in the mouth of the peoples and his deeds will be the food for storytellers.) [p. 93.20–21]

If there is any question of borrowing, *Grípisspá* must be the borrower and since Gunnlaugr Leifsson died in 1218 or 1219, his imitator cannot be placed earlier than the first part of the thirteenth century.

The interview with Grípir is the first incident in Sigurd's life. Retreating beyond it, we come to his birth and early childhood.

---

[32]Quoted from *Gottfried's von Monmouth Historia Regum Britanniae,* ed. San-Marte [Alwin Schulz] (Halle: Eduard Anton, 1854).

On this subject Codex Regius is remarkably taciturn. The prose passage preceding *Grípisspá* ("Frá dauða Sinfjǫtla" "On the Death of Sinfjǫtli") relates the birth in the following spare terms: "King Sigmund resided for a long time in Denmark in the realm of Borghildr after marrying her. Then Sigmund traveled south to Frankland to his realm there. Then he married Hjǫrdís, the daughter of King Eylimi. Sigurd was their son. King Sigmund fell in battle at the hands of Hundingr's sons. Hjǫrdís was married to Álfr, the son of King Hjálprekr. Sigurd grew up there as a child."

The beginning of chapter 13 in *Vǫlsunga saga* provides a modest supplement to this account:

> It is now told that Hjǫrdís gives birth to a male child and the boy is brought to King Hjálprekr. The king was delighted at the sight when he saw the piercing eyes in his face and said no one would be his equal and he was sprinkled with water and given the name Sigurd. All agree that he had no equal in conduct and stature. He was fostered very lovingly there at the court of King Hjálprekr. And when all the greatest men in ancient tales are named, then Sigurd will be first in strength and accomplishments, boldness and courage, which he possessed in greater measure than any man in the north. Sigurd grew up there at the court of Hjálprekr and everyone loved him. He betrothed Hjǫrdís to King Álfr and determined her bridal fee. Sigurd's foster father was named Reginn, the son of Hreiðmarr. He taught him skills, table games and runes and many tongues, as was customary for princes, and many other things.

To the extent that this additional material is not the work of the saga author himself, it presumably filters down from "Sigurðar saga." Because it contains no narrative action, nothing need be said about it. The paucity of incident becomes interesting only in comparison with the accounts of Sigurd's childhood in *Þiðreks saga*, the *Nibelungenlied*, and *Das Lied vom Hürnen Seyfrid*.

CHAPTER 3

The Sequel to
Sigurd's Death

The center of the legend of Brynhild and Sigurd is provided by the three poems *Forna, Skamma,* and *Meiri.* From this center the legend unfolds in two directions, backward in time to reveal Sigurd's early adventures and forward to reveal the lot of Brynhild and, more particularly, Gudrun after Sigurd's death. We have surveyed Sigurd's prehistory and may now turn to the events subsequent to his murder. These are told largely in the form of laments, *Guðrúnarkviður* I, II, and III and *Oddrúnar-grátr.* A fifth poem, entitled *Helreið Brynhildar,* describes Brynhild's descent to the underworld and her reflective conversation with a witch. These poems are static and add no new story material, but they must nonetheless be reviewed for hints on the development of the legend. Our understanding of the Eddic elegies goes back not to the golden age of Nibelung research (1900–1920), but to a critical breakthrough in two brilliant papers published by Wolfgang Mohr in 1938 and 1939. Heusler had considered the poems in question to be a late indigenous development, an "isländische Spätblüte," but Mohr demonstrated that they have close stylistic and lexical affinities to the Scandinavian ballads and German counterparts for which Hermann Schneider had coined the term "novellistische Spielmannslieder."[1] Since

[1] Andreas Heusler, "Heimat und Alter der eddischen Gedichte: Das isländische Sondergut," *Archiv,* 116 (1906), 249–81; rpt. in his *Kleine Schriften,* ed. Stefan Sonderegger, II (Berlin: de Gruyter, 1969), 165–94. Wolfgang Mohr, "Entstehungsgeschichte und Heimat der jüngeren Eddalieder südgermanischen Stoffes," *ZDA,* 75 (1938), 217–80, and "Wortschatz und Motive der jüngeren Eddalieder mit südgermanischem Stoff," ibid., 76 (1939), 149–217.

the appearance of Mohr's studies there has been no doubt that the Eddic elegies are a very late literary phenomenon based on Dano-German models, but the relative dating of the individual poems and their relation to the late "Sigurd" poems (*Skamma* and *Meiri*) continues to be a vexed question.

Guðrúnarkviða I

Guðrúnarkviða I follows *Brot af Sigurðarkviðu* in Codex Regius and is preceded by a short prose paragraph: "Gudrun sat over Sigurd as he lay dead. She did not weep like other women, but she was ready to burst with grief. Both women and men went to comfort her, but it was not easily done. People say that Gudrun had eaten of Fáfnir's heart and because of this she understood the speech of birds. The following is also told of Gudrun. . . ." What follows is a poem of twenty-seven stanzas relating how Gudrun sat over Sigurd paralyzed by grief and what efforts were made to release her feelings.[2] Each woman expresses her sympathy by recounting her bitterest experiences. Gjaflaug, Gjúki's sister, tells of the loss of five husbands, three daughters, three sisters, and eight brothers, but Gudrun's tears remain blocked. Herborg, queen of Hunland, offers an even more lugubrious tale of woe: her husband and seven sons fell in battle in the south and her mother, father, and four brothers went down in a storm at sea. She herself was captured and obliged to serve a harsh mistress. This too fails to release Gudrun's tears. Gullrǫnd, Gjúki's daughter and Herborg's foster daughter, now intercedes and removes Sigurd's shroud so that Gudrun can see his face. She dissolves in a flood of tears, and Gullrǫnd states that theirs was the greatest love on earth. Gudrun bursts into a lament, which is at the same time a eulogy of Sigurd, a comment on her own loneliness, and a reproach to the brothers who broke their oaths and murdered Sigurd. The complaint concludes with a reminiscence of the joy that prevailed before Sigurd set off with Gunnarr on his ill-fated

[2]The fullest treatments of *Guðrúnarkviða* I are Mohr, "Wortschatz und Motive," pp. 167–76, Rose Zeller, *Die Gudrunlieder der Edda,* Tübinger germanistische Arbeiten, Sonderreihe: Studien zur nordischen Philologie, 26 (Stuttgart: Kohlhammer, 1939), pp. 64–82, and Einar Ól. Sveinsson, *Íslenzkar bókmenntir í fornöld,* I (n.p.: Almenna Bókafélagið, 1962), 493–99.

wooing of the wretched creature Brynhild. Brynhild responds by cursing Gullrǫnd for releasing Gudrun's tears and tongue. Gullrǫnd reciprocates the curse and Brynhild lays the blame on her brother Atli, who coveted her suitor's gold. The concluding stanza pictures Brynhild with her eyes flashing fire and breathing poison as she looks at Sigurd's wounds. A brief postlude in prose anticipates the following events: "Gudrun went away to the forest in the wilderness and went all the way to Denmark and stayed with Þóra, Hákon's daughter, for three and a half years. Brynhild did not want to live after Sigurd. She had eight of her thralls and five of her bondwomen killed. Then she stabbed herself to death as is told in *Sigurðarkviða in skamma*."

The content of *Guðrúnarkviða* I is slight. Its framework of competitive laments is paralleled by a Danish ballad (*DgF* 286: "Hustrus og Moders Klage") and is presumably borrowed.[3] Gjaflaug, Herborg, and Gullrǫnd would appear to be fictional characters devised ad hoc to fill the frame.[4] Nothing is known from other sources of the woeful destinies attributed to the first two.[5] The details of Sigurd's death are not significantly illuminated, though stanza 21 hints that Gunnarr's killing of Sigurd was also motivated by a desire for his gold, perhaps no more than an unfounded charge provoked by Gudrun's grief and anger. Verbal echoes of other Eddic poems have been noted and there is a fair consensus that the poet must have known *Guðrúnarkviða* II and *Þrymskviða*, perhaps also *Helgakviða Hundingsbana* II, *Reginsmál*, and *Fáfnismál*.[6] The key issue is the relationship to *Skamma*, and here the opinions are hopelessly divided. In 1908 the revised edition of Karl Müllenhoff's *Deutsche Alter-*

[3]See Mohr, "Entstehungsgeschichte und Heimat," pp. 246–51, and Zeller, p. 78.

[4]An etymological case for Gjaflaug's antiquity was made by Erik Noreen, "Några anmärkningar om Guðrúnarkviða I," *Festskrift til Finnur Jónsson* (Copenhagen: Levin & Munksgaards Forlag, 1928), pp. 252–54.

[5]Mohr, "Entstehungsgeschichte und Heimat," p. 248, adduced ballad parallels, and Helga Reuschel, "Melkorka," *ZDA*, 75 (1938), 297–304, drew an interesting comparison between Herborg's bondage and the story of Melkorka in *Laxdœla saga*.

[6]See Noreen, pp. 253–54; Zeller, pp. 68–75; Jan de Vries, "Das zweite Guðrúnlied," *ZDP*, 77 (1958), 179; and Sveinsson, p. 499. However, Mohr, "Wortschatz und Motive," pp. 150–51 and 154, believed that *Guðrúnarkviða* II is secondary to *Guðrúnarkviða* I.

tumskunde (V, 372–73) assigned the priority to *Skamma*, but in the same year Gustav Neckel's *Beiträge zur Eddaforschung* (p. 298) reversed the priority. Again in 1939 Zeller claimed the priority for *Skamma* (p. 73), but in the same year de Vries ("Het Korte Sigurdlied," pp. 14–16) once more reversed the order. Henrik Ussing (*Om det indbyrdes forhold*, pp. 109–11) and Einar Ól. Sveinsson (pp. 499 and 517) both took the view that *Guðrúnarkviða* I influenced *Skamma*.

The verbal correspondences are so close that there can be no doubt about the interdependence, but no parallel passage reveals the direction of the borrowing. More general considerations must therefore be used. *Guðrúnarkviða* I does not appear in a group with the other elegies, but between *Brot* and *Skamma*. The reason seems to be chronological since the action of *Guðrúnarkviða* I precedes Brynhild's suicide in *Skamma*. Had *Guðrúnarkviða* I followed *Skamma*, it would have been necessary, editorially speaking, to revive Brynhild for the purpose. If we now imagine that the *Skamma* poet composed his work with *Guðrúnarkviða* I as precisely in mind as the verbal echoes suggest, it is curious that he left no room for Gudrun's lament aside from a despairing clap of the hands that causes the drinking vessels to jingle and the geese to cackle (stanza 29). It seems more likely that the poet of *Guðrúnarkviða* I availed himself of this gesture (echoed in stanza 16) to develop a full lament for Gudrun as a counterpart to Brynhild's lament in *Skamma*. At the same time he availed himself of the time lapse in *Skamma* between Sigurd's death and Brynhild's suicide to devise a new scene. A second indication of a specific derivation from *Skamma* is the blame Brynhild places on Atli in stanza 25:

Veldr einn Atli   ǫllo bǫlvi

(Atli alone causes   all the evil)

Not only does this line echo *Skamma* 27.7–8 ("ein veldr Brynhildr / ǫllo bǫlvi"), but, as we have seen in Chapter 1, *Skamma* is the only version of the story that assigns responsibility for Brynhild's tribulations to Atli. The idea in *Guðrúnarkviða* I can originate only in the specific context of *Skamma* 36–38, which tells the story of Atli's pressure on his sister. Furthermore, Brynhild's reminiscence of her first view of Sigurd (*Guðrúnar-kviða* I, 26.1–4) reenacts the same scene in *Skamma:*

> Þá er við í hǫll   húnscrar þióðar
> eld á iǫfri   ormbeðs litom.

> (When in the hall   of the Hunnish folk
> We saw on the prince   snakebed's fire [gold].)

Her first sight of Sigurd in *Skamma* 39.1–4 was similarly brightened by gold:

> Þeim hétomc þá,
> er með gulli sat   á Grana bógom.[7]

> (I pledged myself to him
> Who sat with gold   on Grani's back.)

The phrasing in *Guðrúnarkviða* I must be viewed as a curious skaldic twist on *Skamma*. In the light of this evidence, the terms used to describe the departure of the wooing expedition in *Guð-rúnarkviða* I, 22.5–6 ("oc þeir Brynhildar / biðia fóro"—"and they set out to woo Brynhild") must also be modeled on the corresponding line in *Skamma* 3.1–2 ("Unz þeir Brynhildar / biðia fóro"—"until they set out to woo Brynhild").

Even more difficult to construe is the relationship between *Meiri* and *Guðrúnarkviða* I. Zeller (p. 77) suggested that the serial attempts to console Gudrun in the latter poem may be modeled in part on the similar attempts to console Brynhild in *Meiri* (*Vǫl-sunga saga,* chap. 31 [29]); the influence may run the other way, however. It is quite conceivable that the *Meiri* poet took the condolent framework for his dialogue sequence from the more modest innovation in *Guðrúnarkviða* I, in which the situation is adequately explained by the ballad background. It is of course

---

[7]On these parallels see Zeller, p. 81. The latter echo shows that the gold in *Skamma* 39 was thought to be ornamental and was not identified as Fáfnir's treasure. This confirms Finnur Jónsson's understanding of the passage in "Sagnformen i Sigurðarkviða en skamma," *ANF,* 34 (1918), 279 (note).

difficult to argue that the poet of *Guðrúnarkviða* I did not know *Meiri*, but it is worth noting that the legendary presuppositions are all from *Skamma* and not *Meiri*. Atli is blamed for the coercion of Brynhild, not Buðli, who took over this role in *Meiri*. Atli becomes the scapegoat (stanza 25: "Veldr einn Atli / ǫllo bǫlvi"), not Grimhild, on whom the onus so manifestly rests in *Meiri*, for example, according to the evidence of *Grípisspá* 51:

> Þá er Guðrúno   grimt um hiarta,
> *er* brœðr hennar   þér til bana ráða,
> oc at ǫngo verðr   ynði síðan
> vitro vífi;   veldr því Grímildr.

> (Then Gudrun   is grim at heart
> When her brothers   plot your death,
> and no joy   remains thereafter
> for the wise woman;   Grimhild is the cause.)

Grimhild's responsibility for all the ills is confirmed by Brynhild in *Meiri* (*Vǫlsunga saga* 71.26–27: "Hun velldr aullum uppaufum þess bauls, er oss bitur." "She is responsible for all the sources of the evil that afflicts us."). In view of these sentiments and the explicit phrasing ("valda bǫlvi"—"cause evil"), it would be contradictory for a poet using *Meiri* to make Atli the sole culprit with the words "Veldr einn Atli / ǫllo bǫlvi." Given the clear reminiscences of *Skamma* and the absence of allusion to the version of the story represented by *Meiri*, we might reasonably suppose that *Guðrúnarkviða* I was composed at some point between these poems. However, we will see below that *Guðrúnarkviða* I must postdate *Guðrúnarkviða* II, while *Guðrúnarkviða* II presupposes *Meiri*. *Guðrúnarkviða* I must therefore have been composed later than *Meiri* but without reference to it.

The most interesting literary feature of the elegy is the emergence of Gudrun from her subsidiary role in the "Sigurd" poems into the foreground. We have stated that the "Sigurd" poems might be titled more accurately the "Brynhild" poems. They are preoccupied with her fate and treat her plight sympathetically, while Gudrun, as late as *Meiri*, is something of an intruder, who takes another woman's man with the aid of Grimhild's potions and wiles. In *Guðrúnarkviða* I the attitude has changed and Gudrun becomes the focus of our sympathies, leaving Brynhild to suffer the reproaches of her rival and of Gullrǫnd for her role in the murder of Sigurd. The interest has shifted from the strong woman to the passive victim, perhaps under the influence of ballad attitudes. The resulting vilification of Brynhild is analogous to Kriemhilt's literary fortunes in Germany. In the *Nibelungenlied* she remains a credible heroine despite the title *vâlandinne* (she devil), but in the later Middle Ages she suffers a decline in public esteem because of her part in the murder of her brothers.[8]

Helreið Brynhildar

Sigurðarkviða in skamma is followed directly by *Helreið Brynhildar*, the setting for which is given in another brief prose preface: "After Brynhild's death two pyres were built, one for Sigurd, which burned first, and Brynhild was cremated on the other; she was in a wagon adorned with costly weavings. It is told how Brynhild fared with the wagon on the road to Hel and crossed a yard where a certain witch dwelled." The idea of Brynhild's wickedness, which surfaces in *Guðrúnarkviða* I, underlies the following conversation. The witch forbids her passage, saying that it would be more fitting for her to mind her weaving than to visit another woman's husband (in the underworld). Furthermore, she has just washed human blood from her hands. Brynhild retorts that there is nothing to reproach her for even if she has engaged in viking activities. The witch rejoins that Brynhild was born the most ill-fated of creatures and that she destroyed Gjúki's children and home. Brynhild now launches into an account of her career, presumably by way of justification. The story begins with an otherwise unknown episode in which a king carries off the *hamir* (changeable guises) of eight sisters (presumably Brynhild and seven sisters). She was twelve when she swore oaths to the "young prince." (Should the "young prince" be construed as the king who carried off the *hamir* and should it be

[8]See the references in Wilhelm Grimm, *Die deutsche Heldensage*, 3d ed. (Gütersloh: C. Bertelsmann, 1889), pp. 124, 158, 181, 187, 314, 361, and 477.

understood that he exacted a betrothal in exchange for their return? Or is the "young prince" Agnarr, whom she presently supports in battle?[9]) Brynhild goes on to relate that she was called
"Hildr under the helmet" by everyone in Hlymdalir. She killed
Hjálm-Gunnarr and gave victory to the brother of Auða (Agnarr,
as we know from the prose of *Sigrdrífumál*). In reprisal, Odin
enclosed her in shields and allowed her to be awakened only by a
man who knew no fear. He also raised a wall of fire around her
and decreed that it be crossed only by the man who brought her
the gold on which Fáfnir brooded. Sigurd rode to her foster
father's residence and slept with her in one bed "as if he were my
born brother." Then Gudrun accused her of sleeping with Sigurd
and the whole deception was revealed. The final stanza concludes
with the generalization that women and men are born to sorrow
and the statement that she and Sigurd will end their lives together.

Helreið is a late syncretic piece. It is the only poem in the
Edda, aside from *Fáfnismál* 42–43 ("Hortlied B"), which clearly
equates Brynhild with Sigrdrífa and coalesces the former's flame
wall with the latter's shield wall. Very possibly the author of
Vǫlsunga saga took over the identification from one or both of
these poems though he makes no use of *Helreið*. Boer and Neckel
assumed that Brynhild's foster home in Hlymdalir was borrowed
from *Helreið* 7 into the "Falkenlied" (in my view *Meiri*) and
thence into *Vǫlsunga saga,* but nothing stands in the way of
supposing that *Helreið* took the location from *Meiri* (*Vǫlsunga
saga* 66.16 and 68.27).[10] It could even have been in *Forna,* which
Neckel (p. 93) considered the main source for *Helreið*. Neckel (p.
96) and de Vries ("Het Korte Sigurdlied," p. 23) were inclined to
assume an influence from *Helreið* on *Skamma,* but Sveinsson (p.
525) inclined the other way. In no Eddic poem are the literary
relationships more tenuous. What appears to have escaped the
notice of most scholars is a somewhat clearer connection with
Snorra Edda, the only other source in which Sigrdrífa/Brynhild is
given the name Hildr: "Þa vaknaþi hon ok nefndiz Hildr; hon er

[9]See Friedrich Panzer, *Studien zur germanischen Sagengeschichte,* II: *Sigfrid*
(Munich: Beck, 1912), 232–33.
[10]R. C. Boer, "Sigrdrifumál und Helreið," *ZDP,* 35 (1903), 309 and 323, and
Gustav Neckel, *Beiträge zur Eddaforschung mit Exkursen zur Heldensage*
(Dortmund: Ruhfus, 1908), pp. 86 and 97–98.

kavllvð Brynhildr, ok var valkyria"[11] ("Then she woke up and identified herself as Hildr; she is called Brynhild and was a valkyrie"). This phrasing looks as though it derives from *Helreið* 7:

Héto mic allir   í Hlymdǫlum
Hildi undir hiálmi,   hverr er kunni.

(In Hlymdalir   everyone called me
Hildr under the helmet,   all who knew me.)

Snorri (or his redactor) could have used the name Sigrdrífa outright, but welcomed the name Hildr in *Helreið* because it did not absolutely commit him to the identification of Brynhild with Sigrdrífa.

Gustav Neckel, Finnur Jónsson, and Wilhelm Lehmgrübner viewed *Helreið* as an apologia for Brynhild.[12] As such it may stand in deliberate opposition to *Guðrúnarkviða* I. But a further motivation for the composition of the poem may have been some belated speculation on Brynhild's youth. *Meiri* was full of intriguing references to her days as a shield maiden (*Vǫlsunga saga* 59.7–10, 60.5–8, 60.11, 68.6–8, 68.11–13). By equating her with the valkyrie Sigrdrífa in the "Erweckungslied," the poet of *Helreið* was able to solve the mystery and fill Brynhild's youth with valkyrie lore. The *hamir* taken from Brynhild and seven sisters remind us that Sváva/Sigrún was also a valkyrie equipped to fly with eight companions (*Helgakviða Hundingsbana II*, Neckel-Kuhn, p. 154.3–4) and the Helgi legend may thus have contributed to the picture of Brynhild's youth along with the adventures of Sigrdrífa. In short, *Helreið* is an effort on a very modest scale to create the sort of *enfance* for Brynhild that was provided in such rich detail for Sigurd in the various poems devoted to his early adventures.

---

[11]*Edda Snorra Sturlusonar*, ed. Finnur Jónsson (Copenhagen: Gyldendal, 1931), p. 130.13–14. Only B. Sijmons, "Sigfrid und Brunhild: Ein Beitrag zur Geschichte der Nibelungensage," *ZDP*, 24 (1892), 8–9; and Wilhelm Lehmgrübner, *Die Erweckung der Walküre* (Halle: Niemeyer, 1936), pp. 38–39, seem to have registered the connection.

[12]Neckel, p. 90; Finnur Jónsson, *Den oldnorske og oldislandske litteraturs historie*, 2d ed., I (Copenhagen: Gad, 1920), 295; and Lehmgrübner, p. 20.

Guðrúnarkviða II

At the conclusion of *Brot* there is a prose insert with the heading "Frá dauða Sigurðar" ("On the Death of Sigurd"). In reporting various versions of Sigurd's death it includes the following sentence: "And it is told in the *Old Lay of Gudrun* (*Guðrúnarkviða in forna*) that Sigurd and Gjúki's sons had ridden to the assembly when he was killed." This account of *Guðrúnarkviða in forna* matches what we find in the poem now titled *Guðrúnarkviða* II (stanza 4.1) and the two are therefore taken to be identical. The background of *Guðrúnarkviða* II is provided in yet another prose insert, "Dráp Niflunga" ("The Slaying of the Niflungs"). As the title suggests, this piece anticipates Atli's slaying of Gunnarr and Hǫgni, but it also contains a note on Gudrun's marriage: "Gunnarr and Hǫgni took all the gold, Fáfnir's legacy. There was strife between the Gjukungs and Atli. He blamed the Gjukungs for the death of Brynhild. The matter was settled by their agreeing to give him Gudrun in marriage and they gave her a potion of forgetfulness to drink before she would consent to marry Atli." Thus *Guðrúnarkviða* II follows *Guðrúnarkviða* I chronologically; it is no longer a lament over the fallen Sigurd, but an account of how Gudrun was persuaded to marry again. The setting for the poem, supplied by the prose preface, is curious: "King Þjóðrekr was with Atli and had lost almost all his men. Þjóðrekr and Gudrun recounted their sorrows to one another. She said to him . . ." A situation in which Þjóðrekr (Dietrich) is in the company of Atli and in communication with Gudrun (Kriemhilt) is known to us only from the *Nibelungenlied* and *Þiðreks saga*. We are therefore invited to imagine a conversation between Þjóðrekr and Gudrun after her marriage to Atli and presumably after some mass fighting involving Huns, Burgundians, and Þjóðrekr's followers. But there is no suggestion in the poem itself that Þjóðrekr participates as speaker or listener, and Zeller reasonably concluded that the setting is carried over from *Guðrúnarkviða* III, where it makes sense.[13] It has no bearing on the date or legendary status of *Guðrúnarkviða* II.

---

[13]*Die Gudrunlieder*, p. 38. See also Otto L. Jiriczek, *Deutsche Heldensagen* (Strasbourg: Trübner, 1898), p. 158.

The poem comprises forty-four stanzas, all spoken by Gudrun or reported from other speakers in her words. She recalls an idyllic childhood before her marriage to Sigurd, whom she commemorates in a series of exalted comparisons. All was cut short when her brothers begrudged her the most distinguished husband and killed Sigurd at an assembly. She spoke with Grani, who hung his head knowing that his master was dead. Gunnarr too was dejected and Hǫgni told her of Sigurd's death. She grieved over the body, then went to the hall of Hálfr and stayed in Denmark for three and a half years with Þóra, Hákon's daughter, who distracted her with pictorial weaving. Then Grimhild located her and called a meeting to appease her. Though offered great treasure, she remained skeptical until Grimhild administered a magic potion. Even then she declined to accept Grimhild's proposal that she marry Atli, despite redoubled offers and threats. She foresaw Atli's destruction of Gunnarr and Hǫgni; Grimhild wept at the prospect, but persisted until the marriage was finally arranged. Gudrun then journeyed to Hunland (*Vǫlsunga saga* 89.15–21 adds a short account of the wedding feast). The poem concludes with Atli's recital of nightmares that presage her murder of him and his sons.

Guðrúnarkviða II is clearly a transition piece designed to bridge the gap between Sigurd's death and Gudrun's revenge.[14] Its place in the chronology of the Eddic collection is much disputed, but there is fair agreement that it preceded and influenced *Guðrúnarkviða* I.[15] Jan de Vries ("Das zweite Guðrunlied," p. 179) made what appears to me to be the decisive argument. The closest parallel involves Gudrun's failure to express her sorrow:

> gerðit hon hiúfra   né hǫndom slá,
> né qveina um   sem konor aðrar.

> (She did not lament   or wring her hands,
> Or whine aloud   like other women.) [*Guð*. I.1.5–8]

---

[14]Sveinsson, p. 489.

[15]Karl Müllenhoff, *Deutsche Altertumskunde,* ed. Max Roediger, V (Berlin: Weidmannsche Buchhandlung, 1908), 371; F. Jónsson, *Den oldnorske og oldislandske litteraturs historie,* I, 287–88; Zeller, pp. 44, 48, 68–75; de Vries, "Das zweite Guðrúnlied," p. 179; Sveinsson, p. 499. Neckel, p. 295; and Mohr, "Wortschatz und Motive," pp. 150–51 and 154, consider that *Guðrúnarkviða* I is primary.

gerðiga ec hiúfra   né hǫndom slá,
né kveina *um*   sem konor aðrar,

(I did not lament   or wring my hands,
Or whine aloud   like other women.)   [*Guð*. II.11.5–8]

As de Vries pointed out, the reticence in *Guð*. II, where it is a proper heroic stance, becomes the theme for *Guð*. I. In other words, *Guð*. II provided the framework for the poet of *Guð*. I, who filled it in with ballad material. He announces and authenticates his theme by quoting *Guð*. II in the first stanza. This sequence makes the title *in forna* comprehensible; from the point of view of the Eddic compiler the poem is old in relation to *Guð*. I.

More problematical is the relationship of *Guð*. II to *Skamma*. Neckel (*Beiträge*, p. 320) believed that *Guð*. II influenced *Skamma*, but later (pp. 453–54) he changed his mind. Zeller (pp. 43–44, 48, 62) concurred with this later view. To compound the uncertainty, Jan de Vries stated in 1939 ("Het Korte Sigurdlied," pp. 16–17) that *Guð*. II influenced *Skamma*, but in 1958 ("Das zweite Guðrúnlied," pp. 178–79) he stated the opposite (without reference to his earlier view). The verbal similarities are most conveniently summarized in de Vries's first statement. The closest parallel is the following:

Hvarf sér óhróðugr   andspilli frá

(He went dejected   from the talk)   [*Skamma* 46.1–2]

Hvarf ec ein þaðan,   annspilli frá

(I went alone   from the talk)   [*Guð*. II.11.1–2]

But the evaluation of the parallel was not made easier when Zeller (p. 44) pointed out that the phrase also occurs in a stanza from *Meiri* (*Vǫlsunga saga* 77.15–16):

Ut geck Sigurdr   anspialle fra

(Sigurd went out   from the talk)

The poet of *Guðrúnarkviða* II could have taken the locution from the poets of *Skamma* and *Meiri*, or they from him.

The evidence of a connection with *Meiri* is much more secure and has been argued most clearly by Zeller.[16] The machinations of Grimhild and specifically the magic potion administered to Gudrun in *Guðrúnarkviða* II can hardly derive from any source other than *Meiri*. We are thus left with these probable influences:

Guðrúnarkviða II ⟶ *Guðrúnarkviða* I
Skamma ⟶ *Guðrúnarkviða* I
Meiri ⟶ *Guðrúnarkviða* II

Because it seems fairly certain that *Skamma* is older than *Meiri*, the following chronology emerges:

Skamma—Meiri—Guðrúnarkviða II*—Guðrúnarkviða* I

Guðrúnarkviða III

The last two episodic poems have very little pertinence to the story of Brynhild and Sigurd and deserve mention only for completeness. The eleven stanzas of *Guðrúnarkviða* III are prefaced by a correspondingly brief statement in prose: "One of Atli's bondwomen was named Herkja; she had been his concubine. She told Atli that she had seen Þjóðrekr and Gudrun together. Atli was very melancholy. Then Gudrun said..." There follows an inquiry into Atli's melancholy state and his explanation of the charge. Gudrun swears that she has had no illicit commerce with Þjóðrekr, other than one embrace when they recounted their sorrows to one another. He had come with thirty men, all of whom died; they had deprived (? MS corrupt) her of her brothers. She bids Atli make preparations for an ordeal with boiling water in the presence of seven hundred witnesses. Calling on her deceased brothers, she plucks the stone from the cauldron and displays an unscathed hand. Atli is overjoyed and calls on Herkja to submit to the same test. Her hands are scalded and she is sunk in a swamp as a punishment for the false accusation.

The presence of Þjóðrekr (Dietrich) at Atli's court and the loss of his men in the fighting against the Burgundians (*Nibelungen-*

---

[16]*Die Gudrunlieder*, pp. 55–56. See also Neckel, p. 225, and Mohr, "Wortschatz und Motive," p. 158.

lied 2318 and *Þiðreks saga* II.328.13–21) reflects a specifically German tradition which may have traveled to Iceland by the same late route as *Þiðreks saga*.[17] The slandering of a queen and her vindication by ordeal is a motif embedded in a rich tradition of legendary history and ballad.[18] By any measure, then, *Guðrúnarkviða* III is a late and inorganic offshoot from the Norse legend. It has no tangible connection with earlier or later action and is not easily pressed into the available frame. We must imagine some intervening time between the death of Gudrun's brothers and her revenge and immediate suicide (*Atlakviða*) or attempted suicide ("Frá Guðrúno"). Furthermore, the special relationship between Gudrun and Þjóðrekr makes little sense in view of the latter's role as Atli's ally and participation in the killing of Gudrun's brothers (stanza 5). This situation is predicated on the German version, in which Gudrun/Kriemhilt seeks vengeance against her brothers for the death of her husband and enlists Dietrich's aid in the effort. An alliance between Dietrich and Gudrun/Kriemhilt is at odds with her loyalties in the Norse legend and the poet of *Guðrúnarkviða* III has done nothing to remedy the contradiction. The extrinsic position of the poem is emphasized by an absence of verbal connections with the other Norse poems of the cycle. The only plausible reminiscence links *Guð.* III.4.1–2 ("Nema ec hálsaða / heria stilli"—"Except that I embraced the prince of the hosts") with *Guð.* I.13.7–8 ("sem þú hálsaðir / heilan stilli"—"as you embraced the upright prince"), but not much can be made of such a thin echo. Neither content nor phrasing suggests any knowledge of *Skamma* or *Meiri*. About all that can be said with any certainty is that the undigested German context of the poem suggests a very late arrival on the Scandinavian scene.

Oddrúnargrátr

The final poem in the cycle is *Oddrúnargrátr*, a piece that no longer touches either Sigurd or his widow Gudrun directly. The

---

[17]On the German background of the meeting between Gudrun and Þjóðrekr, see Jiriczek, pp. 158–61, and Zeller, pp. 91–93.

[18]See Svend Grundtvig in *Danmarks gamle folkeviser*, I (Copenhagen: Thiele, 1853), 177–204 (introduction to no. 13 "Ravengaard og Memering"); Hugo Gering, *Kommentar zu den Liedern der Edda*, III, pt. 2: *Heldenlieder* (Halle: Buchhandlung des Waisenhauses, 1931), 317–19; Zeller, pp. 93–95.

customary prose introduction sets the stage in the following terms: "There was a king named Heiðrekr. His daughter was named Borgný. Her lover's name was Vilmundr. She was unable to give birth until Atli's sister Oddrún came to her. Oddrún had been the lover of Gjúki's son Gunnarr. Concerning this tale the following is told." Oddrún hears of Borgný's difficulty in giving birth and comes to her friend's assistance. She learns that Borgný has been carrying on a secret affair with Vilmundr. The delivery is induced by magic charms, and Borgný gives birth to twins by "Hǫgni's killer" (are we to understand that Vilmundr participated in the killing of Hǫgni?). Borgný calls on Frigg and Freyja to reward Oddrún for her release, but Oddrún rejects her gratitude: her aid is motivated not by Borgný's deserts, but by her own vow to help one and all. Borgný appeals to her on the basis of close friendship, but Oddrún reminds her of the time she reproached her for her liaison with Gunnarr. There follows a recital of woes in the style of *Guðrúnarkviða* I. Her father's (Buðli's) last wish was that she should marry Gunnarr, while Brynhild should be a valkyrie. But Brynhild remained in her bower at her weaving until Sigurd came to her hall. A battle was fought and her hall broken into, and it did not take long before she knew of the deception. Brynhild took harsh revenge and committed suicide for the sake of Sigurd. Then Oddrún became Gunnarr's lover. The Gjukungs offered Atli gold and compensation (for the death of Brynhild), fifteen estates, and Sigurd's treasure if he would agree to Oddrún's marriage, but he refused. Others interceded with the objection that Oddrún and Gunnarr were already a couple, but Atli maintained that Oddrún would commit no villainy. He nonetheless sent spies, who found them together and reported to Atli despite offers of gold. They did not however tell Gudrun (who would have acted to protect her brothers). The Gjukungs visited Atli and were slain; Hǫgni's heart was excised and Gunnarr placed in the snake pit. From the remoteness of Læsø Oddrún heard him strike the harp summoning her to his aid, but before she could arrive, Atli's mother had delivered the fatal stroke in the form of a serpent. Oddrún concludes her lament with a statement of bewilderment that she remains alive after the death of Gunnarr, whom she loved like herself.

The motif of delayed birth, which provides the background for this lament, has its closest parallels in Danish ballads.[19] Despite this late ballad context, the poem was once thought to be as old as the eleventh century; Neckel, however, argued for the twelfth or thirteenth.[20] Neckel's arguments in such matters rested to some extent on verbal correspondences, but it is difficult to establish to everyone's satisfaction the degree of verbal coincidence necessary to prove borrowing. Formulaic equivalence is always a possibility. Even if borrowing is agreed on, the two texts involved have competing claims to priority. Less precise arguments may therefore carry more weight. In the case of *Oddrúnargrátr*, the clearest affiliations are with the other elegies and episodic poems. The primary purpose may have been to provide a lament for Gunnarr equivalent to Gudrun's laments for Sigurd. Oddrún's recital of woe has a precise counterpart in *Guðrúnarkviða* I and to some extent in *Helreið*. The idea that Atli blames the Gjukungs for the death of Brynhild and requires compensation (stanza 21) parallels the situation in *Guðrúnarkviða* II, specifically stated in "Dráp Niflunga." The direction of the borrowing seems fairly clear in this case because the conciliation of Atli is the underlying concept of *Guðrúnarkviða* II and only a peripheral concern in *Oddrúnargrátr*. Finally, the erotic tensions and the central position of an illicit affair are reminiscent of *Guðrúnarkviða* III, although the priority scarcely seems possible to determine.

The most important poem in establishing the literary location of *Oddrúnargrátr* is *Skamma*. It has always been assumed that *Oddrúnargrátr* is the older of the two because it is summarized in *Skamma* 58:[21]

Muntu Oddrúno   eiga vilia,
enn þic Atli mun   eigi láta;

[19] *Danmarks gamle folkeviser*, nos. 84–85. See Mohr, "Entstehungsgeschichte und Heimat," pp. 263–64. The international context was first suggested by Wilhelm Jordan, "Oddruns Klage," *Germania*, 13 (1868), 257–70. See the listings in Stith Thompson, *Motif-Index of Folk-Literature*, V (Bloomington, Indiana: Indiana University Press, 1957), 403 (T574: "Long Pregnancy"). The only Norse parallel appears to be the six-year pregnancy of Vǫlsungr's mother (*Vǫlsunga saga* 4.16–5.4), which ends with a caesarean delivery and her death.
[20] Neckel, pp. 307 (with references to early datings by Finnur Jónsson and Eugen Mogk), 446, and 466. Heusler, "Heimat," p. 253; rpt. *Kleine Schriften*, II, 168, also settled on the eleventh century.
[21] Neckel, p. 313; de Vries, "Het Korte Sigurdlied," pp. 8–11; Sveinsson, p.

ìþ munoð lúta   á laun saman,
hon mun þér unna,   sem ec scyldac,
ef ocr góð um scǫp   gerði verða.

(You will wish   to wed Oddrún,
But Atli will   not allow you;
You will meet   in secret tryst,
She will love you   as I should
If good fortune   favored us.)

In reality, the relationship is rather more complicated. Let us
begin by comparing three passages:

Segia mun ec þér, Gunnarr   —siálfr veiztu gorla—,
hvé ér yðr snemma   til saca réðot;
varðcat ec til ung,   né ofþrungin,
fullgœdd fé   á fleti bróður.

(I will tell you, Gunnarr,   —you know it yourself—,
How you long ago   gave rise to strife;
I was not too young   nor too oppressed (?),
Fully dowered   in my brother's hall.)   [*Skamma* 34]

Mær var ec meyia,   móðir mic fœddi,
biǫrt, í búri,   unna ec vel brœðrom;
unz mic Giúki   gulli reifði,
gulli reifði,   *gaf Sigurði.*

(Maid was I among maids,   my mother raised me,
Bright in the bower,   my brothers I loved well;
Until Gjúki   showered me with gold,
Showered me with gold   and married me to Sigurd.)
                                    [*Guðrúnarkviða* II.1]

Var ec up alin   í iǫfra sal
—flestr fagnaði—   *at fira ráði.*
Unða ec aldri   oc eign fǫður,
fimm vetr eina,   svá at minn faðir lifði;

---

512. Only Lehmgrübner, p. 36, suggested that *Oddrúnargrátr* was spun out of
Skamma.

þat nam at mæla   mál iþ efsta
siá móðr konungr,   áðr hann sylti:
Mic bað hann gœða   gulli rauðo
oc suðr *gefa   syni Grímildar.*

(I was raised   in the hall of princes
—All rejoiced—   at the bidding of men.
I enjoyed life   and my father's wealth
Only five winters   while my father was alive.

He began to speak   his final words,
The doughty king,   before he died:
He had me showered   with red gold
And married in the south   to Grimhild's son.)

[*Oddrúnargrátr* 14–15]

If verbal echoes mean anything at all, the passages from *Guð-rúnarkviða* II and *Oddrúnargrátr* must be connected. Since Oddrún is the secondary figure, it seems much more likely that her happy childhood and marriage are modeled on Gudrun's than the reverse, all the more so because the model stanza was conspicuously placed at the beginning of *Guðrúnarkviða* II and was likely to be fixed in the mind of an imitator. As we have seen above, *Guðrúnarkviða* II must be dependent on and later than *Meiri,* which in turn depends on *Skamma*. Hence the chronology: *Skamma—Meiri—Guðrúnarkvida* II—*Oddrúnargrátr.* In fact, the passages quoted from both *Guðrúnarkviða* II and *Oddrúnargrátr* above may ultimately owe the idea of a happy maidenhood to Brynhild's brief reminiscence in *Skamma* 34. This evidence contradicts the theory that *Skamma* 58 excerpted *Oddrúnargrátr*.

Testing the age of *Oddrúnargrátr* further, we may inquire into the connections with *Meiri.* There are no verbal echoes unless we consider that Oddrún's parting words (33.6–8: "unna þóttomz, / sverða deili, / sem siálfri mér"—"I thought to love / the giver of swords / like my very self") are modeled on Sigurd's wrenching declaration to Brynhild (*Vǫlsunga saga* 76.19: "Ek unna þer betr enn mer"—"I loved you better than myself"). But there are broader similarities. Buðli's voice in determining the fates of his daughters Oddrún and Brynhild (stanza 16) belongs to *Meiri* and not to *Skamma,* in which Atli plays the guardian's role. Buðli's

casting of Brynhild as a valkyrie (16.3: "óscmey") derives from
the shield-maiden lore of *Meiri* or perhaps *Helreið*, which is still
later. The idea in *Meiri* was that Brynhild wished to persist in her
shield-maiden activities, but Buðli obliged her to pick a husband.
Since the poet of *Oddrúnargrátr* shifts the marriage designs to
accommodate his new heroine Oddrún, Brynhild remains a free
agent and Buðli's will in *Oddrúnargrátr* coincides with her own
declared preference in *Meiri*.

The clearest echo of *Meiri* is found in stanza 17, which tells us
that Brynhild remained in her bower and wove ("Brynhildr í búri /
borða racþi"). The scene is taken from the description of
Brynhild in *Meiri* ("Falkenlied") as she sits in her chamber weaving pictures of Sigurd's deeds prior to his visit (*Vǫlsunga saga*
58.4–8):

> Hun sat i eine skemu vid meygiar sinar. Hun kunne meiʀa hagleik
> enn adrar konur. Hun lagde sinn borda med gulle ok saumadi a þau
> stormerki, er Sigurdr hafde giorth, drap ormsinns ok upptauku fiar-
> rins ok dauda Regins.

> (She sat in a chamber with her maidens. She was more skillful than
> other women. She worked with gold and wove the great deeds that
> Sigurd had accomplished, the slaying of the serpent and the seizing
> of the treasure and the death of Reginn.)

As in *Meiri,* Sigurd now arrives on the scene and catches sight of
Brynhild's "borg" (17.7–8: "þá er bani Fáfnis / borg um þátti"—
"when Fáfnir's slayer caught sight of the fastness"), the tower of
Vǫlsunga saga 58.11 and 22. What follows, however, is not a
formal wooing, but a battle and a breaching of Brynhild's fortress
(stanza 18.1–4):

> Þá var víg vegit   vǫlsco sverði,
> oc borg brotin,   sú er Brynhildr átti;

> (Then a battle was fought   with foreign sword
> And the fortress breached   that Brynhild had.)

In the discussion of chapter 168 in *Þiðreks saga* below, it will
become apparent that this episode reflects the German tradition

of Sigurd's prior betrothal to Brynhild, according to which Sigurd broke into her residence. Thus, *Oddrúnargrátr* 17 echoes the prior betrothal as it stood in *Meiri*, and *Oddrúnargrátr* 18 echoes the equivalent German version. The poet has harmonized. Stanza 18 concludes with a rather cryptic summary of what ensued:

> vara langt af því,   heldr válítið,
> unz þær vélar   vissi allar.

The subject of "vissi" is Brynhild: "It did not take long for Brynhild to learn of the whole deception." What is alluded to so tersely is the drugging of Sigurd, his proxy wooing in Gunnarr's shape, and the revelation of the deception in the quarrel of the queens. It seems apparent, then, that the poet knew the full *Meiri* version with prior betrothal, potion of forgetfulness, and shape shifting. He also knew the German version of the prior betrothal and coalesced it with the more romantic wooing of *Meiri*.

There seems little doubt that *Oddrúnargrátr* presupposes information available only in *Meiri*. It must therefore postdate *Meiri* and *Meiri*'s source *Skamma*. How then do we account for the apparent excerpt of *Oddrúnargrátr* in *Skamma* 58? It is possible that Gunnarr's affair with Oddrún was common knowledge and could be referred to without presupposing a separate poem, but it seems unlikely that such an apocryphal accretion to the legend had any oral circulation outside *Oddrúnargrátr*. We could speculate that *Skamma* 58 is a later interpolation, but an interpolation is not a pleasing remedy. Or we might imagine that both poems were the work of the same poet or of two poets in close communication with one another. There is no obvious solution, but all the evidence suggests that *Oddrúnargrátr,* like the other episodic poems, is a late excrescence on the narrative core of the three Eddic "Sigurd" lays. All these elegies and reflections are a secondary phenomenon. They subscribe to the later forms of the legend and do no service in illuminating the older layers. Their interest lies in the development of a new literary fashion.

CHAPTER 4

Þiðreks saga

We have now exhausted the early Norse sources on Brynhild and Sigurd and are ready to turn to the German versions. The most primitive of these has come down to us only in the Norse reworking known as *Þiðreks saga*, a compilation of heroic adventures organized around the figure of Dietrich von Bern. Much of the narrative records otherwise unknown north German traditions and sheds welcome light on this poorly illuminated literary province,[1] but the fullest section, on the fall of the Burgundians ("Niflunga saga"), is based on the same written south German epic (Heusler's "Ältere Not") that served as the source for the second part of the *Nibelungenlied*. This source can be reconstructed in broad outline from a comparison of the *Nibelungenlied* and *Þiðreks saga*, and we can trace how it was recast by the north German redactor in terms of his native traditions and again to a lesser extent by the Norse translator in accordance with his knowledge of the Scandinavian version.[2] Other parts of the com-

---

[1] A helpful survey of the heroic stories in northern Germany may be found in Heinrich Hempel, "Niederdeutsche Heldensage," *Die Nachbarn: Jahrbuch für vergleichende Volkskunde*, 3 (1962), 7–30; rpt. in his *Kleine Schriften*, ed. Heinrich Matthias Heinrichs (Heidelberg: Winter, 1966), pp. 134–52.

[2] On "Niflunga saga" and the "Ältere Not" see Léon Polak, "Untersuchungen über die Sage vom Burgundenuntergang," *ZDA*, 54 (1913), 427–66; Andreas Heusler, "Die Heldenrollen im Burgundenuntergang," *Sitzungsberichte der Preussischen Akademie der Wissenschaften*, phil.-hist. class (1914), pp. 1114–43; rpt. in his *Kleine Schriften*, II, ed. Stefan Sonderegger (Berlin: de Gruyter, 1969), 518–45; Roswitha Wisniewski, *Die Darstellung des Niflungenunterganges in der Thidrekssaga: Eine quellenkritische Untersuchung*, Hermaea 9 (Tübingen: Niemeyer, 1961); T. M. Andersson, "The Epic Source of Niflunga saga and the Nibelungenlied," *ANF*, 88 (1973), 1–54.

pilation are much less clear and do not allow for such distinctions. We do not know what part of the work was done in Germany and what part fell to the Norse adapter or in what form the narrative was transmitted.

The prologue to *Þiðreks saga* gives the following account of the composition (I.2.13–21): "This saga is composed according to the account of Germans, to some extent from their poems intended for the entertainment of nobles and originally composed immediately after the events that are told in this saga, and even if you take a man from every town in all of Saxony, they will all tell this tale the same way because of their old poems. And their verse is styled in such a way that we can recognize that it is verse in our tongue." The message is reinforced in the concluding lines of "Niflunga saga" (II.328.5–11): "We have been told about this by men who were born in Bremen or Münster and none knew anything about the other, but all told it the same way, for the most part as it is told by the old poems in the German tongue concerning the deeds of great men and the great events that took place in this country." These statements illustrate perfectly the modern folkloristic observation that singers will claim to perform a tale exactly as they heard it or recited it previously even though their recital is manifestly at variance with other versions.[3] What they fail to provide is a clear picture of how the narrative passed from German verse (or a mixture of German verse and prose) into a Norse saga.

The theorizing on the transmission of the material to Scandinavia can be boiled down to three options:[4] (1) German traders or minstrels brought their oral repertory to Bergen and the stories were set down by someone in the Norwegian audience: (2) a German manuscript or manuscripts were brought to Norway and adapted into Norse; (3) a Norwegian traveler in northern Germany collected the material and brought it home with him.

---

[3] Albert B. Lord, *The Singer of Tales,* Harvard Studies in Comparative Literature 24 (Cambridge, Mass.: Harvard University Press, 1960), p. 28.

[4] The simplest summaries of the problem may be found in Ernst Walter, "Zur Entstehung der Thidrikssaga," *Jahrbuch des Vereins für niederdeutsche Sprachforschung,* 83 (1960), 23–28, and Helmut Voigt's "Nachwort" to *Die Geschichte Thidreks von Bern,* Thule 22, trans. Fine Erichsen (Düsseldorf and Cologne: Eugen Diederichs Verlag, 1967), pp. 464–78.

The second option has been argued persuasively by Heinrich Hempel.[5] I add the following point in support of his conclusion. During the fighting in "Niflunga saga," Họgni kills Írungr in an encounter described in the following terms (II.320.8–14):

Oc nu hlœypr jrungr annat sinni ihollena at hogna. Oc nu varaz hogni við. oc snyr igegn honum. oc legr sinu spioti under hans skiolld i hans briost sua at sundr tecr bryniona oc bukinn sua at um herðarnar kom út. oc þa letr irungr sigaz við steinveginn. oc þesse steinuegr heitir irungs vegr en i dag.[6]

(And now Írungr rushes into the hall at Họgni a second time. Họgni becomes aware of him and turns to meet him and thrusts his spear under his shield and into his chest so that it splits his byrnie and body and comes out at the shoulders. And then Írungr sinks against the stone wall and this stone wall is still called Írungr's Wall today.)

It will be noted that Írungr's fall is reported in conjunction with a local place name in the north German town of Soest, where the battle between Huns and Burgundians is fought according to *Þiðreks saga*. The details of the encounter, specifically the passage of spear or sword through or under the shield and through the byrnie and the projection of the spear, correspond closely to stanzas 2062.2–4 and 2064.1–3 in the *Nibelungenlied:*

der Hâwartes man

wart von Hagenen swerte   krefteclîchen wunt
durch schilt und durch di brünne,   des er wart nimmer mêr
gesunt.

Hagen vor sînen füezen   einen gêr ligen vant.
er schôz ûf Îringen,   den helt von Tenelant,
daz im von dem houbte   diu stange ragete dan.

[5]"Sächsische Nibelungendichtung und sächsischer Ursprung der Thidrikssaga," in *Edda, Skalden, Saga: Festschrift zum 70. Geburtstag von Felix Genzmer*, ed. Hermann Schneider (Heidelberg: Winter, 1952), pp. 138–56; rpt. in his *Kleine Schriften*, pp. 209–25. See also Karl Droege, "Zur Thidrekssaga," *ZDA*, 66 (1919), 46, and Jan de Vries, "Hunebedden en Hunen," *Tijdschrift voor nederlandsche taal- en letterkunde*, 49 (1930), 80.

[6]On this passage in general see Rudolf Meissner, "Iringes Weg," *ZDA*, 56 (1919), 77–98 (esp. 84–94).

(Hawart's retainer was severely wounded by Hagen's sword (passing) through shield and byrnie; he never recovered from it. Hagen found a spear lying at his feet. He took aim at Iring, the hero of Denmark, so that the shaft projected from his head.)

This correspondence indicates that the passage in *Þiðreks saga* is taken over from the south German epic that also underlies the *Nibelungenlied*. It was furthermore taken over by someone familiar with the place names and local history or pseudohistory of Soest. This literary operation—the adaptation of a south German written source in terms of local north German lore—can only be attributed to a resident of Soest or the environs, not to a visiting Norwegian and much less to a Norwegian working from oral informants in Bergen. If this procedure is indicative of *Þiðreks saga* as a whole, the compilation was presumably made in Soest and merely translated with some adjustments in Norway. It then becomes immaterial whether the German manuscript was brought to Norway by a German or a Norwegian.[7] The remarks on German oral tradition in the prologue and at the conclusion of "Niflunga saga" must be seen as authentication, not as evidence of field work among German storytellers.

The Norse translator who worked on the German compilation naturally recognized that the tales of German Siegfried were in some ways identical to his native traditions about Sigurd. There is some evidence at the outset of "Niflunga saga" that he even tried to "naturalize" the story to match his own traditions, though he soon discovered that the discrepancies were too great and was obliged to abandon the scheme.[8] The possibility of a Norse coloring in the Sigurd portion of *Þiðreks saga* therefore exists and must be considered when using the text to document German tradition. The basic story is surely German, but the chance of Norse impingement in detail must be taken into account. Unlike

[7]Eyvind Fjeld Halvorsen, "Didriks saga af Bern," *Kulturhistorisk leksikon for nordisk middelalder*, III (Copenhagen: Rosenkilde and Bagger, 1958), 73–76, points out that it is more reasonable to assume that the translation was made in court circles, as was customary in the mid-thirteenth century, and to assume manuscript rather than oral transmission.

[8]T. M. Andersson, "The Epic Source of Niflunga saga and the Nibelungenlied," p. 20.

"Niflunga saga," which is told in a single block, the tale of Sigurd is told in three separate sections: Sigurd's birth and youth (I.282–319), marriage (II.37–43), and death (II.258–68).

Sigurd's Birth and Youth

King Sigmund of Tarlungaland (Karlungaland),[9] the son of King Sifjan, sends messengers to woo Sisibe, the daughter of King Niðungr of Spain. Niðungr welcomes the suit, but is reluctant to send his daughter abroad with strangers. The messengers return with news of their gracious reception, and Sigmund sets out for Spain shortly thereafter. He is treated with every mark of honor, and the marriage is celebrated with great opulence and splendor for five days, after which Sigmund returns home with his new bride. When he has been at home for a week, his brother-in-law King Drasólfr dispatches messengers urging him to join in a military campaign in Púlinaland. Sigmund consents and gathers forces. Leaving his wife and realm in the keeping of his two counselors Artvin and Hermann, counts in Svávaland, he departs to perform great deeds in Púlinaland. When the two counts have ruled for a time, Artvin approaches Sisibe with the proposal to seize the realm and take her to wife. She indignantly refuses and bids him desist on pain of being hanged when she reports the conversation to Sigmund. Artvin confers with Hermann, who renews the suit on Artvin's behalf to no avail. Sigmund and Drasólfr now complete their campaign with varying success and return home. On the news of their approach, Artvin and Hermann take counsel and determine to preempt any denunciation contemplated by Sisibe. They take leave of her under the pretext of riding out to meet the king. They then take him aside and poison his mind with the fabrication that Sisibe has taken a slave as lover and become pregnant, in the meantime silencing their own objections by threatening to slander them. Sigmund protests at first, but Hermann swears to the truth of Artvin's tale. Sigmund ponders whether she should be hanged or sent back to her father with her eyes put out and feet severed. Artvin counsels that she be sent to Svávaskógr (the Black Forest?[10]) to live with her tongue cut out, a solution that Sigmund finds to his liking.

[9]William J. Paff, *The Geographical and Ethnic Names in the Þiðriks saga: A Study in Germanic Heroic Legend,* Harvard Germanic Studies 2 (Cambridge, Mass.: Harvard University Press, 1959), pp. 185–87.

[10]Paff, pp. 180–81.

The counts return to Sisibe and lure her to Sváváskógr with the fiction that she is to meet her husband there. When they come to a deserted spot, Artvin proposes to cut out her tongue and leave her to die, but Hermann relents at the last moment and suggests that they take the tongue from a dog instead. As the two counts confront one another over the issue, Sisibe gives birth to a baby boy, whom she carefully encloses in a glass vessel. In the meantime, Artvin and Hermann come to blows; Artvin is vanquished, but as he falls, he kicks the glass vessel into a stream. In anguish the queen expires, Hermann brings her body back to court, reveals what has happened, and is banished.

Eventually the glass vessel washes ashore and the baby (who has begun to grow) bursts it. He is rescued by a hind and nursed for a year, by which time he is as big as a four-year-old. The story now turns to Mímir, a great smith who has been married nine years without begetting offspring, much to his sorrow. He has an evil brother named Reginn whose villainy is such that he has turned into a serpent. His nature shows no improvement in this new shape, and he is bent on killing everyone except his brother Mímir. One day Mímir goes to the woods to burn charcoal and the little boy runs up to him followed by the hind, thus indicating the circumstances of his fostering. Mímir clothes him and takes him home with the intention of bringing him up as his own son. He names him Sigfreðr (the saga writer begins with this German form and later changes to the Norse form Sigurðr). When the boy is nine years old, he is so big and strong that no one has seen his match. He is also a roughneck and manhandles Mímir's apprentices. One day when he appears dragging the chief apprentice Ekkiharðr, Mímir determines to put his strength to good use in the smithy, but Sigurd's first blow with the hammer drives the anvil into the stone support below flush with the top. Mímir realizes that whatever else becomes of Sigurd, he will be of no use in the business.

Mímir now ponders how to rid himself of his unwanted foster son and enlists a serpent in the forest to kill him (the text seems to start anew here and does not identify the serpent as his brother Reginn). He bids Sigurd go out to burn charcoal and he accordingly builds an enormous fire. Then he sits down and consumes the food and drink that Mímir had intended for nine days. With such hearty rations under his belt he is ready to take on any man in the world and at this precise moment the serpent appears. Given the chance to test his ambition, Sigurd seizes a burning tree from the fire and clubs the serpent to death. In the evening his hunger revives, and he prepares a stew from the serpent's flesh. When he tests the stew with his

finger, he burns it and thrusts it into his mouth to cool it. The taste of
the juice enables him to understand two birds in a tree. One of them
observes that he would do well to kill Mímir, who has plotted his
death and is the serpent's brother; if Sigurd does not anticipate him,
Mímir will avenge his brother by killing him. Sigurd now bathes
himself in the serpent's blood and his skin turns to horn wherever it
comes in contact with the blood, but he is unable to reach between
his shoulders. Thus vulcanized, he goes home carrying the serpent's
head with him. The apprentices take to their heels at his appearance,
and Mímir must confront him alone. Sigurd threatens to make him
gnaw the head like a dog, but Mímir offers to make amends for his
wrongdoing with gifts of a helmet, shield, and byrnie, weapons he
has made for Hertniðr in Hólmgarðr (Novgorod). In addition he
offers a horse named Grani from Brynhild's stud and a sword named
Gramr. Sigurd agrees and Mímir turns over the promised weapons
including the sword, with which Sigurd promptly cuts him down.

He next sets out for Brynhild's residence. When no one appears to
open the iron gate, Sigurd staves it in and enters. Confronted by
seven sentries, he draws his sword and kills them all. The knights in
residence now realize what is afoot and attack him in concert.
Brynhild learns of the action and states that Sigurd Sigmundarson
must have arrived and would be welcome even if he killed seven
knights in addition to seven thralls. She goes out to stop the fighting
and inquires into his name and ancestry. He gives the name Sigurd,
but knows nothing of his lineage. Brynhild provides the missing
information and bids him welcome. Sigurd now requests the horse
mentioned by Mímir and Brynhild dispatches men to catch it. They
fail and Sigurd is hospitably entertained that night. In the morning he
goes out with twelve men who once more try in vain to subdue the
horse. However, when Sigurd takes the bit, the horse approaches
voluntarily and submits to his new rider. Sigurd thanks Brynhild for
her hospitality and sets out again, never spending more than one
night at any place until he comes to Bertangaland (Brittany).[11] Here
he takes service with King Ísungr, who makes him his counselor and
standard-bearer.

(There follows a long section (I.322–II.37) in which Þiðrekr and
his champions challenge Ísungr, Sigurd, and Ísungr's eleven sons to
battle.) After a series of single combats Þiðrekr meets Sigurd. Sigurd
stipulates that he not use the sword Mímungr, but Þiðrekr evades
the condition with a false oath and Sigurd, finding his shield and
armor gradually whittled away, is obliged to concede defeat and
enter Þiðrekr's service.

[11]Paff, pp. 35–39.

Sigurd's Marriage

King Þiðrekr now accompanies Gunnarr (one of his champions) to Niflungaland, where Sigurd marries Grimhild, the sister of Gunnarr and Hǫgni, and receives half the realm. The wedding feast is celebrated with great splendor and lasts five days. As they sit at the feast, Sigurd proposes that Gunnarr should woo Brynhild of Sægarðr. He offers his services since he knows the way (II.38.14: "ek veit þangat allar leiðir") and Gunnarr readily agrees. They journey to Brynhild's residence, where she welcomes Þiðrekr and Gunnarr warmly, but gives Sigurd a cool reception because she knows that he now has a wife. The previous time they had met, he had sworn oaths that he would marry no other woman and she had sworn to marry no other man. Sigurd now woos her on Gunnarr's behalf, but she reproaches him for his faithlessness and states that she would choose him above all other men. Sigurd replies that they must accept the status quo and urges Gunnarr's suit; he married Grimhild rather than Brynhild because she had a brother and Gunnarr and he had sworn to be brothers to one another. Brynhild reconciles herself to his advice since she cannot have his love. The wedding is arranged, but Brynhild resists Gunnarr in the bridal bed, binds him hand and foot with their belts, and hangs him on a nail until early morning before releasing him. The same pattern is repeated on the second and third nights. Gunnarr now confers with Sigurd, who advises him that there can scarcely be found a man to subdue her so long as she is a virgin, but as soon as her virginity is taken, she will be no stronger than other women. Gunnarr asks Sigurd to perform the necessary task and relies on his discretion. That night they arrange matters so that Sigurd takes Gunnarr's place in bed and Gunnarr departs in Sigurd's clothes to mislead the observers. Sigurd waits until everyone is asleep, then "takes her virginity in a trice." In the morning he exchanges rings with her and manages to exchange clothes with Gunnarr again so that no one is the wiser. Now Gunnarr returns to Niflungaland with his wife and rules in peace with his brother-in-law Sigurd and his brothers Hǫgni and Gernoz.

Sigurd's Death

Gunnarr, Hǫgni, and Sigurd reign in great prosperity at Verniza (Worms).[12] They are wealthier than all other kings and inspire fear in their enemies. Sigurd was preeminent among them and his skin was

[12]Paff, pp. 214–15.

as hard as a boar's hide or horn, so that no weapon could harm him except between the shoulders. One day Brynhild enters the hall and finds Grimhild sitting there. She challenges her and asks why she is so arrogant as not to rise before her queen. Grimhild replies that she does not rise because Brynhild now occupies the highseat that once belonged to Grimhild's mother and she has every right to it. Brynhild retorts that regardless of whether Grimhild's father and mother once owned highseat, palace, and land, these things are now hers and Grimhild might do better to track the hind in the forest after her husband. Grimhild responds that her husband is a cause for honor and not contempt, but that if Brynhild wishes to discuss honor, she might begin by telling who took her virginity and who was her first husband. Brynhild replies that there is no shame in reporting that Gunnarr was her first husband. Grimhild proclaims the answer a lie and identifies the man who took her virginity as Sigurd. Brynhild denies it, but Grimhild verifies the charge with the gold ring that Sigurd took from Brynhild. Brynhild recognizes the ring and realizes what has happened. She regrets that the matter has been divulged in the presence of so many, turns red as blood, says not a word, and leaves the hall.

Brynhild now sees Gunnarr, Hǫgni, and Gernoz riding to the palace and goes out to meet them weeping and tearing her clothes. She asks Gunnarr for vengeance because Sigurd broke his oath by revealing the bed substitution to Grimhild, who has denounced her in the presence of all. Hǫgni replies that she should not weep, but pretend that nothing has happened. Brynhild points out that Sigurd first came to them like a beggar and is now so proud and powerful that he will soon hold them all in thrall. When he first visited her, he did not even know his father or mother or his lineage. Gunnarr bids her take comfort; Sigurd will not be their lord for long, nor Grimhild her queen. They subsequently pretend that no words have passed between them and Sigurd remains absent at the hunt for some time. When he returns, the brothers welcome him warmly.

Some days later Hǫgni proposes a new hunt and secretly orders the steward to salt the food and give Sigurd the saltiest portion. He also arranges for the drink to be delayed during the hunt. The next morning they eat early. Sigurd asks the reason, is told of the hunting plan, and is invited to join the party. He accepts and they set out, Hǫgni's instructions having been followed exactly. Grimhild goes to bed so as to avoid Brynhild. In the meantime, Hǫgni lingers behind and Brynhild urges him to assure that Sigurd will not return that evening, offering him rewards of gold and silver. Hǫgni replies that he cannot be certain of success, but he undertakes to do his best. He then rejoins the hunting party. They run down a wild boar and after Hǫgni kills it, they are so hot and tired that they are ready to burst. They cast themselves down by a stream to drink and Hǫgni, getting to his feet before the others, thrusts his spear between Sigurd's shoulders and into his heart. Before dying Sigurd elegizes that he did not expect such conduct of his brother-in-law; if he had, all four would have been dead before the deed was accomplished. Hǫgni triumphantly announces that the four of them spent all morning hunting a boar, but that he alone has killed a bear or a bison, though it would have been harder for them to bring down Sigurd than a bear or a bison, had he been prepared. Gunnarr proposes that they take the bison home to his sister Grimhild. As they return, Brynhild sees them from the hall bearing Sigurd's body. She goes out to congratulate them and urge that Grimhild be given her husband's corpse to embrace as she deserves. They accordingly throw Sigurd's body into her bed and she awakens to find him dead. From his unscathed shield and helmet she infers that he has been murdered. Hǫgni claims that a wild boar killed him, but Grimhild retorts that he was himself the boar and she weeps bitterly. The killers go to the hall in good spirits (Brynhild is no less cheerful), leaving Grimhild to prepare the corpse for burial. The author concludes with a eulogy of Sigurd, whose name will never die in German or among the Norsemen.

The story told in Þiðreks saga is manifestly what we find in the poems of the Edda or Vǫlsunga saga, but it differs in detail. We may begin by cataloging the similarities and dissimilarities, taking one section of the saga at a time—youth, marriage, and death.

The circumstances of Sigurd's birth are made over entirely on the basis of a folktale known variously as the Constance, Crescentia, or Genevieve story.[13] As a result, the tale of Sisibe's slandering and Sigurd's birth in the wilds looks late and adventitious.[14] Whether it has any foundation in the original story is de-

[13]The background of this section in Þiðreks saga has been studied most fully by Heinrich Hempel, Nibelungenstudien, I: Nibelungenlied, Thidrikssaga und Balladen (Heidelberg: Winter, 1926), 179–99 and 230–64, and Andreas Wild, Sisibesage und Genovefalegende (Bamberg, 1970). The closest parallel is the story "Siegfried und Genofeva" in Jakob and Wilhelm Grimm, Deutsche Sagen (Berlin: Nicolai, 1816), II, 280–85 (no. 532). On the story in general see Margaret Schlauch, Chaucer's Constance and Accused Queens (New York: New York University Press, 1927); this work has only an incidental reference to Þiðreks saga on pp. 103–4.

[14]Heinrich Hempel, "Sigurds Ausritt zur Vaterrache," Kleine Schriften, p. 191.

batable. Perhaps the misfortunes of Hjǫrdís, the death of her husband on the battlefield, her refuge in the forest, and abduction to Denmark (or some analogous account) were sufficient to inspire the more elaborate tale of woe as we find it in *Þiðreks saga*. In any event it is interesting that the saga intervenes in the thinnest part of the Eddic narrative (Sigurd's birth); the procedure suggests a *horror vacui* and a wish to fill in the unexploited spaces.

When the story turns to Sigurd's fostering, the similarities to the Eddic account appear. They may be summarized as follows:

Edda (Vǫlsunga saga)	*Þiðreks saga*
Sigurd is fostered by Reginn the smith.	Sigurd is fostered by Mímir the smith.
Reginn has an evil brother, the serpent Fáfnir.	Mímir has an evil brother, the serpent Reginn (but cf. I.347.6: "er vęringiar kalla faðmi"—"whom the Norsemen call Fáfnir").
Sigurd cleaves Reginn's anvil.	Sigurd drives Mímir's anvil into the stone support.
Reginn incites Sigurd against Fáfnir (with the intention of avenging Fáfnir?).	Mímir incites Reginn against Sigurd.
Sigurd kills Fáfnir.	Sigurd kills Reginn.
Sigurd tastes Fáfnir's heart and understands the birds.	Sigurd tastes Reginn's flesh and understands the birds.
The birds advise him to kill Reginn.	The birds advise him to kill Mímir.
Reginn forges the sword Gramr.	Mímir makes Sigurd a gift of the sword Gramr.
Sigurd kills Reginn.	Sigurd kills Mímir.

The similarities show that the same story underlies both texts, but the differences are sufficient to prove that the redactor of *Þiðreks saga* is not simply retelling the Norse version. The skeleton of the narrative is without doubt a German variant akin to but not identical with the Norse account. The shared outline relates that Sigurd was fostered by a smith with a brother in the form of a serpent, that he killed the serpent, tasted its flesh, and understood the speech of birds. These advised him to kill the smith, advice that he was not slow to follow. In addition, the smith provided a sword and Sigurd either tested the sword (preparatory to killing the serpent) or demonstrated his strength by delivering a tremendous blow on the anvil.

To be sure, many similarities may be secondary and attributable to Norse features introduced into *Þiðreks saga* by the Norse redactor. The serpent in *Þiðreks saga*, which does not appear to be identical with Fáfnir, may be transformed into Mímir's brother as a concession to Norse tradition; it is easy to imagine a serpent adventure in German tradition without the fraternal connection.[15] The tasting of the serpent's flesh and the counsel of the birds may be a similar concession, although it is not apparent why the Norse adapter converted the heart motif into a stew if he did not find the latter in his German source.[16] The presentation of the sword Gramr may also be purely Norse, but if this is so, it is again surprising that the sword has been made over from a dragon-slaying instrument into a conciliatory gift. Perhaps the Norse redactor simply added Gramr to other gifts mentioned in the German source.[17] The only elements reasonably secure for both German and Norse traditions are Sigurd's childhood in the custody of a smith, his acquisition of a sword from his foster father, and his killing of the serpent. The most obvious discrepancy between the traditions is the failure of the German versions (*Þiðreks saga, Nibelungenlied, Das Lied vom Hürnen Seyfrid*) to equate the killing of the serpent with the acquisition of a treasure. Nor is there any reference to Sigurd's vengeance for his father.[18] On the

[15]This is Hempel's view in *Nibelungenstudien*, p. 128.

[16]Hempel, *Nibelungenstudien*, pp. 128–29, attributed the counsel of the birds to Norse influence, as had R. C. Boer, *Untersuchungen über den Ursprung und die Entwicklung der Nibelungensage*, I (Halle: Verlag der Buchhandlung des Waisenhauses, 1906), 102–3, and Friedrich Panzer, *Studien zur germanischen Sagengeschichte*, II: *Sigfrid* (Munich: Beck, 1912), 45. However, Gustav Neckel, "Sigmunds Drachenkampf," *Edda*, 13 (1920), 206–7, argued that this motif belonged to the German original. Hermann Schneider, *Germanische Heldensage*, I (Berlin and Leipzig: de Gruyter, 1928; rpt. 1962), 150–51, returned to the older view.

[17]Hempel, *Nibelungenstudien*, p. 130, considered both Gramr and Grani to be Norse intrusions, as did Schneider, I, 151 (from "Sigurðar saga").

[18]Gustav Neckel, "Die Nibelungenballaden," *Aufsätze zur Sprach- und Literaturgeschichte, Wilhelm Braune dargebracht* (Dortmund: Ruhfus, 1920), pp. 85–137, and Hempel, "Sigurds Ausritt," *Kleine Schriften*, pp. 184–94, made a

other hand, *Þiðreks saga* shows a considerable elaboration of Sigurd's life with the smith, his premature strength, enormous appetite, and rambunctious behavior, all in line with the folktale known as "Bear's Son" and "Strong John."[19] Another new motif is the invulnerable hide produced by a bath in the dragon's blood, an aspect of the German tradition confirmed by the *Nibelungenlied* and *Das Lied vom Hürnen Seyfrid*.

If we sort out the events of Sigurd's youth in *Þiðreks saga* according to their provenance from Norse or German tradition, we must compare our text to the *Edda (Vǫlsunga saga, Vǫls. s.)*, on the one hand and *Das Lied vom Hürnen Seyfrid (HS)* on the other. What accords with the former is likely to be Norse, what accords with the latter is likely to be German. A chart of the relevant motifs may be drawn up as follows:

Þiðreks saga	*Tradition*	*Analogue*
Smith Mímir	German	*HS* 4
Evil brother Reginn in the form of a serpent	Norse	*Vǫls. s.* 33.2–36.9
Mímir raises Sigurd.	service: German fostering: Norse	*HS* 4 *Vǫls. s.* 31.25
Sigurd abuses apprentices.	German	*HS* 5
Sigurd buries anvil.	German	*HS* 5
Mímir enlists serpent.	German	*HS* 5–6
Mímir sends Sigurd to burn coal.	German	*HS* 6
Sigurd builds a fire.	German	*HS* 9
Sigurd clubs serpent with burning tree.	German	*HS* 8
Serpent stew	?	
Finger test	German / Norse	*HS* 10 / *Vǫls. s.* 46.2–3
Sigurd understands the birds.	Norse	*Vǫls. s.* 46.5

case for a German tradition of Sigurd's vengeance. See also Otto Holzapfel, *Die dänischen Nibelungenballaden: Texte und Kommentare*, Göppinger Arbeiten zur Germanistik 122 (Göppingen: Alfred Kümmerle, 1974), pp. 51–52.

[19]Panzer, II, 41–46.

Advice to kill Mímir	Norse	*Vǫls. s.* 46.7–47.2
Bath in dragon's blood	German	*HS* 10–11
Mímir's gifts	?	
Sigurd kills Mímir.	Norse	*Vǫls. s.* 47.5–6

These correspondences cannot of course be taken entirely at face value; *HS* may have lost certain older motifs found in Norse tradition (for example the fostering function of the smith and his death) and is therefore not a perfect index to the German tradition. However, it is adequate to show that the account of Sigurd's youth in *Þiðreks saga* is predominantly German and covered with only a thin Norse veneer.

The final adventure of Sigurd's early years is his mysterious visit to Brynhild in chapter 168 of *Þiðreks saga*. In the most recent and best contribution to the puzzles in this chapter, Hans Fromm divides the action into four episodes:[20]
1. Sigurd's irruption into Brynhild's *borg* and killing of seven watchmen
2. Brynhild's identification of Sigurd
3. The welcome and hospitality afforded Sigurd
4. His winning of the horse Grani

This interlude is so isolated that there has been little agreement on what segment of the extant tradition it belongs to. De Boor proposed that it derives from the winning of a treasure in the German "Hortlied" best illumined by *Das Lied vom Hürnen Seyfrid*.[21] Fromm returned to the idea that it reflects in some fashion the prior betrothal between Sigurd and Brynhild that we find in *Vǫlsunga saga* and have learned to associate with *Meiri*. Sigurd's forcible entry into Brynhild's *borg* in *Þiðreks saga* matches *Oddrúnargrátr* 18.1–4:[22]

> Þá var víg vegit   vǫlsco sverði,
> oc borg brotin,   sú er Brynhildr átti.

---

[20]"Kapitel 168 der Thidrekssaga," *DVLG*, 33 (1959), 237–56. Fromm summarizes earlier criticism on pages 237–39.
[21]"Kapitel 168 der Thidrekssaga," in *Edda, Skalden, Saga*, pp. 157–72.
[22]See Panzer, II, 226–27, and Hermann Schneider, "Verlorene Sigurddichtung," *ANF*, 45 (1929), 10.

(Then a battle was fought   with foreign sword
And the fortress breached   that Brynhild had.)

This passage is echoed in the Faroese ballad "Brynhildar táttur" (cited by Fromm, p. 241), which combines the crossing of a flame wall with the breaking down of a door. This juxtaposition of flame wall and forced entrance is duplicated by the Eddic poem *Skírnismál* 9 and 11–13 (plus prose insert), where there is no broken door, but a confrontation with an inhospitable watchman. On the basis of a detailed comparison of Sigurd's wooing with *Skírnismál*, Fromm (p. 243) believes that the poet of *Skírnismál* took the scene from some late version of the Sigurd legend, for which we can therefore assume the watchman or watchmen also implied in *Oddrúnargrátr* 18 ("Þá var víg vegit"). The forced entrance and battle waged against the defenders of the *borg* in *Þiðreks saga* 168 can thus be associated with the wooing of Brynhild as documented in "Brynhildar táttur," *Skírnismál*, and, by implication, *Oddrúnargrátr* 18.

The second episode in chapter 168 is Brynhild's identification of Sigurd; she learns of the battle with the watchmen and concludes, "that must be Sigurd the son of Sigmund." This passage echoes "Brynhildar táttur" (cited by Fromm, p. 247), in which Brynhild must ask the name of her visitor instead of knowing it by magical intuition, and *Vǫlsunga saga* 48.10–12, in which Brynhild (= Sigrdrífa) is aroused from her trance and asks what has awakened her—"or has Sigurd the son of Sigmund come here, who has Fáfnir's helmet and carries his killer (Gramr) in his hand?" The second element in chapter 168 can therefore also be explained as a relic of the wooing of Brynhild (Sigrdrífa).

The third episode is Brynhild's proffering of hospitality (I.318.1: "you are welcome to our hospitality"). Fromm traces the motif to *Vǫlsunga saga* 49.4–5 ("Brynhild filled a vessel and brought it to Sigurd") and "Brynhildar táttur" (cited by Fromm, p. 248). The drinking vessel in *Vǫlsunga saga* (and the second prose insert of *Sigrdrífumál*) derives from the fifth stanza of *Sigrdrífumál*, recurs in *Skírnismál* 16 (Fromm, p. 242), and may be found as well in the opening scene of *Meiri* ("Falkenlied") recorded by *Vǫlsunga saga* 59.26–28 ("then she arose and four maidens with her and brought him a golden vessel and bade him drink''). Fromm's conclusion (p. 250) that the hospitality is well anchored in the tradition of the prior betrothal seems amply justified.

The final point in chapter 168 is Brynhild's gift of a horse.[23] This episode is difficult to reconcile with the wooing sequence. Fromm (pp. 250–51) assumes that the account transfers the role of Sigurd's mother in procuring a horse, as documented by "Regin smiður,"[24] to Brynhild, but the solution is not compelling. The chief difficulty in interpreting chapter 168 in terms of a prior betrothal is of course the author's failure to mention any such betrothal. The objection was formulated most sharply by de Boor.[25] To be sure, the author of *Þiðreks saga* presupposes the betrothal further along in the narrative (II.38.20–39.3), but, argued de Boor, all the more reason not to suppress the betrothal in chapter 168 if it was once mentioned there. We would have to make the unlikely assumption that the author somehow forgot the most vital aspect of the episode.

This logic does not exhaust the possibilities, however. It is credible that the saga writer omitted mention of the prior betrothal rationally. The omission may in fact be connected with the Norse revision of a German exemplar that we have had occasion to observe elsewhere.[26] We may reasonably believe that the prior betrothal was a basic feature of German tradition, but we have seen that this feature gained firm footing in Scandinavia only with the composition of *Meiri*. If the adaptation in *Þiðreks saga* was executed prior to the composition of *Meiri* or carried out in Norway without a knowledge of *Meiri*, we must assume that it was done by a writer for whom the norm was a version akin to *Forna* without the prior betrothal. He would therefore naturally suppress the betrothal in order to accommodate the German story to

---

[23]See Neckel, "Die Nibelungenballaden," pp. 118–21.

[24]E.g., F 38–41 in *Føroya kvæði (Corpus Carminum Færoensium)*, ed. N. Djurhuus and Chr. Matras (Copenhagen: Munksgaard, 1951), p. 166.

[25]"Kapitel 168 der Thidrekssaga," in *Edda, Skalden, Saga*, p. 161.

[26]Hermann Schneider, *Die deutschen Lieder von Siegfrieds Tod* (Weimar: Hermann Böhlaus Nachfolger, 1947), p. 21, toyed with the idea that the prior betrothal was a German import in Scandinavia, but drew back in favor of the hypothesis that the erotic relationship between Brynhild and Sigurd developed spontaneously in both traditions. Cf. Fromm, "Kapitel 168 der Thidrekssaga," p. 254. See also Hempel, *Nibelungenstudien*, pp. 134–37.

his own tradition. As a replacement for this lost motif and as a justification for Sigurd's visit to Brynhild, he inserted ad hoc the acquisition of Grani. The exact status of this gift in Norse tradition is not clear; it may have been bestowed by Sigurd's mother as in "Regin smiður" or by King Hjálprekr as in *Vǫlsunga saga* 32.14–15. Perhaps the very fluidity of the motif made it possible for the Norse adapter of *Þiðreks saga* to reallocate it as he saw fit. What he failed to realize when he displaced the prior betrothal in chapter 168 was that it would return to haunt him later in the story, namely in chapter 227, in which Sigurd woos Brynhild on Gunnarr's behalf and is reproached for his faithlessness. Here the prior betrothal could not be so easily suppressed because it was the substance of the dialogue. As a result, the redactor was obliged to retrieve the betrothal as best he could:

> jt fyʀa sin*n* er þav hœfðu hitz þa hafði han þ*vi* heitið hen*n*i m*eð* æiðu*m* at h*ann* skylldi œngrar ko*n*o fa næma hen*n*ar oc ho*n* et sama at gipptaz ongu*m* man*n*i oðru*m*.

> (The previous time they had met, he had promised her with oaths that he would marry no other woman but her and she likewise to marry no other man.) [II. 38.23–39.3]

I conclude that the German exemplar of chapter 168 contained the prior betrothal and that it was consciously eliminated by the Norse redactor in an ultimately unsuccessful attempt to adjust the German story to a Norse tradition without the prior betrothal.

We may now move to the following section on Sigurd's marriage, a passage in which the correspondences between German and Norse legend are once more clearer. The following summary of the chief correspondences observes the chronology in *Þiðreks saga* and juxtaposes the equivalent Eddic themes without regard to the differing sequence in which they occur:

Þiðreks saga	*Edda (Vǫlsunga saga)*
Sigurd marries Grimhild.	Sigurd marries Gudrun.
Sigurd proposes that Gunnarr should woo Brynhild.	Grimhild proposes that Gunnarr should woo Brynhild.
Sigurd offers to help because he knows the way.	Sigurd knows the way (*Skamma* 3).

Brynhild receives Sigurd ungraciously because she knows he has another wife and has broken his oaths to her.	Prior betrothal (*Meiri*)
Brynhild reproaches Sigurd for his faithlessness.	Brynhild reproaches Sigurd for his faithlessness (*Meiri*).
Sigurd exchanges clothes with Gunnarr, subdues Brynhild in bed, and deflowers her.	Sigurd clears the flame wall in Gunnarr's shape and shares her bed for three nights.
Exchange of rings	Exchange of rings

The shared outline in this section includes Sigurd's betrothal to Brynhild, his subsequent marriage to Gunnarr's sister, and the assistance lent Gunnarr in winning Brynhild by overcoming hindrances for which Gunnarr is no match (the flame wall in the *Edda* and Brynhild's superhuman strength in *Þiðreks saga*). The most conspicuous feature that emerges from a comparison of the two texts is the special degree of correspondence between *Þiðreks saga* and the portions of *Vǫlsunga saga* attributable to *Meiri*. This correspondence involves the prior betrothal and Brynhild's reproach to Sigurd for breaking his betrothal oaths. However, the similarities go beyond the coincidence of plot elements and extend to the verbal level. The words with which Brynhild reproaches Sigurd during his wooing on Gunnarr's behalf in *Þiðreks saga* answer to the words with which Sigurd plights his troth in the prior betrothal according to *Meiri:*

Þiðreks saga II.38.23–39.3	*Vǫlsunga saga* 60.14–16
jt fyʀa sinn er þav hœfðu hitz þa hafði han þvi heitið henni með æiðum at hann skyldi œngrar kono fa næma hennar oc hon et sama at gipptaz ongum manni oðrum.	". . . ok þess sver ek vid gudinn, at ek skal þik eigha eda eingha konu ella." Hun mellti slikt.
(The previous time they had met, he had promised her with oaths that he would marry no other woman but her and she likewise to marry no other man.)	(". . . and I swear by the gods that I will marry you and no other woman." She swore the same.)

Furthermore, the content of the dialogue during the proxy wooing in *Þiðreks saga* corresponds closely to the final dialogue between Brynhild and Sigurd in *Meiri*. Sigurd urges Brynhild to marry (or love) Gunnarr (*Þiðreks saga* II.39.4–5 and *Vǫlsunga saga* 76.2–3), Brynhild declares Sigurd to be preeminent above all men or her first choice in the world (*Þiðreks saga* II.39.8–10 and *Vǫlsunga saga* 76.16–18[27]), but Sigurd invokes the status quo and urges resignation (*Þiðreks saga* II.39.10–14 and *Vǫlsunga saga* 75.27–29). This conjunction is especially significant if we bear in mind that *Meiri* and *Þiðreks saga* are the only texts in the legendary material in which it comes to a direct confrontation between Brynhild and Sigurd and an open discussion of the broken oaths. When these oaths are similarly formulated in both texts and the discussion proceeds along similar lines, an explanation is required.

R. C. Boer believed that the wooing scene in *Þiðreks saga* was an accurate reflection of German tradition, but Polak, followed by Heusler, believed that *Þiðreks saga* was based on *Meiri*.[28] Hempel also argued for Norse influence,[29] but we have seen that the prior betrothal belongs to the German version underlying *Þiðreks saga*. There is therefore no reason to attribute the references to this betrothal in the wooing scene to Norse influence. At the same time, we have seen that *Meiri* was subject to a whole series of German influences. It is therefore plausible that the *Meiri* poet drew on the reproachful discussion between Brynhild and Sigurd in the German wooing scene to construct the showdown in their final dialogue. Viewed in this way, Sigurd's wooing on Gunnarr's behalf in *Þiðreks saga* is an original German feature, while the dialogue between Brynhild and Sigurd in *Meiri,* which is manifestly secondary, owes its inspiration to their earlier exchange at

[27]Hempel, *Nibelungenstudien*, p. 131, notes an even closer parallel between *Þiðreks saga* II.39.8–10 and *Vǫlsunga saga* 55.10–11 (the betrothal to Sigrdrífa).

[28]Boer, I, 36–37; Léon Polak, *Untersuchungen über die Sigfridsagen*, Diss. Berlin (Berlin: Universitäts-Buchdruckerei, 1910), pp. 108–14; Andreas Heusler, "Die Quelle der Brünhildsage in Thidreks saga und Nibelungenlied," *Aufsätze zur Sprach- und Literaturgeschichte, Wilhelm Braune dargebracht* (Dortmund: Ruhfus, 1920), p. 57; rpt. in his *Kleine Schriften*, I, 75.

[29]*Nibelungenstudien*, p. 131. Hermann Schneider, "Verlorene Sigurddichtung," p. 29, and Wilhelm Lehmgrübner, *Die Erweckung der Walküre* (Halle: Niemeyer, 1936), p. 79, derived the scene from "Sigurðar saga."

the time of the proxy wooing in the German source of *Þiðreks saga* or some analogous version.

Only the last section of Sigurd's biography in *Þiðreks saga*, the story of his death, remains. The correspondences to the Eddic version may be tabulated as follows:

Þiðreks saga	*Edda (Vǫlsunga saga)*
Brynhild and Grimhild quarrel in the hall.	Brynhild and Gudrun quarrel in the bath.
Grimhild proves her contention by exhibiting the ring Sigurd took from Brynhild.	Gudrun proves her contention by exhibiting the ring Sigurd took from Brynhild.
Brynhild incites Gunnarr.	Brynhild incites Gunnarr.
She warns of Sigurd's growing power.	She harks back to Sigurd's growing power (*Brot* 8–9).
Hǫgni kills Sigurd.	Gotþormr (*Skamma* 21) or the brothers jointly (*Brot* 7) kill Sigurd.
Sigurd is slain outside.	Sigurd is slain outside (*Brot*) or in his bed (*Skamma*).
Sigurd's body is thrown into Grimhild's bed and she awakens next to him.	Gudrun awakens next to her dead husband (*Skamma*).
Brynhild rejoices.	Brynhild rejoices (*Brot* 10, *Skamma* 30).

This segment of the narrative in *Þiðreks saga* gives the impression of being purely German. The correspondences in the Eddic version are a common inheritance and do not suggest a Norse reworking of the German tale; so much is confirmed by the supporting evidence of the *Nibelungenlied,* in which a Norse overlay is not possible. Thus the queens' quarrel in the hall stands closer to the quarrel before the church in the *Nibelungenlied* than to the quarrel in the bath in *Vǫlsunga saga.* Brynhild's warning about Sigurd's growing power echoes the so-called *Machtmotiv* in the *Nibelungenlied* 870, in which Hagen notes that Siegfried's death would mean a great acquisition of land for Gunther; according to *Þiðreks saga* II.37.21–22, Sigurd is actually given half the realm. Hǫgni's killing of Sigurd (in place of Gotþormr in *Skamma* and the joint killers in *Brot*) corresponds to Hagen's role as murderer in Adventure 16 of the *Nibelungenlied*. The location of the slaying in the forest during a hunt (complete with salted food—see below Chapter 5) is similarly duplicated in the *Nibelungenlied*. Finally, the casting of Sigurd's corpse into Grimhild's bed recurs in slightly mitigated form in the *Nibelungenlied;* here Hagen orders that the corpse be deposited before her door (stanzas 1003–4). The occasional surfacing of a more delicate sensibility in the *Nibelungenlied* may also account for the absence of Brynhild's outright rejoicing in this text, though a hint of her malicious disregard for Kriemhilt persists in 1100.2:

> swaz geweinte Kriemhilt,   unmære was ir daz.
>
> (She was indifferent to Kriemhilt's mourning.)

On the whole, we may surmise that the redactor of *Þiðreks saga* found it easy to compose the concluding section on Sigurd's death because the German source was sufficiently removed from his own tradition so as not to invite efforts at harmonization. He simply translated what he had before him.

In summary, the German original of *Þiðreks saga* is based on a native German tradition quite independent of the Norse counterpart, though genetically connected with it. The Norse redactor of the German original occasionally retouched the text in order to accommodate it to the Scandinavian version, but these interventions are superficial and can usually be detected. When allowance is made for them, we can reconstruct the German story underlying *Þiðreks saga* in the following manner:

1. Sigurd grows up with the smith Mímir.
2. Sigurd abuses Mímir's apprentices and demolishes his anvil.
3. Mímir arranges to have Sigurd killed by a serpent.
4. Sigurd clubs the serpent to death with a burning tree.
5. Sigurd becomes invulnerable by bathing in the serpent's blood.
6. Sigurd breaks into Brynhild's residence and betrothes himself to her.
7. He subsequently weds Gunnarr's sister Grimhild.
8. He then urges Gunnarr to woo Brynhild and offers his assistance because he knows the way.
9. At Sægarðr (the Norse redactor's substitution for a too familiar Islant in the German text?) Sigurd woos Brynhild on Gunnarr's behalf.

10. The wedding is celebrated, but Brynhild hangs her ardent husband on a nail for three consecutive nights.

11. Gunnarr appeals to Sigurd, who exchanges clothes with him, takes his place in bed, and deflowers Brynhild.

12. They exchange rings.

13. Brynhild and Grimhild quarrel in the hall and the deception is revealed.

14. Brynhild incites Gunnarr.

15. Hǫgni plots revenge and arranges for a hunt with salt food and an absence of drink.

16. Hǫgni kills Sigurd as he drinks at a fountain.

17. They return with the body and Brynhild bids them cast it in Grimhild's bed.

18. Grimhild infers from unscathed shield and helmet that he has been murdered, but Hǫgni attributes the killing to a boar.

19. Brynhild rejoices.

20. Grimhild prepares the corpse for burial.

If we take a general view of the version in *Þiðreks saga,* we are struck by the latitude given Sigurd and the shrinkage in Brynhild's role.[30] This is evident in the proportions of the narrative. Sigurd's birth and youth are given some thirty-four pages in Bertelsen's edition, his dealings with Brynhild and his marriage only eleven, and his death another eleven. In addition, an extended passage integrates Sigurd into the adventures of Þiðrekr. In the light of this inflated *enfance,* Brynhild appears as a chance figure in Sigurd's career, especially since their romantic interlude is awkwardly narrated in retrospect. The situation differs sharply from the *Edda,* in which the three central poems *Forna, Skamma,* and *Meiri* were preeminently Brynhild poems and Sigurd's youth was given considerably less profile in a series of verse fragments with little poetic impact. What led to the shift? It certainly has much to do with the genre to which *Þiðreks saga* belongs and which is more concerned with arms and the man than with romantic passions. *Þiðreks saga* is often classed with the native Scandinavian *fornaldarsǫgur* (legendary sagas) precisely because it is a quasi-biographical narrative of male adventure. There is much heraldry, tourneying, and denting of helmets. The

---

[30]Heusler commented on the relative importance of Brynhild and Gudrun, but the reweighting of Brynhild's and Sigurd's roles is even more obvious. Heusler, "Die Quelle der Brünhildsage," *Kleine Schriften,* I, 89.

erotic component, so conspicuous elsewhere in the legend, is lost sight of in the new epic of brawn and broadswords. Exactly the same development seems to have been characteristic of the genuine *fornaldarsaga* "Sigurðar saga." Here too Sigurd's youthful feats were expanded in relation to his later entanglement with Brynhild. If we cast about for a purely literary explanation of Sigurd's late fame, it may be found in the displacement of classical heroic poetry by the later tale of adventure with its emphasis on supernatural prowess in a biographical frame.

CHAPTER 5

The Sources of the
Nibelungenlied Part I

Each branch of the Nibelung legend is beset by a particular complex of difficulties. The Eddic version is complicated by problems of relative dating, the scrambled transmission of Sigurd's youth, and the conjectural reconstruction of the lost gathering in Codex Regius. The version in *Þiðreks saga* is complicated by the necessity of separating the Norse translator's revisions from the German original. Our understanding of the inherited story in the *Nibelungenlied* is impeded by an epic amplitude in which old elements are obscured in new romantic and chivalric details added by a German poet whose taste was profoundly modified by the contemporary flowering of "courtly" romance and lyric which dominates French and German literature around 1200. Stern surgery is required to separate the layers and expose the tradition that underlies the new growth. No less disheartening than the textual problem are the complexity of German philological study and the analysis of many details in the *Nibelungenlied* to the point of paralysis. The critic interested in the legendary background of the poem must cope with not only text and analogues, but also an unwieldy meta-literature. At the same time, he must contrive to prevent the mass of critical opinion from blurring the main line of the argument. In an effort to satisfy this last requirement, I have relegated the scholarly debate to a few essential footnotes and a discussion of the main competing theories in the following chapter.[1]

[1] It is of course customary to groan under the bibliographical burden, e.g., H.-

Despite the general familiarity of the story and the cumbersome detail involved in a paraphrase of the *Nibelungenlied,* we cannot dispense with a certain amount of retelling. The richness of the text obliges us to recall the story from the outset, however tedious such a recapitulation may be. To minimize the tedium and the demands on memory, I shall subdivide the plot into three sections of roughly equivalent length corresponding to the three divisions of *Þiðreks saga.* The first section deals with Siegfried's youth prior to the wooing of Brynhild (Adventures 1–5 and 8, or 371 stanzas). The second section tells the story of Brynhild up to the time of her quarrel with Kriemhilt (Adventures 6–7 and 9–13, or 442 stanzas). The third section recounts the death of Siegfried and the aftermath (Adventures 14–19, or 329 stanzas). This particular division of the text has no inherent justification, especially the anticipation of Adventure 8 in the first section, and I adopt it only to facilitate retention. Each summary will be followed by a discussion of the attendant legendary problems. The numbers in parentheses preceding each paragraph refer to the particular adventure reviewed.

Siegfried's Youth

(1) Kriemhilt, not Siegfried, is given precedence.[2] She grows up in Burgundy, a preeminent beauty, but destined to cause the death of

Fr. Rosenfeld, "Nibelungensage und Nibelungenlied in der Forschung der letzten Jahre," *NM,* 26 (1925), 145: "Nächst Goethes Faust hat wohl keine andere deutsche Dichtung eine solche Literatur gezeitigt wie das Nibelungenlied." In our area it is in fact sufficient to study the contributions of Boer, Heusler, Polak, Neckel, Panzer, de Boor, Hempel, Schneider, Wieselgren, Mohr, Hans Kuhn, and individual articles by Fromm and Bumke. The remaining literature adds little. The standard bibliography on the *Nibelungenlied* is Willy Krogmann and Ulrich Pretzel, *Bibliographie zum Nibelungenlied und zur Klage,* 4th ed. (Berlin: Erich Schmidt, 1966), but this selection reflects the modern descriptive bias and is deficient on the legendary background of the *Nibelungenlied* (pp. 58–68). For a guide to reviews of research see the Selected Bibliography.

[2]Heusler began his book *Nibelungensage und Nibelungenlied: Die Stoffgeschichte des deutschen Heldenepos,* 6th ed. (Dortmund: Ruhfus, 1965) with a comment on the poem's Kriemhilt orientation and the appropriateness of the title *Nibelungenlied* that has become common usage (p. 5): "Der treffendere Name begegnet erst bei einem Nachzügler: 'das Buch von Kriemhilden.'" The fullest discussion of the *Nibelungenlied* as a Kriemhilt novel is Werner Schröder, "Die Tragödie Kriemhilts im Nibelungenlied," *ZDA,* 90 (1960–61), 41–80 and 123–60;

many a hero. She is in the care of her three noble brothers Gunther, Gernot, and Giselher (only brief mention is made of their mother Uote and father Dancrat). Among their more important retainers are Hagen, Ortwin, and Volker. One night Kriemhilt dreams of training a falcon, which, to her great grief, is torn apart by two eagles. Her mother interprets the falcon as a noble man whom Kriemhilt stands to lose. Kriemhilt brushes aside any thought of a man in her life, but her mother bids her not protest too much because only the love of a man will make her completely happy. Kriemhilt continues to reject the thought, but the poet identifies the falcon as her future husband, whom her relatives slay and whom she avenges.

(2) The story now turns to Siegfried, the son of Sigemunt and Sigelint at Xanten on the lower Rhine. He undertakes many adventures abroad and is a miracle of honor and beauty. His training is conducted with suitable care and his native instincts are virtuous. When he is old enough to frequent the court, he becomes a popular figure there. At the age when he begins to bear weapons, he also turns his attention to the ladies. Sigemunt arranges a great feast to celebrate the knighting of his son and the festivities last for seven days.

(3) Siegfried now learns of Kriemhilt's fabled beauty and inaccessibility; she attracts many suitors, but wants none of them. His family and retainers urge him to wed, and he settles on Kriemhilt without delay. His parents are alarmed at the thought, but Siegfried is determined to follow the dictates of his heart. Sigemunt acquiesces reluctantly and warns of the arrogance of Gunther and Hagen. Siegfried replies that he will take by force what he cannot get by persuasion. Sigemunt urges an armed expedition, but Siegfried declares that he will set out with eleven companions (stanza 59; increased to twelve in stanza 64). His parents equip him in style, and he departs amid apprehensive farewells. On the seventh morning he arrives at Worms and is received attentively by the Burgundian retainers, who direct him to Gunther's hall. In the meantime, Gunther has heard of the strangers' arrival and is curious about their identity. Ortwin advises him to consult Hagen. Having been called to the scene, Hagen views the group from the window and surmises

---

rpt. in his *Nibelungenlied-Studien* (Stuttgart: Metzler, 1968), pp. 48–156. Günter Kochendörfer, *Das Stemma des Nibelungenliedes und die textkritische Methode,* Diss. Freiburg (Freiburg: Johannes Krause, 1973), however, has argued that the whole first Adventure was missing in the archetype. If true, this conclusion has implications for our understanding of the *Nibelungenlied* as a Kriemhilt novel (Kochendörfer, p. 123).

that the leader must be Siegfried, though he has never seen him before. He relates (stanzas 88–100) how Siegfried rode out alone and came upon the young princes Schilbunc and Nibelunc dividing the Nibelung treasure at the foot of a mountain. They ask for assistance in the division and give him the sword Balmunc in compensation. When the division is not to their satisfaction, they call on twelve giants, whom Siegfried dispatches with Balmunc. In addition, he subjugates seven hundred Nibelung warriors together with their land and kills Schilbunc and Nibelunc. Their retainer, the dwarf Alberich, attempts to avenge them, but succumbs as well and is obliged to swear oaths of allegiance, surrender a cloak that makes the wearer invisible (*Tarnkappe*), and act as guardian of the treasure, which has now passed into Siegfried's possession. Finally, Siegfried also kills a dragon and becomes invulnerable by bathing in the blood. On the basis of these credentials Hagen suggests that Siegfried be received with scrupulous courtesy. He is welcomed accordingly, but responds by challenging Gunther to a combat in which both their realms will be at stake. The Burgundians are baffled by this unexpected demonstration; Gunther demurs, Gernot conciliates, and Ortwin bursts out angrily. Gernot restrains Hagen, Ortwin, and the others by forbidding them to speak, then pacifies Siegfried, whose thoughts have turned to Kriemhilt and who has therefore become more amenable. He is subsequently entertained with great honor at the Burgundian court for a full year, during which he yearns for Kriemhilt constantly without ever seeing her.

(4) Unexpectedly messengers arrive at court to declare war against the Burgundians on behalf of King Liudeger of Saxony and Liudegast of Denmark. Gunther and his retainers are at a loss and Siegfried inquires into their obvious dismay, offering his services. When he learns of the declaration, he volunteers to head an army of a thousand men and confront the enemy. The emissaries are dispatched with the message that Danes and Saxons may attack at their own peril. Liudegast and Liudeger are distressed to learn of Siegfried's presence at the Burgundian court and assemble an army forty thousand strong. The Burgundians mobilize similarly, but Siegfried bids Gunther remain at home while he conducts the campaign. Once in Saxon territory, he reconnoiters the opposing army alone and encounters Liudegast on a similar mission. He takes him prisoner, kills thirty followers bent on freeing him, and leads him back captive to his army. There follows a general engagement in which Siegfried is appropriately conspicuous. When Liudeger recognizes Siegfried by his shield, he orders his standards lowered and surrenders. Mes-

sengers return to Worms to deliver a report of the victory, and in particular a private account of Siegfried's signal prowess to the breathless Kriemhilt. The army now arrives with its prisoners, the wounded on both sides are cared for, and Liudegast and Liudeger are graciously released. Siegfried asks leave to depart, but is prevailed on to remain because he cherishes the wish to see Kriemhilt.

(5) Gunther organizes a great feast and guests flock from far and wide. He is aware of Siegfried's feelings for Kriemhilt and therefore falls in with Ortwin's suggestion that the feast be graced by the presence of the ladies of the court. The beauty of Kriemhilt and Siegfried is described in evocative similes, and Gernot arranges the introduction. The handsome couple is the center of everyone's attention during the twelve days of festivities that ensue. Liudegast and Liudeger offer Gunther an immense treasure in exchange for reconciliation, but Siegfried advises that they be released with a handclasp as security for a promise of nonaggression. The feast is now disbanded with a great display of liberality. Siegfried too wishes to depart, but Giselher dissuades him and he remains for the sake of Kriemhilt, whom he now sees daily.

To complete the picture of Siegfried's nonage, we must skip Adventures 6 and 7 and look ahead to Adventure 8. In the *Nibelungenlied* version, the latter forms an interlude in the wooing sequence, but elsewhere in the legend it belongs to the tales of Sigurd's youth. I include it here to facilitate the comparison.

(8) Having accompanied Gunther on his wooing expedition to Islant and feeling threatened by Brynhild's powerful following, Siegfried dons his *Tarnkappe* and secretly sets sail for the land of the Nibelungs. With magic swiftness he arrives at his destination in the remainder of that day and one night. He draws the boat up on the sand and approaches a fortress (*burc*). Finding the gate closed, he pounds on it and rouses a giant standing guard. He demands entrance, disguising his voice so as not to be recognized. The encounter develops into a violent combat, but Siegfried, delighted by such faithful guardianship despite the danger to his life, eventually subdues and binds the giant. In the meantime his treasure keeper Alberich rushes to the attack, but is also subdued. Siegfried now identifies himself and asks Alberich to procure a thousand men. No sooner said than done, and they arrive splendidly outfitted back in Islant. Brynhild sees the sails in the distance and Gunther identifies the arriving force as his own. She welcomes them in style and preparations for the departure are made. She leaves the realm in the keeping of an uncle, never to return.

It has generally been believed that the opening Adventures of the *Nibelungenlied* are not much fettered by tradition and that the poet created his own courtly preface,[3] but I shall argue that the poet draws extensively on older material. Adventure 1 centers on Kriemhilt's falcon dream. Undoubtedly this dream is identical to Gudrun's hawk dream in *Vǫlsunga saga*, and Heusler assigned it to the beginning of his "Brünhildenlied," but the common prehistory of the motif has otherwise not been much emphasized.[4] As long as the hawk dream in *Vǫlsunga saga* was explained from a separate "Traumlied," it did not figure in the core of the tradition and could be dismissed as an excrescence of no particular significance.[5] But if, as I believe, the hawk dream was part of the long poem *Meiri*, built to a considerable extent on a German model, it becomes an integral part of the traditional narrative, and the perspective changes. Instead of considering that the *Nibelungenlied* poet devised a childhood for Kriemhilt and happened to include a falcon dream available somewhere in the poetic lore, we must suppose that he capitalized on a solid piece of tradition for Kriemhilt's coming of age. The falcon dream was presumably located in a German version underlying both *Meiri* and the *Nibelungenlied*.

A second aspect of Adventure 1 suggests a foundation in tradition: Kriemhilt's reluctance to marry. Her maidenly reserve has been tacitly understood as part of the borrowing from Heinrich von Veldeke's *Eneide* (vv. 9735–9990) and the adaptation of the conversation in which Lavinia responds skeptically to her mother's lecture on love.[6] The question has not been pushed to

[3]E.g., Emil Kettner, *Die österreichische Nibelungendichtung* (Berlin: Weidmannsche Buchhandlung, 1897), pp. 164–65.

[4]*Nibelungensage und Nibelungenlied*, p. 122. Friedrich Panzer, "Nibelungische Ketzereien: 4. Das Traumlied in der Völsungasaga," *BGDSL*, 75 (1953), 255–72 and *Das Nibelungenlied: Entstehung und Gestalt* (Stuttgart and Cologne: Kohlhammer, 1955), p. 282, settled the issue simply by supposing that *Vǫlsunga saga* borrowed from the *Nibelungenlied*.

[5]Franz Rolf Schröder, "Kriemhilds Falkentraum," *BGDSL*, 78 (1956), 319–48, doubted the existence of the "Traumlied" and traced the motif in *Vǫlsunga saga* ultimately to an Old French ballad through German and Danish intermediaries. The weakness of this theory is that it assumes chance inclusion of the ballad scene in both the *Nibelungenlied* and *Vǫlsunga saga*.

[6]Henric van Veldeken, *Eneide*, ed. Gabriele Schieb and Theodor Frings, I (Berlin: Akademie-Verlag, 1964), 688–707. On the parallel see, for example, Panzer, *Das Nibelungenlied*, p. 281.

the point of asking why the *Nibelungenlied* poet chose to borrow
this particular scene. The answer may lie in the tradition. I shall
argue later that Siegfried's wooing of Kriemhilt in Adventure 3 is
modeled in some detail on the traditional wooing of Brynhild. In
fact the *Nibelungenlied* poet has a characteristic habit of real-
locating motifs from one part of the narrative to another.[7] Confronted with the wooing of Kriemhilt, the poet found he had no
traditional framework for the sequence, except perhaps that she
was foisted on Siegfried by deception as in *Meiri*. At the same
time, he had suppressed Siegfried's prior betrothal to Brynhild
and was therefore free to transfer the motifs connected with this
episode to the wooing of Kriemhilt. Similarly, reluctance to wed
is traditionally associated not with Kriemhilt, but with Brynhild
(or her mysterious double Sigrdrífa). Odin's curse on Brynhild /
Sigrdrífa in *Vǫlsunga saga* 48.22–23 is that she will never be
victorious again and will be obliged to marry (a passage derived
from the prose of *Sigrdrífumál*). The curse presupposes that she
is a reluctant bride. In *Meiri* ("Falkenlied") Sigurd determines to
woo Brynhild, but Alsviðr warns him that no one has found favor
with her and that she wishes to perform warlike deeds (*Vǫlsunga
saga* 59.7–10). Accordingly, she resists Sigurd's suit with the argument that she is a shield maiden (*Vǫlsunga saga* 60.5–8 and
11). Here too Brynhild is obviously loath to marry. It seems altogether possible that the theme of the reluctant bride, attached to
Brynhild in the tradition, was in the back of the *Nibelungenlied*
poet's mind when he modeled Kriemhilt's debut on Lavinia's
protestations in the *Eneide*. We shall see that the theme is not lost
from view in Kriemhilt's later development.

Traditional echoes persist more faintly in Adventure 2. In
stanza 21 foreign exploits are alluded to in passing:

> er versuochte vil der rîche   durch ellenthaften muot.
> durch sînes lîbes sterke   er reit in menegiu lant.

(He tested many realms with bold spirits. To prove his strength he
rode out in many lands.)

---

[7]T. M. Andersson, "The Epic Source of Niflungasaga and the Nibelungenlied,"
ANF, 88 (1973), 16–17.

Whether this is a reference to the traditional adventures (vengeance, treasure, dragon) or no more than a heroic flourish is not clear, but the knowledge of specific exploits in Germany is suggested by an additional stanza in redaction C:[8]

> Ê daz der degen küene   vol wüehse ze man,
> dô het er solhiu wunder   mit sîner hant getân,
> dâ von man immer mêre   mac singen unde sagen;
> des wir in disen stunden   müezen vil von im gedagen.

(Before the bold warrior was grown to full manhood, he had accomplished such miracles that one may sing and tell of them forever after; for this reason we must now omit much of his story.)

What the C redactor is telling us is that he could expatiate at length on Siegfried's youthful heroics if he were so minded. He, at least, interpreted the preceding stanza as referring to such exploits. The second possible echo of tradition is Siegfried's early courting of beautiful women (stanza 26). This attentiveness is generally taken to reflect his precocious devotion to courtly love, but it is difficult to see how such amours serve to legitimize him. It seems as likely that the remark is a courtly deflection of Siegfried's prior betrothal to Brynhild, a motif the *Nibelungenlied* poet first suppresses, then retrieves in this oblique manner.

Kriemhilt's reluctance to marry in Adventure 1 is the first hint that she may have borrowed traits from the Brynhild of earlier tradition. This borrowing becomes the basis of the wooing of Kriemhilt in Adventure 3. We know from other branches of the tradition that Siegfried did not in fact woo Kriemhilt (Gudrun); she was offered to him by her family or forced upon him at the expense of his oaths to Brynhild. This unceremonious match had

[8]Ursula Hennig, ed., *Das Nibelungenlied nach der Handschrift C*, Altdeutsche Textbibliothek, 83 (Tübingen: Niemeyer, 1977), p. 5. The interpolation may be seen in the light of those reversions to a tradition still current at the time the redactor of C made his revisions; see Helmut Brackert, *Beiträge zur Handschriftenkritik des Nibelungenliedes*, Quellen und Forschungen zur Sprach- und Kulturgeschichte der germanischen Völker, N. F. 11 (135) (Berlin: de Gruyter, 1963), pp. 141–43. Helmut de Boor, "Die Bearbeitung m des Nibelungenliedes (Darmstädter Aventiurenverzeichnis)," *BGDSL* (Tübingen), 81 (1959), 193–94, suggested that this stanza was the point of departure for the expanded account of Siegfried's adventures in redaction m of the *Nibelungenlied*.

no place in the *Nibelungenlied* poet's courtly climate. He was intent on finding a framework in which the wooer exerted himself in some romantic fashion, a context in which the hero wins the bride, not vice versa. What was more natural than to transfer this context from another part of the same story, Siegfried's arduous wooing of Brynhild? The narrative was available for reconversion because the poet had passed over it in silence so as to spare his hero's reputation. He therefore found himself with one wooing available for reallocation and a second wooing that required restructuring. The former was substituted for the latter and the wooing of Brynhild in the inherited tale became the wooing of Kriemhilt in the courtly revision. But since the wooing of Brynhild in German tradition (*Þiðreks saga*, chap. 168) was anything but courtly, it required considerable adjustment. The staving in of the princess' door and the killing of her watchmen did not provide the proper tone. The *Nibelungenlied* poet took over her inaccessibility and the hostile confrontation with her guardians, but in a considerably modified form.

We have seen that in conversation with her mother Kriemhilt rejects the idea of marriage. This theme is sounded again at the outset of Adventure 3. Kriemhilt's beauty attracts a host of visitors to Gunther's court, but many a hero experiences the maiden's "hôhgemüete" (stanza 45). De Boor glossed the word with the courtly sense of cheerful, festive temper, but the context suggests Kriemhilt's pride and aloofness (cf. stanza 680). This sense is borne out by the following stanza (46), in which we learn that Kriemhilt finds none of her suitors to her liking. The rejection of suitors is not a feature connected with Gudrun in the analogues, but it is a standing attribute of Brynhild's.[9] Her words in *Skamma* 35.1–2 are explicit:

Né ec vilda þat,   at mic verr ætti,
áðr þér Giúcungar   riðot at garði...

(Nor did I wish   that a man should marry me
Until you Gjukungs   rode into my courtyard.)

---

[9] I take seriously an idea that seems to have crossed Heusler's mind when he considered the fatal consequences ascribed to Kriemhilt's beauty in stanza 2 of the *Nibelungenlied* (*Nibelungensage und Nibelungenlied*, p. 123).

In *Vǫlsunga saga* 68.11–13 (based on *Forna* or perhaps *Meiri*) Brynhild makes the same representations about her military priorities that she makes to Sigurd on the occasion of the prior betrothal. In *Skamma* she consents only under family pressure and in *Meiri* she must at least partially acquiesce to paternal dictates. The maiden's disinclination is thus a peculiarity shared by the Eddic Brynhild with the German Kriemhilt.

The theme of Kriemhilt's inaccessibility is followed by a puzzling passage (stanzas 50–60) in which Siegfried's parents demonstrate great anxiety over his intention since they fear the hostility of Gunther and his men.[10] This is puzzling because there is no good reason why a suitor with such distinguished credentials as Siegfried should receive anything but the most cordial treatment at the Burgundian court. The alleged danger of the enterprise may be a reflex of the conventional hazards of the *Brautwerbung,* mechanically transferred to a context in which the hazards are not so obvious. But another possibility is that the emphasis on danger is carried over from the traditional perils experienced by Siegfried in his wooing of Brynhild, the forced entry into her fortress and the battle with her retainers. There is thus some suggestion that the themes with which Adventure 3 begins, Kriemhilt's rejection of wooers and the alarm expressed over Siegfried's expedition, were transferred from the older tradition of Siegfried's betrothal to Brynhild. This transfer sheds light on the new emergence of Kriemhilt at Brynhild's expense in the revised conception of the *Nibelungenlied* poet. The tradition concerned with Brynhild's prior betrothal was mined to furnish new narrative material for Kriemhilt. This crossing of roles also affords some insight into a psychological shift. Just as Brynhild forfeits some of her narrative prerogatives to her rival in the *Nibelungenlied,* she also forfeits some of her old stature. Brynhild is the avenger of her wrong in the *Edda,* but this wrong is obscured in the *Nibelungenlied* and the great avenging role falls to Kriemhilt. The Eddic tradition solved the problem of Gudrun's conversion from characterlessness in the Sigurd story to ferocity in *Atlakviða* and *Atlamál* by giving her a bite of Fáfnir's heart (*Vǫlsunga saga* 66.2–4); the

---

[10]R. C. Boer, *Untersuchungen über den Ursprung und die Entwicklung der Nibelungensage,* II (Halle: Verlag der Buchhandlung des Waisenhauses, 1907), 5.

Nibelungenlied sharpened her profile by giving her a portion of Brynhild's role.

The next motif in Adventure 3 is Siegfried's resolve to set out on the dangerous mission with only eleven men (stanza 59). The modest retinue may be another loan from the *Brautwerbung* pattern, but it may also be a reflex of the lonely adventures of Sigurd's youth, in particular his solitary wooing expeditions in *Vǫlsunga saga* 47.22–23 and 57.3–4.[11] The teichoscopy at Worms and Hagen's account of Siegfried's youth follow. This retrieval of Siegfried's youth in retrospect constitutes something of a structural anomaly, but if, as I have proposed, the poet has been thinking in terms of Siegfried's early betrothal to Brynhild in the process of constructing the romance of Kriemhilt, the story has in fact not progressed much beyond Siegfried's youthful adventures and there is less backtracking in Hagen's account than there appears to be. It begins with another explicit reference to Siegfried's solitariness (stanza 88.1):

> Dâ der helt al eine   ân' alle helfe reit

> (The hero rode all alone and without any help)

Siegfried as loner is one of the persistent images of the legend. Next in order come the story of the Nibelung treasure acquired from Schilbunc and Nibelunc and the slaying of the dragon. However different the details, clearly these traditions are equivalent to Heusler's Eddic "Hortlied" and in Germany as well as in Scandinavia Siegfried's tragic story was prefaced by heroic exploits.

When Hagen's digression is completed, Siegfried is graciously welcomed and responds by challenging Gunther peremptorily to do battle for his kingdom. This is a perennial knot in discussions of the *Nibelungenlied*.[12] Why should Siegfried, this model of

---

[11] Panzer, *Das Nibelungenlied*, p. 291: "Hier taucht zuerst der land- und vaterlose Märchenheld empor, der bisher nur künstlich heroisiert und verhöfischt wurde." Cf. Karl Droege, "Zur Geschichte des Nibelungenliedes," *ZDA*, 48 (1906–1907), 472.

[12] On Siegfried's conduct at Worms see Joseph Körner, *Das Nibelungenlied* (Leipzig and Berlin: Teubner, 1921), p. 112; Carl Wesle, "Brünhildlied oder Sigfridepos?" *ZDP*, 51 (1926), 36–37; Hans Naumann, "Die jüngeren Erfindungen im Heldenroman," *ZD*, 40 (1926), 31–33, and "Stand der Nibelungenforschung,"

etiquette in his native Netherlands, treat his meticulous hosts to such an outrage? To be sure, he has warned his father that he will take by force what he cannot get *in bono*, but he makes no effort to woo peaceably. If he had, there is every reason to believe that his suit would have been well received. He attacks Gunther without provocation and presumably to the detriment of his own best interests. No sufficient reason has ever been adduced. Once more we are led to explore the tradition. Pursuing our supposition that the narrative of Siegfried's wooing is modeled on the wooing of Brynhild in the inherited tale, we note that a hostile clash with the prospective bride's guardians is a feature of this account in both *Þiðreks saga* 168 and, by implication, *Oddrúnargrátr* 18. Siegfried's aggression remains senseless in the context of the *Nibelungenlied*, but the tradition of an armed challenge provides at least an adequate historical explanation no matter how defective the psychology.

We turn now to Adventure 4 and the Dano-Saxon war. This episode has often been judged to be the *Nibelungenlied* poet's innovation. Panzer derived the narrative details from French epic and contemporary history, and I have suggested that they may owe something to the Saxon war in Chrétien's *Cligés*.[13] The question is whether the campaign is a complete fabrication or is partially based on a prior tradition.[14] Such a tradition is suggested

ibid., 41 (1927), 10–11; Mary Thorp, "Two Literary Problems in the Nibelungenlied," *JEGP*, 37 (1938), 164–66; Dietrich von Kralik, *Die Sigfridtrilogie im Nibelungenlied und in der Thidrekssaga*, I (Halle: Niemeyer, 1941), 102–4; Wolfgang Mohr, rev. of *Die Sigfridtrilogie* by Dietrich von Kralik, *Dichtung und Volkstum*, 42 (1942), 103–4; Hermann Schneider, *Die deutschen Lieder von Siegfrieds Tod* (Weimar: Hermann Böhlaus Nachfolger, 1947), pp. 14–16; Bodo Mergell, "Nibelungenlied und höfischer Roman," *Euphorion*, 45 (1950), 309–11; Panzer, *Das Nibelungenlied*, pp. 308–11; Karl Heinz Ihlenburg, *Das Nibelungenlied: Problem und Gehalt* (Berlin: Akademie-Verlag, 1969), pp. 54–56; Otfrid Ehrismann, "Siefrids Ankunft in Worms: Zur Bedeutung der 3. aventiure des Nibelungenlieds" in *Festschrift für Karl Bischoff zum 70. Geburtstag*, ed. Günter Bellmann, Günter Eifler, Wolfgang Kleiber (Cologne and Vienna: Böhlau, 1975), 328–56.

[13]Friedrich Panzer, *Studien zum Nibelungenliede* (Frankfurt: Moritz Diesterweg, 1945), pp. 42–54 and 92–95, and *Das Nibelungenlied*, pp. 314–21; T. M. Andersson, "Chrétien's *Cligés* as a Source for the *Nibelungenlied* II–IV" in *Saga og språk: Studies in Language and Literature*, ed. John M. Weinstock (Austin, Texas: Jenkins Publishing Company, 1972), 153–64.

[14]Bibliographical references in Boer, II, 14–16; Kralik, p. 114; Panzer, *Studien zum Nibelungenliede*, p. 93.

by the references to a Danish campaign in *Vǫlsunga saga* 75.22–23 and *Norna-Gests þáttr* (above Chapter 1, n. 46). The passage in *Vǫlsunga saga* derives from *Meiri,* which may owe the episode, along with several others, to a German tradition that would also have been available to the *Nibelungenlied* poet.

Adventure 5 on the celebration of the victory and Siegfried's introduction to Kriemhilt appears to have no foundation in tradition, but Adventure 8 (Siegfried's expedition to the land of the Nibelungs) clearly does. It has similarities to chapter 168 in *Þiðreks saga:* Siegfried's arrival at a fortress, pounding on the gate, armed encounter with a gatekeeper, renewed encounter with another guardian who supervenes, recognition, and hospitable reception. If chapter 168 is read as a version of the prior betrothal with Brynhild (Fromm), Adventure 8 may be derived from the same tradition. If chapter 168 is interpreted as an alternate version of Siegfried's winning of the treasure (de Boor), Adventure 8 may be associated with this tradition. Bumke mediated between the explanations by suggesting that the hoard adventure and prior betrothal had already been amalgamated in the common source of chapter 168 and Adventure 8.[15] Because Fromm convinces me that chapter 168 reflects the betrothal tradition and because I have argued that the betrothal was related in the German original and suppressed only by the Norse redactor of *Þiðreks saga,* I choose to connect Adventure 8 with this tradition. When the *Nibelungenlied* poet decided against the prior betrothal, he reallocated the pertinent narrative in part to Siegfried's wooing of Kriemhilt (the hostile encounter with her guardians) and in part to his summoning of troops from Nibelungenland (the forcible entry into a fortress).

Adventure 8 is anything but transparent. What should be retained is that it reflects traditional material, in whatever state of confusion. Like Hagen's digression in Adventure 3, it demonstrates the poet's disinclination to leave any portion of the tradition unused.[16] This economy is understandable in view of his epic

---

[15]Joachim Bumke, "Sigfrids Fahrt ins Nibelungenland," *BGDSL* (Tübingen), 80 (1958), 253–68. Panzer, on the other hand, regarded Adventure 8 as an invention of the *Nibelungenlied* poet (*Das Nibelungenlied,* p. 334).

[16]Heusler, p. 87: "Die mittelalterlichen Dichter waren so dafür, nichts umkommen zu lassen!"

ambitions and his need to swell the dimensions with any resources available to him. It also reinforces our supposition that if the poet knew a tradition according to which Siegfried was first betrothed to Brynhild, he would be likely to harness the tradition in some way. The test was not pertinence, as the extraneous nature of Adventure 8 illustrates, but inclusiveness. In this early part of the *Nibelungenlied* we observe the poet in a characteristic narrative quandary. He makes certain artistic decisions, but often finds it difficult to hold to them consistently.[17] Thus he decides that he does not wish to preface the epic with a straightforward account of Siegfried's early youth as a waif of superhuman strength with a series of grotesque adventures to his credit. Instead, he wished to give him the same social advantages that were a more natural part of Kriemhilt's status in tradition. But given his economy, he discovered in retrospect that he could not sacrifice the rich traditions connected with Siegfried's youth. He therefore retrieved them in Adventures 3 and 8, ignoring the clash in tone between the courtly young gentleman of Adventure 2 and the rambunctious bearder of dragons, dwarves, and giants in 3 and 8.

Similarly, he made the artistic decision not to burden his hero with a prior betrothal to Brynhild, presumably because this would discolor his image and compromise his status as Kriemhilt's devoted suitor. Here too he reneged, feeling unable to part with the narrative material that tradition associated with the prior betrothal. He therefore reapplied some of this material to amplify the wooing of Kriemhilt. Again there is a clash in tone between Siegfried's newly acquired mannerliness and the aggressive suitor of tradition. The incongruency results from the poet's failure to reconcile fully his courtly modernization with what he perceived to be his obligations to tradition.[18]

The central matter in Part I of the *Nibelungenlied* is the wooing of Brynhild and Siegfried's marriage to Kriemhilt. This narrative is covered by Adventures 6–7 and 9–13.

---

[17]The principle is clarified by Olive Sayce, "Abortive Motivation in Part I of the *Nibelungenlied*," *MA*, 23 (1954), 36–38.

[18]The best general exposition of this problem is Friedrich Neumann, "Schichten der Ethik im Nibelungenliede," *Festschrift Eugen Mogk zum 70. Geburtstag* (Halle: Niemeyer, 1924), pp. 119–45; rpt. in his *Das Nibelungenlied in seiner Zeit* (Göttingen: Vandenhoeck & Ruprecht, 1967), pp. 9–34.

Siegfried's Marriage

(6) News of Brynhild and the athletic contests on which she stakes her hand arrives at the Burgundian court and Gunther determines to woo her. Siegfried advises against the plan in view of the price she exacts for failure, and Hagen recommends that Gunther should at least enlist Siegfried's aid since he knows Brynhild's circumstances. Gunther applies to Siegfried accordingly and Siegfried stipulates Kriemhilt's hand as a reward for his service. Gunther agrees and they seal the compact with oaths. The preparations begin. Siegfried packs his *Tarnkappe* and Gunther inquires whether they should embark a retinue of thirty thousand men. Siegfried, true to his personal tradition of solitary adventure and in contradiction to his later importation of one thousand Nibelungs, replies that they should undertake the expedition four men strong (Siegfried, Gunther, Hagen, and Dancwart). A passage of no fewer than twenty-nine stanzas (343–71) follows in which Kriemhilt undertakes to furnish the appropriate clothing for the expedition, a task which absorbs some seven weeks. The departure itself precipitates tears and a suggestion by Kriemhilt that another courtship might be less hazardous. She consigns her brother's welfare to Siegfried's care. The little group now sets sail with Siegfried acting as helmsman because he knows the course. Twelve days bring them to Brynhild's castle Isenstein, which Siegfried identifies for Gunther at a distance. At the same time, he states that the only hope for success lies in the fiction that he is Gunther's vassal. The reason for this fiction is not divulged, but all agree to abide by it.

(7) As they approach Isenstein, the maidens of the castle gaze at them from the windows. Gunther asks Siegfried if he is acquainted with any of them, and he counters by asking Gunther to pick out the one he would choose for a wife. Gunther settles on a white-robed damsel, whom Siegfried identifies as Brynhild herself. When they land, Siegfried performs vassal's service by helping Gunther into the saddle. They are received by Brynhild's retainers, who ask to take their arms. Hagen bridles at the suggestion, but Siegfried instructs him on the local custom. Their presence is then announced to Brynhild, who inquires into the identity of the strangers. A retainer informs her that one of their number resembles Siegfried and goes on to describe Gunther, Hagen, and Dancwart (emphasizing the latter's youth in preparation for the statement in Part II that he was only a child when Siegfried was killed). Brynhild responds that if Siegfried has come to win her love, he will pay with his life. When she goes out to meet the group, she accordingly addresses Siegfried first, but

he defers to Gunther, whom he introduces as his lord and her wooer. She specifies the nature of the contests: stone cast, broad jump, and javelin. Siegfried reassures Gunther in an aside and he takes up the challenge. Brynhild arms and Siegfried secretly dons his *Tarnkappe*. His three companions are much intimidated by the size and weight of Brynhild's arms and they devoutly wish to have their own weapons in hand. Brynhild patronizingly fulfills their wish. As the contest is about to begin, Siegfried approaches invisible in his cloak and whispers directions to Gunther, who is to make the motions while Siegfried performs the deeds. Brynhild begins by casting the spear, which penetrates the shield and levels her opponents. But Siegfried rebounds, reverses the spear so as not to injure Brynhild with the tip, and topples her with no less powerful a cast. She then hurls the stone twelve "klåfter" and leaps even further, but Siegfried outdoes her, carrying Gunther as he jumps. She colors with anger, but bids her men recognize Gunther's sovereignty. Siegfried removes his disguise and pretends not to know that the contests have already taken place. When he has allowed himself to be enlightened by Hagen, he urges Brynhild to set out, but she demurs, wishing to convene a council of her relations first. Hagen is alarmed by the assembling forces, but Siegfried promises a counterpoise of a thousand warriors. (Siegfried's expedition to Nibelungenland in Adventure 8 has been described above and we can pass on to Adventure 9.)

(9) When the voyage back to Worms has been under way for nine days, Hagen proposes that a messenger be sent ahead and designates Siegfried for this service. Siegfried is reluctant only until Kriemhilt's name is invoked. He is then charged and departs. As he comes into view alone, Gernot and Giselher are apprehensive about the fate of their brother, but their fears are quickly dispelled by Siegfried's report. The same report is delivered for Kriemhilt's special benefit, and she rewards him with twenty-four gold rings in mock acknowledgment of his messenger's service. These he immediately distributes among Kriemhilt's retinue. Preparations are now made for a magnificent reception to honor Gunther and his bride.

(10) The reception and accompanying festivities are described in abundant detail. Siegfried reminds Gunther that Kriemhilt has been promised in return for his services. Kriemhilt consents with bashful bliss and the betrothal takes place. Brynhild observes the couple and bursts out in tears. When Gunther inquires into her grief, she expresses dismay that Kriemhilt should be married to a vassal. Gunther offers to explain the matter in due course, but Brynhild

threatens not to sleep with him unless she is told. Gunther now divulges that Siegfried is a king in his own right, but she remains dejected. The time comes for the newly-wed couples to go to bed and the husbands approach their brides with varying success: Siegfried with utter satisfaction and Gunther with none at all. Brynhild resists him and insists again on knowing what lies behind the vassal fiction. Gunther resorts to force, but is no match for Brynhild, who binds him hand and foot and hangs him on a nail. In the morning she releases him against a promise of good behavior. That day the weddings are consecrated in church and the festivities continue. Gunther informs Siegfried of his nuptial fiasco and Siegfried once again volunteers his services, this time by entering the bedchamber in his *Tarnkappe* and subduing Brynhild in Gunther's place. Gunther accedes, stipulating only that he stop short of intercourse. That evening Siegfried vanishes from Kriemhilt's side and carries out his plan. After a prolonged struggle Brynhild concedes defeat and Siegfried departs, taking with him her ring and belt. Gunther is now able to consummate the marriage, and Brynhild is magically deprived of her surplus strength. The feast continues for two full weeks and concludes with a massive display of liberality.

(11) Siegfried and Kriemhilt prepare to return to Xanten. Her brothers offer to share their lands and riches, but Siegfried's self-sufficiency leads him to decline. Kriemhilt is offered a retinue and begins by singling out Hagen and Ortwin. Hagen objects violently to being transferred out of Gunther's service and Kriemhilt must settle for a lesser retinue of thirty-two women and five hundred men. They are welcomed magnificently by Sigemunt and Sigelint, who cede the crown to their son. After ten years Kriemhilt gives birth to a son named Gunther and Brynhild gives birth to a son with the reciprocal name Siegfried. At the same time, Sigelint dies, leaving Kriemhilt in full sway. She and Siegfried rule in glory and abundance.

(12) Back in Worms Brynhild reverts to the old theme of Siegfried's vassalage and wonders why he has done no service. She expresses the wish to see Kriemhilt, but Gunther hesitates because of the distance. Brynhild replies that a vassal is obligated to obey his lord's every command and forces Gunther to comply. He dispatches messengers accordingly and in three weeks they arrive at Nibelunc's castle in Norway bearing the invitation. Siegfried seeks advice from his retainers and agrees to the trip, on which he is accompanied by Kriemhilt, his father Sigemunt, and a thousand followers. The messengers return with the acceptance and display their reward, which prompts an indelicate interest in the Nibelung treasure on Hagen's part.

(13) Siegfried's party arrives in Worms and another massive reception is staged. The feasting and ceremonial activities continue for eleven days.

For this section of the narrative the *Nibelungenlied* poet is generally dependent on a source analogous to the source or sources on Brynhild's wooing reflected in the *Edda* and *Þiðreks saga*. The details are taken directly from the source, vary the source in the interest of altered emphases, or borrow from the subsequent story. This last category (what I shall call intraborrowing) becomes increasingly important. It is possible that the poet in fact composed the second part of the epic first because he had a fuller source for this section (the "Ältere Not").[19] The latter part of his epic would then have been available as a model when he worked on the first. On the other hand, he may also have borrowed certain epic ideas from the "Ältere Not" before developing this older poem into Part II of the *Nibelungenlied*. Nothing compels us to believe that his borrowings were from the final form rather than the underlying source.

News of the exotic warrior maiden Brynhild comes to Gunther's ears a little mysteriously (325: "Novel tidings came across the Rhine"). The mystery is of course dispelled if we imagine that in the original Siegfried, made knowledgeable by a prior visit to Brynhild and betrothal to her, communicates the information as he does in *Þiðreks saga* II.38.6–14. We shall see that such prior knowledge on his part is constantly implied in Adventures 6 and 7. The vague rumors concerning Brynhild include the tests to which she subjects her suitors. Two of the tests (stone cast and broad jump) are innocently athletic, but the spear contest entails single combat with the lives of the contestants at stake. The match is therefore not a mere game, and the combat element keeps alive the tradition of Brynhild as a warrior maiden who prefers warfare to marriage (*Skamma* 37 and *Vǫlsunga saga* 60.5–12 and 68.8–13). This tradition has been altered to accord with the folktale studied by Panzer, but Brynhild's warrior status

---

[19]See Droege, p. 500; Werner Richter, "Beiträge zur Deutung des Mittelteils des Nibelungenliedes," *ZDA*, 72 (1935), 11; Helmut K. Krausse, "Die Darstellung von Siegfrieds Tod und die Entwicklung des Hagenbildes in der Nibelungendichtung," *GRM*, 21 (1971), 375–76.

must have suggested this particular folktale to the poet.[20] The folktale overlay does not appear in *Þiðreks saga* and therefore cannot be proved for the source of the *Nibelungenlied*. There is no direct evidence for the argument that the *Nibelungenlied* poet either inserted or inherited the bridal games, but he clearly had no objection to the burlesque mode and there is no reason to doubt that the games are his innovation. Since *Þiðreks saga* confines Siegfried's proxy wooing to verbal representations, a scene supported by analogous phrasing in *Meiri*, we might well assume the same situation in the *Nibelungenlied* source. At the same time, the evidence of *Þiðreks saga* II.41.14–18 indicates that the source endowed Brynhild with supernatural strength, thus allowing the *Nibelungenlied* poet to elaborate this concept based on a powerful folktale queen quite naturally.[21]

[20]On the "Brautwerbermärchen" see Wolfgang Golther, "Ein mingrelisches Siegfriedmärchen," *ZVL*, 13 (1899), 46–50; Friedrich Panzer, *Studien zur germanischen Sagengeschichte*, II: *Sigfrid* (Munich: Beck, 1912), 144–85; "Nibelungische Ketzereien. 1. Das russische Brautwerbermärchen im Nibelungenlied," *BGDSL*, 72 (1950), 463–98; rpt. in *Zur germanisch-deutschen Heldensage: Sechzehn Aufsätze zum neuen Forschungsstand*, ed. Karl Hauck (Bad Homburg vor der Höhe: Hermann Gentner, 1961), pp. 138–72, and *Das Nibelungenlied*, pp. 322–25; A. von Löwis of Menar, *Die Brünhildsage in Russland*, Palaestra, 142 (Leipzig: Mayer & Müller, 1923); C. W. von Sydow, "Brynhildepisoden i tysk tradition," *ANF*, 44 (1928), 164–89; Sven Liljeblad, *Die Tobiasgeschichte und andere Märchen mit toten Helfern* (Lund: A.-B. Ph. Lundstedts Univ.-Bokhandel, 1927); Siegfried Beyschlag, "Deutsches Brünhildenlied und Brautwerbermärchen," *Märchen, Mythos, Dichtung: Festschrift zum 90. Geburtstag Friedrich von der Leyens*, ed. Hugo Kuhn and Kurt Schier (Munich: Beck, 1963), pp. 121–45; Karl-Eugen Wädekin, "Nibelungenlied und deutsch-russische Beziehungen im Mittelalter," *BGDSL*, 73 (1951), 284–304.

[21]Andreas Heusler, "Die Quelle der Brünhildsage," *Kleine Schriften*, I, ed. Helga Reuschel (Berlin: de Gruyter, 1969), 83, and *Nibelungensage und Nibelungenlied*, p. 84, assigned the martial games to the source. Heinrich Hempel, *Nibelungenstudien*, I (Heidelberg: Winter, 1926), 132 and 201, agreed. Wolfgang Mohr in *Dichtung und Volkstum*, 42 (1942), 116–22, assumed a separate *Spielmannsdichtung* as the source for Gunther's wooing. Helmut de Boor, "Die Bearbeitung m des Nibelungenliedes," p. 190, and *Das Nibelungenlied*, 19th ed. (Wiesbaden: Brockhaus, 1967), p. xxvi, also assumed two sources to account for bed conquest and martial games in the *Nibelungenlied*. I find myself closest to the noncommittal view of Wolfgang Golther, "Ueber die Sage von Siegfried und den Nibelungen," *ZVL*, 12 (1898), 299–302, who assumed that *Þiðreks saga* represents the original situation and that the *Nibelungenlied* superimposed the martial games on the bed conquest, but did not specify the exact source of the elaboration. See also H. W. J. Kroes, "Die Kampfspiele des Nibelungenliedes (NL 389–481)," *Neophilologus*, 29 (1944), 161–64.

In arriving at a decision to woo Brynhild, Gunther does not appeal for counsel despite the *Nibelungenlied* poet's predilection for council scenes and despite Gunther's reliance on the advice of others in the analogues (Grimhild in *Vǫlsunga saga* 66.7–9 and Sigurd in *Þiðreks saga* II.38.6–14). There is however a trace of such a council scene in Hagen's advice that Gunther avail himself of Siegfried's help. The reason Hagen alleges for Siegfried's participation is that he knows Brynhild's situation, the first of repeated indications that he has had some prior contact with her. But when Siegfried stipulates Kriemhilt's hand as a reward for his service, this is a radical departure from tradition in the interest of developing the theme of *Minnedienst*. It is in line with the escalation of Sigurd's joint harrying with his sworn brothers (*Vǫlsunga saga* 64.19–22, 65.32–66.2, 75.22–23) into a full-scale military campaign in Adventure 4 designed to win the favor of his future in-laws.

Once the expedition is resolved, Siegfried fetches his *Tarnkappe* (336–38). The significance of the *Tarnkappe* is unclear unless we know the sequel, but it is equivalent to the shape-shifting in which Grimhild instructs Gunnarr and Sigurd on their departure (*Vǫlsunga saga* 67.1–2 and *Grípisspá* 37–39). These two forms of disguise occupy the same narrative slot. Siegfried's rejection of a large retinue and insistence on a company of four echoes the tradition of solitary adventures as we have it in stanza 59 on his departure from Xanten, stanza 88 when he sets out on the hoard adventure, or stanza 180 when he reconnoiters alone in Saxony. The apprehension and tears that accompany the departure (372–74 and 376) match the mood at the Netherlandish court when Siegfried leaves for Worms and represent a stock scene in the *Nibelungenlied* repertory. It may originate ultimately in the Burgundian departure for Hunland in the "Ältere Not" (*Þiðreks saga* II.284.18–20; *Nibelungenlied* 1515–16 and 1520–23), in which the Burgundians leave mourning wives and lovers behind. The scene is old (*Atlakviða* 12 and *Atlamál* 30–31) and could have been generalized from the source of Part II to elaborate the departure scenes of Part I. The company sets sail and Siegfried takes charge since he knows the course (378), a motif that echoes *Skamma* 3.6 and *Þiðreks saga* II.38.14 and again implies some prior knowledge on his part. Further evidence of his familiarity with Brynhild is his recognition of Isenstein.[22] Both old and new is the elaborate fiction that Siegfried is Gunther's vassal. Siegfried insists that the fiction is prerequisite to success, but the point is not fully developed. Why should Brynhild be deluded in this way and why must Gunther be made more attractive to her? The only plausible explanation is that she must be convinced that Gunther is more desirable than Siegfried on the basis of status rather than intrinsic merit. But why does Siegfried come into consideration at all? Clearly because tradition assigned him to Brynhild, and she must somehow be dissuaded. The *Nibelungenlied* poet draws on this tradition in two ways. In the first place, the emphasis on Gunther's standing echoes Sigurd's arguments on Gunnarr's behalf in his conversation with Brynhild in *Vǫlsunga saga* 75.28–76.5 ("and a distinguished king paid your bridal fee") and *Þiðreks saga* II.39.15–16 ("he is an outstanding man and a gentleman of exceptional excellence and a powerful king"). In the second place, his own disenfranchisement plays on his traditional role as a waif with a doubtful genealogy, a theme suppressed in Adventure 2, but allowed to inspire the vassal fiction at this point.[23] The interest of the vassal fiction of course goes far beyond possible outcroppings of tradition. There is in the poet's vision a playful ambivalence between the respect owed to kingly authority and the vassal's innate superiority. Siegfried's masquerade contains an element of deference and an element of scorn as well, as the poet signals directly in stanza 728

[22]For summaries of the evidence in the *Nibelungenlied* that Siegfried has a prior acquaintanceship with Brynhild see Golther, "Ueber die Sage," pp. 187, 207, 296–99, and, most recently, Hermann Reichert, "Zum Sigrdrífa-Brünhild-Problem" in *Antiquitates Indogermanicae: Studien zur indogermanischen Altertumskunde und zur Sprach- und Kulturgeschichte der indogermanischen Völker. Gedenkschrift für Hermann Güntert zur 25. Wiederkehr seines Todestages am 23. April 1973,* Innsbrucker Beiträge zur Sprachwissenschaft, 12, ed. Manfred Mayrhofer, Wolfgang Meid, Bernfried Schlerath, Rüdiger Schmitt (Innsbruck, 1974), pp. 251–52.

[23]On the vassal fiction in the *Nibelungenlied* and Siegfried's servitude in the other sources see Boer, I, 111–13; Léon Polak, *Untersuchungen über die Sigfridsagen* (Berlin: Universitäts-Buchdruckerei, 1910), pp. 74–79; Heusler, "Die Quelle der Brünhildsage," *Kleine Schriften,* I, 91, and *Nibelungensage und Nibelungenlied,* p. 88; Mary Thorp, pp. 166–68; Kralik, p. 89; Hugo Bekker, "The 'Eigenmann'-motif in the *Nibelungenlied,*" *GR,* 42 (1967), 5–15.

when Gunther seems to recognize his own shortcomings and smiles at the absurd thought of imposing on his powerful vassal. The poet hovers between the respect owed royalty on the one hand and aristocratic sympathies on the other.[24] Everything in Adventure 6 is attributable in some measure to tradition, either the source or sources on Siegfried, the narrative of earlier Adventures, or the narrative of the "Ältere Not." Adventure 7 begins in the same vein with yet another hint of Siegfried's foreknowledge: he is able to identify Brynhild as she gazes down from a window. Her own view from this vantage point reenacts the Burgundian survey of Siegfried's arrival in Adventure 3. Teichoscopy is in fact a stock scene in the *Nibelungenlied* and may ultimately owe its existence to a scene in the "Ältere Not" in which Kriemhilt observes the arrival of her relatives (*Þiðreks saga* II.297.10–19; *Nibelungenlied* 1716–17).[25] The first phase of the vassal fiction is played out as Siegfried helps Gunther mount. The guests are relieved of their arms in a scene borrowed from the attempted disarming of the Burgundians when they arrive at the Hunnish court in the "Ältere Not" (*Þiðreks saga* II.298.7–9; *Nibelungenlied* 1745).[26] Brynhild inquires into their identity and is told that one resembles Siegfried. This scene is just as clearly modeled on Gunther's inquiry of Hagen when Siegfried arrives at Worms and can be retraced further to the identification of Hagen on his arrival in Hunland in the "Ältere Not" (*Þiðreks saga* II.302.3–6; *Nibelungenlied* 1752–57).

Brynhild greets Siegfried, suggesting again that he has some prior status at her court, and he specifies the vassal fiction in deferring to Gunther. The situation is unclear: if Brynhild knows about Siegfried, she must also know that he is not a vassal. Yet she makes no protest. This is one of the instances in which the *Nibelungenlied* poet has hit on a new idea that he cannot quite manage. The vassal concept is never fully integrated into the machinery of the plot. Brynhild is deluded in two ways: she is made to believe that Siegfried is a vassal, and she is subdued by

[24]Ihlenburg, pp. 146–47.
[25]Mohr, p. 120.
[26]Mohr, p. 119: "Denn die Forderung 'Waffen sind an der Garderobe abzugeben' und Hagens trotzige Ablehnung stammt natürlich aus dem Burgundenuntergang." Cf. Panzer, *Das Nibelungenlied*, p. 332.

him in disguise. But neither delusion, nor a combination of the two, is the basis of her complaint. It would be plausible, given the latitude of the status question in the text, if she should take double offense at being subdued by a social inferior, but she does not connect the themes in this way. Instead, as we shall see below, she creates a third complaint and charges that Siegfried has claimed a sexual conquest. The two well-founded issues are ignored and an unfounded one is raised. Why devise the vassal fiction at all? Part of the answer may lie once more in the poet's narrative economy; knowing the theme of Siegfried's inferior birth from his source, he was eager not to sacrifice it altogether. At the same time, his own courtly version of Siegfried's birth and his well-developed sense of social hierarchy prevent him from making serious use of the theme. It can only parade as a manifest fiction. The other part of the answer is that the theme of Siegfried's inferior birth was a traditional element in the quarrel scene (Brynhild's words to Grimhild in *Þiðreks saga* II.260.1–3: "You can go off to the forest and track the hind after your husband Sigurd"). The *Nibelungenlied* poet has given up the idea that Siegfried was fostered in the forest and must use some other motif to fill this place in the quarrel. Siegfried's alleged vassal status serves the purpose (*Nibelungenlied* 821, for example). The vassal theme is therefore doubly anchored in tradition—on the one hand as a reinterpretation of Sigurd's dubious birth and on the other as an inherited part of the queens' quarrel.

The winning of Brynhild occurs in two stages in the *Nibelungenlied,* her defeat in the games (equivalent to the crossing of the flame wall in the Norse version) and her defeat in bed (equivalent to the sham nuptials in the Norse version). Which form is older or whether both conceivably go back to a compromise form is not possible to ascertain.[27] The *Nibelungenlied* poet may well have contributed the games on the basis of the *Brautwerbermärchen.* He did not, however, add the vanquishing of Brynhild in bed since this motif is already present in *Þiðreks saga.* Indeed, we will have reason to surmise that he knew it in

[27]See Klaus von See, "Die Werbung um Brünhild," *ZDA,* 88 (1957–58), 1–20, and "Freierprobe und Königinnenzank in der Sigfridsage," *ZDA,* 89 (1958–59), 163–72; R. G. Finch, "Brunhild and Siegfried," *Saga-Book of the Viking Society,* 17 (1967–68), 224–60.

the unbowdlerized version of *Þiðreks saga,* according to which Sigurd deflowers Brynhild. The *Tarnkappe* plays a part in both the game scene and the bed scene. It is equivalent to the shape changing of Eddic tradition, which, however, covers the duration of Sigurd's visit with Brynhild, while the *Tarnkappe* is an intermittent disguise and must be donned twice. Neither motif is more realistic than the other, but the shape-shifting is more adequate for its purpose: Sigurd appears as Gunnarr throughout. The *Tarnkappe* must serve two different purposes, invisibility in the games and disguise in bed. Invisibility is not the same thing as disguise and the latter scene makes little sense; any light would reveal Siegfried's invisibility and expose the deception. It is therefore likely that the motif of invisibility belongs originally to the game sequence and that the disguise in bed was effected by a simple exchange of clothing (however inadequate this may be) as in *Þiðreks saga.* The *Nibelungenlied* poet transferred the *Tarnkappe* from the first context to the second for the sake of simplicity or consistency.[28]

The little comedy at the end of the Adventure, according to which Siegfried knows nothing of the games that have just transpired, is rooted in a playful side of Siegfried's personality which appears in none of the Norse sources or *Þiðreks saga,* but which led Dietrich von Kralik to posit burlesque versions of the tale among the sources of the *Nibelungenlied.* It appears in Siegfried's surreptitious disappearance before the games to don the *Tarnkappe* (stanza 431), his deluding of his Nibelung vassals with a disguised voice (487), his playful vanishing from Kriemhilt's side to aid Gunther (661–62), and his hunting antics in Adventure 16.[29] In retrospect, there are three sorts of tradition in Adventure 7. Most of the substantive motifs (prior knowledge of Brynhild, vassal fiction, and the subduing of Brynhild in bed) go back to earlier versions of the story. The bridal games together with the

[28]On this scene see Heusler, *Nibelungensage und Nibelungenlied,* p. 89; Kralik, pp. 485–90; Joachim Bumke, "Die Quellen der Brünhildfabel im Nibelungenlied," *Euphorion,* 54 (1960), 9–10.

[29]On the poet's humorous vein see Heusler, *Nibelungensage und Nibelungenlied,* p. 89; Kralik, p. 81; Carl S. Singer, "The Hunting Contest: An Interpretation of the Sixteenth Aventiure of the *Nibelungenlied*," *GR,* 42 (1967), 170–73; Hartwig Mayer, *Humor im Nibelungenlied,* Diss. Tübingen (Ulm/Donau: H. Köhler, 1966).

Tarnkappe are taken over from the *Brautwerbermärchen*. The narrative incidentals (teichoscopy, recognition, disarming, and comical flourishes) are borrowed from the "Ältere Not" or are in tune with other sections of Part I.

Adventure 9 is an ornamental canto and offers nothing of substance. It relates the dispatching of messengers to announce the success of the wooing expedition to those awaiting news in Worms. This motif originated in the "Ältere Not," in which Rüdeger sent messengers ahead to announce his arrival with the Burgundians in Hunland (*Þiðreks saga* II.296.23–297.1; *Nibelungenlied* 1713–15). It was also used at the conclusion of Adventure 4 to bring news of the victory over Saxons and Danes. In the present instance Hagen designates Siegfried as messenger. This pattern derives from Adventure 6, in which Hagen elects Siegfried to lead the expedition to Islant. Such a mission is surely below Siegfried's station, but he accepts it because it promises a quicker reunion with Kriemhilt, a repetition of his pliability in Adventure 3 when thoughts of Kriemhilt lead him to desist from his unruly challenge. The apprehension expressed on his arrival concerning Gunther's fate is simply the closing panel of the apprehension that accompanied their departure. Siegfried's special report to Kriemhilt echoes the special report she receives in Adventure 4 (stanzas 225–42), as does the reward that she confers on her noble messenger in a light-hearted scene which belongs among the comic interludes.

Adventure 10 has a more traditional core. It begins with reception festivities modeled perhaps most directly on those in Adventure 4, but ubiquitous in the *Nibelungenlied* and perhaps ultimately derived from the great banquet in the "Ältere Not." There follows the curious passage in which Brynhild observes Kriemhilt and weeps at the thought of her marriage to the vassal Siegfried. This is clearly not part of the last overlay, but a remnant of tradition. It corresponds most nearly to a passage in *Vǫlsunga saga (Meiri)* in which Brynhild is described as downcast (70.8) and silent (70.19). Gudrun asks Sigurd "why is Brynhild so cheerless?" and goes on to emphasize that she has after all gotten the man she wanted. This passage is badly garbled in the saga. It comes after the quarrel of the queens (from *Forna*), and Gudrun therefore knows perfectly well what has saddened Brynhild. The saga author apparently wished to find room for both the river quarrel from *Forna* and the hall quarrel from *Meiri*. He separated them by placing the river quarrel ahead of Brynhild's expression of grief—so that the grief seems motivated by the quarrel—and the hall quarrel afterward. The original situation was surely that the grief preceded the quarrel and was prompted not by the revelation of Brynhild's deception, but by her concern over not getting the husband she wanted, just as Gudrun's words imply (*Vǫlsunga saga* 70.10–12): "Why doesn't she enjoy her wealth and good fortune and general esteem since she has gotten the man she wanted?" What we can posit for *Meiri* is therefore a scene preceding the quarrel in which Brynhild mourns her failure to get Sigurd. This is the narrative slot occupied by Brynhild's tears in the *Nibelungenlied*, but the motif is deflected. Since there has been no question of a betrothal to Siegfried, her sadness must be motivated differently. The new concept of Siegfried's vassal status fills the gap and is used to explain her grief. This ad hoc motivation has always struck critics as specious: Why should Brynhild expend tears on an imagined wrong done her sister-in-law?[30] The lack of conviction in the scene stems from the altered motivation. In the original Brynhild wept for her own marriage and her tears were amply motivated. We can thus deduce for *Meiri* and the German source of the *Nibelungenlied* a scene in which Brynhild bewails her misfortune even before the quarrel with Kriemhilt.

When Gunther inquires into her grief, she demands to know the reason for Kriemhilt's humiliation and threatens not to sleep with Gunther until she is told. This too has a hollow ring about it and may be explained as another deflection of an old motif. In *Meiri*

[30]On Brynhild's tears see Karl Bartsch, "Die dichterische Gestaltung der Nibelungensage," *Gesammelte Vorträge und Aufsätze* (Freiburg and Tübingen: Akademische Verlagsbuchhandlung von J. C. B. Mohr, 1883), p. 101; Heusler, "Die Quelle der Brünhildsage," *Kleine Schriften*, I, 93, and *Nibelungensage und Nibelungenlied*, pp. 90–92 (derives the scene from his second "Brünhildenlied"); Körner, p. 64; Kralik, p. 91 (takes tears at face value); Schneider, p. 27 ("Aber kein vernünftiger Leser des NL hat wohl noch bezweifelt, dass seine [des Dichters] erkünstelte Motivierung falsch ist, und dass es sich um Zornestränen der Verschmähten, Liebesenttäuschten handelt"); D. R. McLintock, "Les larmes de Brünhilt," *Studia Neophilologica*, 33 (1961), 307–13 (quotes Schneider on page 312 and tries to justify the scene on its own terms).

(*Vǫlsunga saga* 79.14–16) Brynhild threatens not to sleep with Gunnarr unless he carries out the murder of Sigurd. This is a threat that fits the magnitude of the enterprise. In the *Nibelungenlied* it is overkill when used to enforce an expression of curiosity. An obvious surmise is that the *Nibelungenlied* poet borrowed ahead and took the threat to withhold marital favors from the later context.[31] This surmise is confirmed by the A redaction (797), in which Brynhild coerces Gunther with the same threat as in *Meiri*.[32] Again we find a coincidence between the narrative ancestry of the *Nibelungenlied* and *Meiri*. Yet a third instance is the double wedding, a motif which seems indicated for *Meiri* by *Grípisspá* 43.

"Double wedding" is of course something of a misnomer since the marriage of Gunther and Brynhild goes awry. Her resistance has no correspondence in the Eddic story and appears to belong only to the German variant. As a result Siegfried's offense is twofold in the German story: he acts both as Gunther's invisible helper in the games and as his stand-in in bed. One offense is of course sufficient for the purposes of the story and it is tempting to suppose that the duplication in the *Nibelungenlied* results from the superimposition of the athletic conquest on the sexual conquest. Confirmation may be found in *Þiðreks saga,* which has the latter motif, but no sign of the games. The subduing of Brynhild in bed is prefaced by one unsuccessful night in the *Nibelungenlied* and three in *Þiðreks saga*. Boer and Heusler considered the triad to be older.[33] The point is minor and difficult to argue. A more important difference is that in *Þiðreks saga* Sigurd deflowers Brynhild; in the *Nibelungenlied* he merely subdues her. Which variant is original? A general argument is that Norse translators are not much given to innovation and that *Þiðreks saga* is more likely to be a faithful mirror than the *Nibelungenlied*. A more immediate argument is that the *Nibelungenlied* shows signs of

---

[31]On borrowing ahead see T. M. Andersson, "The Epic Source," p. 16.

[32]Michael S. Batts, ed., *Das Nibelungenlied: Paralleldruck der Handschriften A, B und C nebst Lesarten der übrigen Handschriften* (Tübingen: Niemeyer, 1971), p. 258 (normalized): "dune beredest, künec, mich / der vil grôzen schanden, / ich minne niemer dich." See Bumke, "Die Quellen," p. 23 (n. 56).

[33]Boer, II, 27, and Heusler, "Die Quelle der Brünhildsage," *Kleine Schriften,* I, 77.

178 The Legend of Brynhild

having suppressed the deflowering, a change readily understandable in light of the poem's status as polite literature. In the first place, the poet protests rather too much. Gunther stipulates abstention specifically (655.1: "Âne daz du iht triutest . . ."), and Siegfried agrees with equal explicitness (656.2: "daz ich ir niht enminne"). Gunther is present to assure himself and the reader that "nothing happens" (667.3: "daz heimlîcher dinge / von in dâ niht geschach"). Similarly indicative is the later motivation of Siegfried's death. He is charged with a claim that he slept with Brynhild. The underlying fact must be that in the source he did indeed sleep with her and this misstep was used to motivate his murder. In the *Nibelungenlied* the deflowering has been eliminated and the nature of the accusation must therefore also be changed. Siegfried can no longer be accused of actually sleeping with Brynhild, only of claiming to have done so. The change is of course awkward since there is no reason, psychological or rational, to suppose that Siegfried did or would be inclined to make such a claim.

In *Þiðreks saga* Grimhild precipitates the catastrophe by asking Brynhild "who took your virginity?" but the crucial issue in the final analysis is not sexual infringement; Brynhild complains to Gunnarr only that Sigurd broke his oath by telling his wife everything. According to *Þiðreks saga,* then, Sigurd's crime is a loose tongue. According to the *Nibelungenlied,* Siegfried's crime is a loose and lying tongue. The version in *Þiðreks saga* makes perfect sense as a model for the *Nibelungenlied.* Originally Gunther asked Siegfried to rob Brynhild of her superhuman strength by deflowering her; the reduction of her strength to normal is a motif that persists in the *Nibelungenlied* 681–82. At the same time, Siegfried undertook not to tell of the arrangement, but broke his promise by betraying the secret to his wife. The *Nibelungenlied* poet suppressed the sexual conquest, but not Siegfried's revelation to Kriemhilt, which in his version is therefore deprived of any factual basis and becomes a false boast (stanzas 855, 857, 867). The Sigurd of *Þiðreks saga* commits an indiscretion in private conversation with his wife and she publicizes the matter in anger. In the *Nibelungenlied* it is not at all clear what he does; perhaps he makes an empty boast, perhaps Kriemhilt draws her own conclusions from the belt and ring given her, or perhaps she

tells a calculated lie. The changes made by the *Nibelungenlied*
poet have obscured the issue.[34]

Adventure 10 concludes with renewed festivities—which correspond to chapter 230 of *Þiðreks saga* and may well have some
foundation in the source—and a display of liberality matching the
conclusion of Adventure 5. For the most part Adventure 10 is
well anchored in tradition, while Adventure 11 contains almost
exclusively parasitic material derived from motifs in the "Ältere
Not." The offer of Kriemhilt's brothers to share their lands, Siegfried's self-sufficient rejection of any share in their wealth, the
appointment of a retinue for Kriemhilt, and Hagen's intervention
against Kriemhilt, all these points anticipate the concerns of Part
II and prefigure the antagonism between Kriemhilt and Hagen.
Specifically, the passage is modeled on Kriemhilt's departure for
Hunland, presumably as it stood in the "Ältere Not" and more or
less as it stands in the *Nibelungenlied* 1271–86. Here too there is
an opposition between Hagen and the royal brothers with regard
to Kriemhilt. In the later passage Hagen deprives Kriemhilt of her
gold over the objections of her brothers (1274.3) and Gernot inter-
feres to distribute the gold among Rüdeger's retainers (1277.4). In

---

[34]There have been numerous efforts to solve the riddle of Siegfried's guilt in the
Nibelungenlied. See Heusler, *Nibelungensage und Nibelungenlied*, p. 90; Hans
Naumann, "Brünhilds Gürtel," *ZDA,* 70 (1933), 46–48; Werner Fechter, *Sieg-
frieds Schuld und das Weltbild des Nibelungenliedes* (Hamburg: J. P. Toth Ver-
lag, 1948); Burghart Wachinger, *Studien zum Nibelungenlied: Vorausdeutungen,
Aufbau, Motivierung* (Tübingen: Niemeyer, 1960), pp. 103–16; Werner Schröder,
"Die Tragödie Kriemhilts," pp. 71–72 (rpt. in his *Nibelungenlied-Studien*, pp.
91–92); Hugh Sacker, "On Irony and Symbolism in the *Nibelungenlied:* Two
Preliminary Notes," *GL&L,* 14 (1960–61), 277–78; Beyschlag, pp. 127–28; Paul B.
Salmon, "Why Does Hagen Die?" *GL&L,* 17 (1963–64), 9–12; Walter Johannes
Schröder, "Der Zank der Königinnen im Nibelungenlied: Zur Interpretation mit-
telalterlicher Dichtungen," *Das Problem der Interpretation. Mainzer Univer-
sitätsgespräche* (Sommersemester 1964), pp. 19–29; Ulrich Pretzel, "Das
Nibelungenlied," *Germanistik in Forschung und Lehre: Vorträge und Diskus-
sionen des Germanistentages in Essen 21.-25. Oktober 1964,* ed. Rudolf Henss
and Hugo Moser (Berlin: Erich Schmidt, 1965), pp. 13–19; Francesco Delbono,
"Sulla strofa Bartsch 854 del *Nibelungenlied* nel contesto della XIV *aventiure,*"
Studi Germanici, 3 (1965), 159–81; Werner Hoffmann, *Das Nibelungenlied*
(Munich: R. Oldenbourg, 1969), p. 31; Karl Bischoff, "Die 14. Aventiure des
Nibelungenliedes: Zur Frage des Dichters und der dichterischen Gestaltung,"
*Akademie der Wissenschaften und der Literatur (Mainz): Abhandlungen der
Geistes- und Sozialwissenschaftlichen Klasse* (1970), no. 8, 3–23; Paul Salmon,
"Sivrit's Oath of Innocence," *MLR,* 71 (1976), 315–26.

the passage in hand, the order is reversed and the brothers make offers to Kriemhilt before Hagen interposes himself. Siegfried's lordliness in refusing the lands offered him corresponds to Rüdeger's attitude in insisting that Etzel will give Kriemhilt more wealth than she can ever hope to spend (1275) and that neither he nor she will touch the Nibelung treasure (1278–79). That Kriemhilt's retinue is modeled on the later passage is suggested by the fact that it is headed by Eckewart in both cases (700 = 1283). Even the size of the retinue is analogous. In one case it comprises thirty-two women and five hundred men (700.3), in the other five hundred men (1284.1) and one hundred women (1286.1).

On the return to Xanten, Sigemunt cedes his crown to Siegfried. This too looks like a loan from the "Ältere Not," in which Etzel's messengers offered the Burgundians a share in the Hunnish realm because he is aging and his young son by Kriemhilt is not old enough to rule. The offer survives in *Þiðreks saga* II.281.9–14, but was dropped in the *Nibelungenlied*.[35] In Adventure 11 Sigemunt is also aging, but Siegfried is clearly old enough to succeed to the throne. The poet borrowed the motif of the transference of power to put Siegfried on a plane of clear equality with Gunther in preparation for the queens' quarrel. The same reasoning explains Sigelint's death and Kriemhilt's promotion to sole dominion; it was essential to establish Kriemhilt's status as Brynhild's precise equal prior to their quarrel. The last motif in Adventure 11 borrowed from the "Ältere Not" is the birth of sons to Kriemhilt and Brynhild, modeled on the birth of Kriemhilt's son Ortliep (*Þiðreks saga:* Aldrian) in Hunland (stanza 1387).

Adventure 12 is a parasitic canto in the same sense as the preceding one and derives its substance from parallels in the "Ältere Not." Brynhild's engineering of an invitation for Siegfried and Kriemhilt sets the stage for the quarrel of the queens and the slaying of Siegfried just as Kriemhilt's engineering of an invitation for her brothers in Part II sets the stage for the confrontation between Hagen and Kriemhilt and the slaughter of the Burgun-

---

[35] I have argued for the presence of this motif in the "Ältere Not" in "The Epic Source," p. 27 (n. 21).

dians.[36] Here the poet finds further use for the vassal fiction: Brynhild justifies the proposed invitation by insisting on Siegfried's service (724 and 728). There is, however, a conflict between this underlying reason and the ostensible reason conveyed to Gunther in 726 and 729–30. Her ostensible reason is that she wishes to see Kriemhilt. The conflict between a real reason and an ostensible one is precisely what characterizes Kriemhilt's persuasion of Etzel to issue an invitation in Part II. In this latter passage the real reason is a desire for revenge (1391–93 and 1396–97), the ostensible reason is a wish to see her brothers (1393, 1397, 1403). The structure of the passages is the same. In each case the passage is divided into a "reflection scene" (724–25 = 1391–99), in which the queen ponders her real reason, and a "conversation scene" (726–33 = 1400–7), in which she alleges the ostensible reason in an effort to persuade her husband. In both cases the ostensible reason is a desire to see her relative or relatives. In both cases the husband protests distance as the impeding factor (727.3 and 1404.2), but in both cases he declares that there are no guests he would rather see (731.2 and 1406.2–3). Undoubtedly these two passages are interdependent. The latter cannot be modeled on the former because it demonstrably derives from the "Ältere Not," which had the same structural division between "reflection scene" and "conversation scene" and the same conflict between real and ostensible reasons.[37] The interrelationship of the two invitation sequences is further supported by the following correspondences:

1. The queen's urging results in the dispatching of messengers (732–57 and 1407–49).

2. The invitation is considered in a council scene (757–62 and 1457–72).

3. The king is counseled to take a retinue of 1000 men (760 = 1472 and *Þiðreks saga* II.284.15).

---

[36]See Wesle, p. 36, and Kralik, pp. 112–13. As de Boor, "Die Bearbeitung m des Nibelungenliedes," p. 180, pointed out, the redactor of m shows his awareness of the parallel in the heading of Adventure 27: "Abinture wie daz kriemelt warp daz ir / brudir kam zün hunē also det brunhilt vor / daz siferit kam zün burgundin" ("Adventure telling how Kriemhilt caused her brother to come to the Huns as Brynhild previously caused Siegfried to come to the Burgundians").

[37]I have dealt with the form of the "Ältere Not" in "The Epic Source," pp. 25–26 (n. 15).

The last traces of intraborrowing are the rewarding of the messengers in line with similar compensations in 243 and 558 and Hagen's expression of interest in Siegfried's treasure, which anticipates his seizure of the treasure in Adventure 20. The thirty-six stanzas of Adventure 13 are devoted entirely to the festive reception of Siegfried and his retinue in Worms and shed no light on the tradition or the poet's compositional procedures.

We turn now to the final phases of the story in Adventures 14–19, that part of the narrative which extends from the quarrel of the queens through the aftermath of Siegfried's death.

Siegfried's Death

(14) One day the queens sit watching a tournament and musing on their respective husbands. Kriemhilt reflects that her husband might fittingly possess the whole realm. Brynhild protests that this is not possible during Gunther's lifetime. Without replying directly, Kriemhilt continues to dwell on Siegfried's preeminence. Brynhild's temper rises slightly and she bespeaks the foremost position for Gunther. Kriemhilt responds that Siegfried is surely Gunther's equal. Brynhild now raises the point, somewhat apologetically, that Siegfried has declared himself to be Gunther's vassal. Kriemhilt bids her desist from such nonsensical talk, but Brynhild points out that she cannot well relinquish the service of so many men. Kriemhilt retorts that she has no choice but to relinquish their service since Siegfried is more distinguished than Gunther: if he were a vassal, it would be surprising indeed that he has withheld his fee so long. Brynhild now proposes to determine whether she or Brynhild enjoys greater honor. Kriemhilt falls in with the test and vows to take precedence at church that day to prove that she occupies a higher position than any other queen. Brynhild replies that if she does not acknowledge her vassal status, she must leave her retinue. Kriemhilt is more than ready. She orders forty-three ladies-in-waiting to dress in their most splendid attire and proceeds to church in grand style.

Here Brynhild bids her stop because a woman in service (838: "eigen diu") may not precede a queen. Kriemhilt inquires how a man's (or vassal's) concubine can become a queen and, in reply to Brynhild's startled question about the word "concubine," she maintains that it was Siegfried who took Brynhild's virginity. Brynhild threatens to take the charge to Gunther, Kriemhilt reproves her arrogance, and Brynhild bursts into tears while Kriemhilt sweeps

The Sources of the *Nibelungenlied* Part I 183

ahead of her and enters the church. When Brynhild emerges from the service, she reflects that it will cost Siegfried his life if he has made such a claim and she questions Kriemhilt accordingly. Kriemhilt verifies her claim by exhibiting the ring Siegfried took from Brynhild. Brynhild maintains that it was stolen from her. Kriemhilt counters with her second proof, the belt taken by Siegfried. At this point Brynhild breaks down in tears again and summons Gunther to witness the accusation. She then repeats Kriemhilt's charge that Siegfried slept with her, points to the tokens, and asks to be vindicated. Gunther proposes that Siegfried step forward and state whether he has made such a boast.

When Siegfried is brought to the scene, Gunther confronts him with Brynhild's charge that he boasted of a conquest. (This is of course inaccurate—Brynhild said only that Kriemhilt accused her of sleeping with Siegfried.) Siegfried readily offers an oath to exculpate himself. Gunther at first welcomes the idea, then interrupts the oath to say that he accepts Siegfried's innocence. Siegfried concludes the scene with some words on the disciplining of wives. Next Hagen approaches a weeping Brynhild and, on learning of the problem, vows that Siegfried will pay for what he has done. The scene continues in an elliptical stanza (865) that seems to involve Brynhild, Hagen, and Gunther in a plot to take Siegfried's life, though Gunther's presence is only implied in the plural "helde." Giselher advises against the murder. Hagen urges that they not abet womanizers and that Siegfried should pay for his boast.[38] Gunther opposes the murder because of Siegfried's faithful service. Ortwin urges it for no obvious reason. Hagen prosecutes the argument by pointing out that they stand to gain a great deal of territory in the event of Siegfried's death. Gunther continues his opposition, alleging the honor that accrues from Siegfried's presence and the overpowering strength with which he would frustrate any attempt against him. Hagen maintains that he can find a way and Gunther expresses interest despite himself. Hagen then proposes to instigate a false declaration of war as a pretext for learning the secret of his vulnerability and Gunther finally agrees.

(15) Four days later the false emissaries arrive with a renewed declaration of war on the part of Liudegast and Liudeger. Siegfried learns of the situation and offers to meet the attack with his own

[38]L. L. Hammerich, "Zu Nibelungenlied 867 (*gouch* 'Bastard'?)," *Neophilologus*, 16 (1931), 96–98. Hammerich translates "Suln wir gouche ziehen?" with "Sollen wir Buhler pflegen?" ("Should we consort with seducers?").

men. Hagen presents himself to take leave of Kriemhilt, who asks him for his good offices in protecting Siegfried from Brynhild's reprisals and from injury in battle. Hagen asks how he can best provide this protection and Kriemhilt reveals that when he became invulnerable by bathing in the dragon's blood, a leaf fell between his shoulders, causing one spot to remain untreated. Hagen urges her to sew a sign on the appropriate part of his coat so that he can shield him effectively. She agrees and Hagen departs. The next morning Siegfried sets out and when Hagen has made note of the mark, he dispatches new messengers to countermand the declaration of war. Gunther thanks Siegfried profusely for his willingness and, following Hagen's treacherous counsel, announces a hunt. Siegfried declares his desire to participate.

(16) Siegfried bids Kriemhilt farewell. She remembers her revelations to Hagen and weeps. In a dream she has seen two boars chasing Siegfried over the heath and she begs him to refrain from the hunt. He answers that he is not aware of having enemies, but Kriemhilt recounts a second dream in which she saw two mountains collapse on him. He embraces her and takes his leave. The hunters set out, but Gernot and Giselher remain at home. It is decided to split up so that each participant can hunt on his own and prove his skill. Siegfried naturally excels and accounts for a young boar ("halpful"), a lion, a bison, an elk, four aueroxen, a "schelch,"[39] various harts and hinds, and a full-grown boar. A horn sounds to conclude the hunt, but on the way back to camp, Siegfried encounters a bear, captures it on foot, ties it up, loads it on his horse, enters camp in his magnificent hunting attire, and looses it in the midst of hunters, dogs, and cooks, creating massive chaos and consternation. The bear makes for the hills, but Siegfried runs it down again and kills it with his sword.

The feasting begins and Siegfried calls for wine. Hagen claims to have mistaken the location of the hunt and to have sent the wine elsewhere. Siegfried chides him and Hagen suggests a nearby spring. Hagen now proposes a race to the spring and Siegfried offers a substantial handicap—he will start from a prone position and run in full armor. He nonetheless arrives first, but out of courtesy declines to drink before Gunther. When Gunther has finished, Siegfried lies down by the spring, Hagen surreptitiously removes his weapons, spies out the mark on his coat, and plunges a spear into the vulnerable spot. Siegfried jumps to his feet, misses bow and sword, but fells

---

[39]Leonhard Franz, "Was war der *schelch*?" *ZDA*, 96 (1967), 74–78, interprets the word to mean wild stallion.

the fleeing Hagen with his shield. Then he collapses as his strength ebbs and reprimands his killers for their faithlessness. Hagen exults at having eliminated the only rival power. With his dying words Siegfried appeals to Gunther to care for his wife. He is placed on a shield and the murderers agree to disguise Hagen's deed by claiming that he was slain by brigands. Hagen proclaims his indifference to Kriemhilt's feelings in view of the distress she has caused Brynhild.

(17) Hagen orders Siegfried's corpse to be placed on Kriemhilt's threshold, where she will find it the next morning on the way to the early service, but before she emerges, a chamberlain discovers the body and informs her. Though he has not made the identification, she remembers her revelations to Hagen and guesses immediately. As she collapses, she shrieks so that the chamber resounds. A look at the body and the shield undamaged by sword strokes tells her clearly that Siegfried has been murdered. She sends for Sigemunt, who joins in the chorus of mourning. Siegfried's band of Nibelungs is ready to take revenge, but Kriemhilt fears their death at the hands of the Burgundians and urges them to desist. The mourning spreads to the whole town and preparations are made for the burial. Gunther approaches Kriemhilt with false condolences, but she challenges the murderers to pass by Siegfried's bier. As Hagen does so, the wounds burst open again, identifying the culprit. Gunther holds to the story of murderous brigands, but Kriemhilt knows well enough who these brigands are. Gernot and Giselher, on the other hand, are genuine participants in the mourning. The burial is performed with massive pomp and vast donations for the benefit of Siegfried's soul. At the last moment Kriemhilt insists that the coffin be opened again so that she can see Siegfried one last time. She is overcome by grief and must be carried away.

(18) Sigemunt and his retinue prepare to leave with Kriemhilt. Giselher urges his sister to remain, but she contends that she cannot endure the sight of her husband's murderers. Eventually she yields to the brotherly entreaties of Giselher and Gernot over Sigemunt's protests. He departs without taking leave and accompanied by the sad farewells of Giselher and Gernot. She remains behind in perpetual mourning with only Giselher for comfort. The final stanza (1100) reintroduces Brynhild one last time to note her arrogance and indifference to Kriemhilt's tears.

(19) After four and a half years Kriemhilt is finally prevailed on to effect a reconciliation with Gunther. At Hagen's instigation she is also persuaded to retrieve Siegfried's Nibelung treasure from Alberich, but she creates alarm by distributing it freely and winning numerous friends. During an absence of her brothers, Hagen there-

fore seizes the treasure and sinks it in the Rhine. As an afterthought stanza 1140 adds that they (Hagen and Gunther presumably) had agreed that neither would reveal the location. Kriemhilt's grief for her husband is thus compounded by the loss of the treasure. She continues in this state for thirteen years.

The quarrel of the queens is one of the best documented and most complicated parts of the legend.[40] There are five separate versions to deal with: *Forna, Meiri* (both must be inferred from *Vǫlsunga saga*), *Snorra Edda, Þiðreks saga,* and the *Nibelungenlied*. These versions have much in common but differ from one another in many respects. The problem is sufficiently complex so that it will be well to preview the solution before proceeding to an analysis of the texts. I begin therefore with an outline that stands to be amplified.

Common form of the quarrel. No prior betrothal. One scene: (1) quarrel over precedence, (2) relative distinction of respective husbands, (3) revelation of Sigurd's invasion of Brynhild's bed

River quarrel (Norse) in *Forna* and *Snorra Edda*. No prior betrothal. One scene: (1) precedence, (2) relative distinction, (3) revelation

Hall quarrel (German). Prior betrothal. Two scenes: Brynhild's grief; quarrel over (1) precedence, (2) relative distinction, (3) revelation

Meiri. Prior betrothal. Two scenes: Brynhild's grief; quarrel over (1) relative distinction, (2) revelation

Þiðreks saga. Prior betrothal. One scene: quarrel over (1) precedence, (2) relative distinction, (3) revelation

Nibelungenlied. Prior betrothal dropped. Four scenes: Brynhild's grief; quarrel over (1) relative distinction, (2) precedence, (3) revelation

We start with a simple form in which there was no prior betrothal between Sigurd and Brynhild to complicate later develop-

[40] An interesting parallel in Procopius, *Gothica* 7.1, involving a quarrel between a queen and a noblewoman in the bath and the ensuing fatal consequences has been commented on frequently: Heusler, *Nibelungensage und Nibelungenlied*, p.

ments. In this version the quarrel was limited to one scene (whether in river or hall is not certain though the oldest text, *Forna,* vouches for the river) and proceeded in three stages. The queens first contest a favored position (upstream in the river or a highseat in the hall). They then support their claims with reference to the relative distinction of their husbands. The final stage occurs when Gudrun / Kriemhilt reacts to Brynhild's denigration of Sigurd by revealing that it was Sigurd who first invaded Brynhild's bed. This version is best preserved in *Forna* (*Vǫlsunga saga* 69.13–70.7) and *Snorra Edda* (ed. Finnur Jónsson, pp. 130.37–131.12).

Forna (Vǫlsunga saga)

The queens go to the river to bathe and Brynhild wades out further. To Gudrun's query she replies that they are no more equal in this matter than in others: her father is more powerful and her husband has performed brave deeds and crossed the flame wall, while Gudrun's husband was King Hjálprekr's thrall. Gudrun angrily defends her husband as unexampled in every respect, pointing out that it is not proper for Brynhild to denigrate him since he was her own first husband ("frumverr"). He killed Fáfnir and crossed the flame wall when Brynhild thought it was Gunnarr, and he took from her the ring Andvaranautr. Gudrun now exhibits the ring, Brynhild recognizes it, pales, goes home, and says not a word in the evening.

Snorra Edda

The queens go out to the river to wash their hair. Brynhild wades further out, saying that she does not want to use the water which runs out of Gudrun's hair because she has a braver husband. Gudrun follows her and maintains that she can wash her hair upstream be-

---

9; Richard Huss, "Die senna der Königinnen in der Volsungasaga und der Nibelungensage," *BGDSL,* 47 (1923), 506–7; Naumann, "Stand der Nibelungenforschung," p. 8; Martin Lintzel, *Der historische Kern der Siegfriedsage,* Historische Studien, 245 (Berlin: Verlag Dr. Emil Ebering, 1934); H. Grégoire, "Où en est la question des Nibelungen?" *Byzantion,* 10 (1935), 223–24; E. O. Winstedt, "Siegfried," *MA,* 21 (1952), 25; K. F. Stroheker, "Studien zu den historisch-geographischen Grundlagen der Nibelungendichtung," *DVLG,* 32 (1958), 235; Jan de Vries, *Heldenlied und Heldensage* (Bern and Munich: Francke, 1961), p. 268.

cause she has a husband with no equal in the world, including Gunnarr; he killed Fáfnir and Reginn and took their inheritance. Brynhild replies that it was more important that Gunnarr crossed the flame wall, while Sigurd did not dare. Gudrun laughs and says that the one who crossed the flame wall and entered her bed was the one who gave her (Gudrun) the gold ring that she now exhibits. Brynhild, on the other hand, wears a gold ring called Andvaranautr and it was not Gunnarr who fetched it from Gnitaheiðr. Brynhild was silent and went home.

These two accounts are set apart from the others by (1) the absence of a prior betrothal, (2) the location in the river, (3) the use of a single scene. There are doubts that they are identical, and Heusler suggested that *Snorra Edda* may have based its account on *Meiri* rather than *Forna*.[41] However, the similarities are so great as to make differing sources improbable, quite aside from the indications that *Meiri* located the quarrel in the hall. The common motifs in *Forna* and *Snorra Edda* are:
1. The queens wade into the stream and vie for position.
2. Brynhild claims that Gunnarr is braver than Sigurd.
3. Gudrun retorts that Sigurd is the braver.
4. Brynhild maintains that Gunnarr crossed the flame wall.
5. Gudrun reveals that it was Sigurd who crossed the flame wall and became Brynhild's first lover.
6. Gudrun exhibits the ring to prove the point.
7. Brynhild departs in silence.

Both texts abridge somewhat since they are prose epitomes. *Snorra Edda* suppresses Gudrun's first inquiry and lets Brynhild claim her husband's superiority unsolicited. *Snorra Edda* further suppresses her claim to have a more powerful father. *Vǫlsunga saga*, on the other hand, conflates points 2 and 4 in the outline above into a single response. Probably in addition *Snorra Edda* suppresses the remark about Sigurd's thralldom, a detail that is

---

[41]"Lieder der Lücke," *Kleine Schriften*, II, 264 and 271. Wieselgren, *Quellenstudien zur Vǫlsungasaga*, pp. 272–75 and 333–38, also equated the quarrel scene in *Snorra Edda* with *Meiri*. Kralik, p. 640, promised a later proof that the quarrel scene in *Vǫlsunga saga* and *Snorra Edda* derived from *Meiri*. Bumke, "Die Quellen," p. 16, interpreted Kralik to mean that the quarrel scene came from "an authentic old source." See also Panzer's general comparison in *Studien zur germanischen Sagengeschichte*, II: *Sigfrid*, 208–12.

bespoken for the original tradition by the reference to the "hind's trail" in *Þiðreks saga* and the denigration of Siegfried as a social inferior, a vassal, in the *Nibelungenlied*. *Vǫlsunga saga* again conflates points 3 and 5 in the outline above. The additional information on Andvaranautr in *Snorra Edda* may or may not have been in *Forna*.

The most difficult problem is the passage in *Snorra Edda* in which Gudrun claims preeminence for Sigurd because he killed Fáfnir and Reginn ("hon atti þaɴ maɴ, er eigi G(vnnarr) ok engi aɴaʀ iveroldu var iafnfrækn, þviat hann vá Fafni ok Regin ok toc arf eptir baþa þa") and Brynhild replies that it was more important that Gunnarr crossed the flame wall, while Sigurd did not dare ("meira var þat vert, er Gvɴaʀ reið vaforlogann, en Sigurþr þorþi eigi"). The source for this exchange appears to be in *Vǫlsunga saga* 71.9–20:

Brynhilldr svarar: "Sigurdr væ æt Fafnne, ok er þat meira vert enn allt riki Gunnars konungs," sva sem kvedit er:

> 24. Sigurdr væ at orme,
>   enn þat siþan mun
>   engum fyrnazt,
>   medan aulld lifir.
>   En hlyre þinn
>   hvarke þordi
>   elld at rida
>   nę yfir stigha.

(Brynhild replies: "Sigurd slew Fáfnir and that is worth more than all of King Gunnarr's realm," as the poet says:

> 24. Sigurd slew the serpent
>   And forever after
>   That will not perish
>   While the world stands.
>   But your brother
>   Neither dared
>   To ride the fire
>   Nor surmount it.)

There are three things wrong with the use of this stanza in *Snorra Edda:*

1. The writer separates the helmings, which obviously belong together, giving the first to Gudrun and the second to Brynhild.

2. Brynhild's statement that Sigurd did not dare to cross the flame wall makes no sense because she has no reason to believe that Sigurd would try to cross it.

3. *Snorra Edda*'s apparent interpretation of "hlyre þinn" as Sigurd is not justified because Sigurd does not figure as anyone's brother.

I have suggested above (Chapter 1, n. 52) that the stanza may belong either to Gudrun in *Forna,* in which case "hlyre þinn" ("your brother") must have read "hlyre minn" ("my brother," i.e., Gunnarr), or to Brynhild in *Meiri.*[42] If it belonged to *Forna,* we must assume that the writer divided it and assigned the first part to Gudrun, the second to Brynhild, at the same time changing the idea that Gunnarr ("hlyre þinn") did not dare to cross the flame wall into the idea that Sigurd did not dare. The change is necessary because *Snorra Edda* uses the stanza in the context of the *Forna* quarrel, during which Brynhild does not yet know that Gunnarr failed to clear the flames, not in the context of *Vǫlsunga saga*'s version of *Meiri*'s hall quarrel, during which Brynhild is already apprised of Gunnarr's failure. The change of course creates a new puzzle: Why should Brynhild imagine that Sigurd made an attempt on the flame wall? Perhaps the thinking is not that Sigurd did not dare, but that he would not have dared had he been in Gunnarr's position.

If, on the other hand, the stanza belonged to *Meiri,* we must assume that the *Meiri* poet created it by combining Gudrun's words in *Forna* (*Vǫlsunga saga* 69.23–70.1: "ok eigi samir þer vel at lasta hann, þviat hann er þinn frumverr, ok drap hann Fafnne ok reid vafrlogann"—"and it is not proper for you to slander him because he is your first husband and he slew Fáfnir and crossed the flame wall") with the new idea that Gunnarr did not dare to cross the flame wall. *Snorra Edda* assigned the first part to Gudrun, as *Forna* had, and the second part to Brynhild

---

[42]Difficult to interpret is the echo of stanza 22 in *Vǫlsunga saga* 67.15–18: "Far treystizt þar / fylkiss recka / elld at riþa / ne yfir stigha" ("Few warriors dared to ride the fire or surmount it").

according to the revision of the *Meiri* poet. At the same time, it
shifted the failure of courage from Gunnarr to Sigurd as explained
above. Whatever the exact solution of this knotty problem, there
is no evidence that the quarrel versions of *Vǫlsunga saga* and
Snorra Edda derived from substantially different sources. At
most *Snorra Edda* may have borrowed one replique from *Meiri*.

The second branch of the quarrel tradition is found in German
texts (*Þiðreks saga* and the *Nibelungenlied*) and the German-
influenced *Meiri*. It is characterized by a location in the hall
(altered to tourney and church in the *Nibelungenlied*), a prior
betrothal between Brynhild and Siegfried, and a new scene in
which Brynhild expresses her grief at not having the husband she
wanted. The background of the prior betrothal appears only
sporadically in *Þiðreks saga* (II.38.20–40.4) and does not figure as
part of the quarrel scene. It is sacrificed entirely in the
Nibelungenlied, though we have seen how it continues to haunt
the premises of Adventures 6 and 7. Only in *Meiri* (*Vǫlsunga
saga* 70.19–71.3) is explicit reference made to Brynhild's first
betrothal during the quarrel. Here Gudrun inquires into her grief,
and Brynhild replies menacingly that Gudrun will suffer the consequences of possessing Sigurd, adding that she begrudges her
both Sigurd and the treasure. Gudrun protests that she knew
nothing of the betrothal, but Brynhild maintains that she and her
family were well aware of the oaths and she promises revenge.
This scene is equivalent to the *Nibelungenlied* 618–24, the passage in which Brynhild weeps at the sight of Kriemhilt and Siegfried and presses Gunther for an explanation of Kriemhilt's marriage to a vassal. The equivalence is shown by the fact that both
scenes are framed in the same way; they begin with the observation of Brynhild's grief and end with her threat of reprisals. Gudrun's question in *Vǫlsunga saga* 70.8, "Hvi er Brynhilldr sva
ukat?" ("Why is Brynhild so cheerless?"), matches Gunther's
inquiry in the *Nibelungenlied* 619.1–2, "waz ist iu, vrouwe mîn, /
daz ir sô lâzet truoben / vil liehter ougen schîn?" ("What is the
trouble, my lady, that you so darken the light of your bright
eyes?"), and 624.1, "Swaz ir der künic sagete, / si hete trüeben
muot" ("Whatever the king said to her, she remained in a de-
spondent mood"). The scene ends in *Vǫlsunga saga* with
Brynhild's vow to take vengeance and in the *Nibelungenlied* with

the vow not to sleep with Gunther unless he explains the situation. The *Nibelungenlied* poet substitutes Gunther for Gudrun / Kriemhilt in the dialogue of the source because the prior betrothal has been eliminated and Brynhild has nothing to reproach Kriemhilt for.

The evidence that this was a separate scene comes largely from the *Nibelungenlied,* in which it is far removed from the queens' quarrel (Adventures 11–13 intervene). We must imagine an original situation in which Brynhild turns melancholy and responds to her rival's inquiries by reproaching her for the possession of Siegfried. She terminates the discussion by vowing vengeance and this vow becomes the immediate motivation for her provocative behavior in the quarrel scene. In the *Nibelungenlied* the situation has been altered. Brynhild's grief is no longer motivated by her loss of Siegfried. Instead the poet motivates her grief with the rather flimsy idea that she resents a social injustice done Kriemhilt. The scene then concludes not with her vow of vengeance, but with a threat of reprisals against Gunther unless he clarifies the mystery, a mystery which is of the poet's own making because he chose to suppress the prior betrothal.

Why did this branch of the legend insert a separate scene depicting Brynhild's grief? The answer seems to be that in this version Brynhild was previously betrothed to Siegfried and could not very well initiate a quarrel with Kriemhilt by maintaining in all innocence that Gunther was the superior man. In order to mend this illogicality, the original poet added a prior confrontation between the queens in which Brynhild vows vengeance. Her later provocation of Kriemhilt is therefore not to be viewed in terms of logicality, but as a deliberate act of malice prefatory to her vengeance. The actual content of the quarrel in the texts with (or implying) the prior betrothal is very close to what we find in *Forna* and *Snorra Edda. Þiðreks saga* has the same sequence of contention over precedence, relative distinction of the two husbands, and the revelation of the deception. *Vǫlsunga saga*'s version of *Meiri* drops the quarrel over precedence because it has already been taken over from the river quarrel in *Forna* and the duplication would be too obvious. The *Nibelungenlied* changes the order slightly and places the debate over the husbands' relative distinction ahead of the debate over precedence (before

the church), at the same time dividing the quarrel into three separate scenes, each corresponding to one phase of the quarrel.[43]

The most altered text is *Vǫlsunga saga*'s version of *Meiri*.
There can be little doubt that it represents the same traditional
quarrel because the constituent motifs are the same: the debate
over distinction (71.6–9: "Una mundu ver ... ef eigi ęttir þu gauf-
gara mann"—"I would be content if you did not have the more
distinguished husband"; "Attu sva gaufgan mann, at uvist er,
hverr meire konungr er..."—"You have such a distinguished
husband that it is uncertain who is the greater king...") and the
citing of Sigurd's dragon slaying and crossing of the flame wall
(71.13–20 [stanza 24] = 70.1 [*Forna*]). But the context is different. Here Gudrun tries to reconcile Brynhild to her marriage
instead of contesting her marital superiority. The author of *Meiri*
has taken the queens' confrontation from *Forna* and converted it
into conciliatory terms, that is, he uses the quarrel in *Forna* in
conjunction with the later efforts to placate Brynhild (Chapter 1
between n. 51 and n. 52). Thus Gudrun finds herself in the position of lauding Gunnarr instead of disparaging him, while
Brynhild praises Sigurd.

The interview between Gudrun and Brynhild in *Vǫlsunga saga*
(Meiri) continues with the latter's excoriation of Grimhild
(71.23–29), whom she perceives as the mastermind of the deception. This animosity is a familiar preoccupation of the *Meiri* poet
and must have been added into the quarrel scene or, more probably, the grief scene to consolidate the motif. The conversation
then shifts back to Brynhild's resentment of Gudrun's marriage.
Gudrun retorts that she has every intention of enjoying her possession of Sigurd and that no one suspects them of having been
too familiar. In other words, this is an oblique form of the charge
that Brynhild has been Sigurd's lover, the final stage in the traditional quarrel as we find it in the other versions. In *Vǫlsunga
saga* it is weakened to an innuendo because the actual revelation
has already emerged in the river quarrel, which the author of

---

[43]This supposition agrees with Hugo Kuhn, "Über nordische und deutsche
Szenenregie in der Nibelungendichtung," *Edda, Skalden, Saga: Festschrift zum
70. Geburtstag von Felix Genzmer*, ed. Hermann Schneider (Heidelberg: Winter,
1952), pp. 284–85; rpt. in his *Dichtung und Welt im Mittelalter* (Stuttgart: Metzler,
1959; rpt. 1969), p. 201.

Vǫlsunga saga took from *Forna*. The later passage simply alludes to the earlier sexual charge. Then the conversation tapers off uncertainly, again because the violent denouement has already been expended in the river and there remains nothing from which to construct a new crest.

We observe in all these texts a common form of the quarrel in which the queens meet, Brynhild claims precedence, they debate the relative merits of their husbands, and Gudrun/Kriemhilt reveals the deception by producing the incriminating ring. In the texts with the prior betrothal this quarrel is prefaced by a scene in which Brynhild reveals her grievances to Kriemhilt in order to motivate her later provocation. The individual texts adjust the situation variously. *Vǫlsunga saga* fuses the grief and quarrel scenes from *Meiri* and alters *Meiri* somewhat in light of the river quarrel previously registered from *Forna*. The author or redactor of *Þiðreks saga* did not commit himself firmly to the prior betrothal and omitted the grief scene designed to reconcile the prior betrothal with the quarrel. The *Nibelungenlied* poet sacrificed the prior betrothal entirely, but chose to recast the grief scene instead of dropping it altogether; it is motivated as an expression of vicarious grief for Kriemhilt instead of a rehearsal of grievances against Kriemhilt. At the same time, the *Nibelungenlied* poet subdivided the quarrel into three separate phases in accord with the epic tendency to multiply scenes.

What follows in Adventure 14 of the *Nibelungenlied* is as vexed as the quarrel scene itself. Siegfried is charged with boasting of Brynhild's conquest although there is no evidence anywhere in the legend or in the *Nibelungenlied* that he made such a boast. He volunteers to swear an oath to this effect, but is then exempted from the oath. The explanation for this confusion is that the *Nibelungenlied* poet is working from a source akin to *Þiðreks saga,* in which Siegfried actually deflowered Brynhild. The courtly poet's more refined taste prevents him from making full use of such a crass motif, and he consequently reduces the actual deflowering to a mere allegation on Kriemhilt's part. An allegation, however, is not sufficient to motivate Siegfried's death; the poet therefore keeps the suspicion alive that he may have made a boast by foreshortening the oath that would have exculpated him. The source of the difficulty in the *Nibelungen-*

lied is that chivalric courtesy barred the real motivation for Siegfried's murder, the prior betrothal and the deflowering of Brynhild, and allowed only a shadow motivation—the allegation of a boast that Siegfried, as construed by the *Nibelungenlied*, could not and would not have made.

Next in the *Nibelungenlied* is the murder council, corresponding to *Brot* 1–3, *Skamma* 10–20, *Vǫlsunga saga* 77.26–80.5, and *Þiðreks saga* II.261.18–262.26. *Brot* may be supplemented by *Vǫlsunga saga* 77.26–78.5. The situation is that Brynhild incites Gunnarr (*Vǫlsunga saga* 78.2–3: "This will be Sigurd's death or yours or mine..."), Gunnarr seeks Hǫgni's advice, Hǫgni counsels against the murder, but they ultimately delegate Gotþormr to do the deed. The situation in *Skamma* 10–20 (*Vǫlsunga saga* 78.6–79.13) is analogous. The only trace of *Meiri* is in *Vǫlsunga saga* 79.13–80.5, including one stanza ("Sumir vidfiska toku..."). Here there appears to be no opposition from Hǫgni, though it may have been deleted in light of the opposition already recorded from *Skamma* (*Vǫlsunga saga* 78.24–79.6). It is also possible that the opposition expressed in *Vǫlsunga saga* 79.10–12, which has no exact equivalent in *Skamma,* comes from *Meiri.* In addition, the *Meiri* passage contains the key sentence (79.17–18): "Gunnarr segir, at þetta er gilld banasauk at hafa tekit meydom Brynhilldar" ("Gunnarr says that it is sufficient grounds for death to have taken Brynhild's virginity"). These words specify clearly the accusation Brynhild must have leveled in making her case for the murder of Sigurd. She enforces her will in *Skamma* 10–11 (*Vǫlsunga saga* 78.10–13) by threatening to leave Gunnarr, but in *Meiri* (*Vǫlsunga saga* 79.14–16) she exerts the necessary pressure by threatening to withhold her sexual favors. In *Þiðreks saga* Brynhild accuses Sigurd of having broken his word, not in the sense of sleeping with her, but of communicating the deception to Gudrun. Hǫgni offers consolation, which can only be interpreted to have ominous implications concerning his intentions. Brynhild rails at Sigurd's birth and arrogance and Gunnarr adds his consolation, stating that Sigurd will not long be their lord, nor Grimhild their queen.

The main difference between the Eddic versions and *Þiðreks saga* is that in the former Hǫgni shrinks from the murder, while in the latter he appears to be in agreement from the outset. The

motivation in all the texts is a jumble of alleged sexual infringement, lack of discretion, growing arrogance, desire for Sigurd's
treasure, and fear of his power. It is therefore difficult to imagine
a pure form in which one motivation was predominant to the
exclusion of all others. As might be expected, the *Nibelungenlied*
stands closest to *Þiðreks saga*. Hagen is the first to respond to
Brynhild's tears (*Nibelungenlied* 864 = *Þiðreks saga* II.262.
14–16). In 865 Gunther appears to have a hand in the murder council although the poet is eager not to compromise royalty and
obscures the fact by not mentioning his name. In 866 Giselher
assumes the role assigned Hǫgni in the Norse version and seeks
to dissuade the conspirators. In 867 Hagen renews the case
against Siegfried on the grounds of his alleged sexual infringement. In 868 Gunther sides with Giselher despite his prior implication in the murder council (865). Ortwin supports Hagen (869).
Gunther continues to demur (872). Hagen intimates a plan (873),
Gunther elicits it (874–75), and finally agrees (876). This account
is easily derived from a source close to *Þiðreks saga*. The
scruples evinced by Giselher and Gunther are in line with the
poet's distilled conception of their characters and his willingness
to make Hagen the scapegoat. The expanded dialogue and
broadened participation are hallmarks of the poet's epic ambitions.

This analysis of Adventure 14 shows it to be firmly rooted in
tradition. Both the quarrel of the queens and the murder council
preserve the main outlines of the legend as we have it in the
comparable texts. Adventure 15, with its counterfeit declaration
of war by Saxons and Danes, is a different matter. It is the poet's
innovation from whole cloth, introduced for the purpose of
motivating the little cross that Kriemhilt sews on Siegfried's coat
to signal the point of vulnerability.[44] Innovation, in this case, is
not tantamount to a flight of free fancy and leads no further than
to a mock repetition of the Dano-Saxon hostilities of Adventure 4.
The episode is another case of intraborrowing aimed at broaden-
ing the dimensions of the tale, but it serves also to darken the
hues in Hagen's portrait and exonerate Gunther partially by making him a passive accomplice.

---

[44]Schneider, pp. 38–39, declined to credit the *Nibelungenlied* poet with this
innovation and assigned it to his source A.

Adventure 16 returns us once more to legendary bedrock. Here the terrain is easier to survey than in Adventure 14 because Siegfried's forest death is paralleled only in *Þiðreks saga* and we need not be detained by the Eddic versions. The account in *Þiðreks saga* may be boiled down to the following (cf. Chapter 2):

> Hǫgni proposes a hunt and orders that the food be salted and the drink delayed. They set out next morning and Grimhild goes to bed to avoid Brynhild's company. Hǫgni lingers behind and is incited anew by Brynhild. When he rejoins the hunters, they track down a boar and Hǫgni kills it. They are so hot and tired after the chase that they lie down by a stream to drink. Hǫgni gets up first and spears Sigurd from behind. Sigurd's dying words are that he did not expect this of his brother-in-law (the Norse redactor's view of the relationship); if he had, all four of them would have succumbed before he fell. Hǫgni exults at having killed (metaphorically) a bear or a bison. Gunnarr proposes that they return the bison to Grimhild. Brynhild congratulates them on their return and bids them bring Grimhild the dead body to embrace as she deserves. They throw the corpse into her bed and she awakens to find her murdered husband. The murder is clearly signaled by unscathed shield and helmet. Hǫgni maintains that a wild boar killed him, but Grimhild identifies him as the wild boar in question and weeps bitterly.

This account is substantially what we find in the *Nibelungenlied,* but the latter predictably expands the dimensions. The departure for the hunt is prefaced by a characteristic farewell scene (918–25) that has its origin in the departure of the Burgundians for Hunland in the "Ältere Not" (*Þiðreks saga* II.284.18–20; *Nibelungenlied* 1515–16 and 1520–23). That the present passage is indeed modeled on this forerunner in the "Ältere Not" is suggested by corresponding prophetic dreams; Kriemhilt's ominous dreams of two boars chasing Siegfried across the heath and two mountains collapsing on him echo Uote's desolate dream of dead birds (*Þiðreks saga* II.283.17–20; *Nibelungenlied* 1509).[45] The second major deviation from *Þiðreks saga* is the decision by Gernot and Giselher to remain at home. This detail is motivated

[45] See Droege, p. 491: "Der dichter scheint mit einer gewissen vorliebe motive, die ihm gefallen, mehrfach, meist zweimal, auszuführen." Droege's list of examples includes the two monitory dreams. Cf. Kettner, pp. 282–84, and Körner, p. 103.

by the special bond that the *Nibelungenlied* poet has created between Kriemhilt and her younger brothers.[46] An account follows of Siegfried's superhuman hunting exploits, of which *Þiðreks saga* gives no hint—only a boar is mentioned and Hǫgni kills it. The episode may be classed with the military exploits in Adventure 4 and the athletic exploits of Adventure 7 as the *Nibelungenlied* poet's elaboration.

The salted food of *Þiðreks saga* has been lost in the *Nibelungenlied,* but Siegfried's call for wine may imply it and Hagen's misshipment of the wine in the *Nibelungenlied* is in any event equivalent to the delay of drink in *Þiðreks saga.*[47] In the latter text the hunters happen on a spring; in the *Nibelungenlied* Hagen leads them to it, perhaps to emphasize the manipulative skills that he has already exhibited to good effect. The dash to the spring is surely a further piece of the hyperbolic homage to Siegfried peculiar to the *Nibelungenlied,* and his courteous deference in allowing Gunther to drink first no less so. The plunging of the spear into Siegfried's back is comparable in both sources, but in the *Nibelungenlied* Siegfried very nearly takes vengeance by felling Hagen with his shield. That this may be an old motif is suggested by the scene in *Skamma* 22–23 (*Vǫlsunga saga* 80.18–22) in which Sigurd casts his sword after Gotþormr and cuts him in two. If so, the detail has been lost in *Þiðreks saga.* Siegfried's dying words in both sources contain a reproach, but the *Nibelungenlied* poet adds an appeal on behalf of his wife.

What may be deduced thus far for the common source of *Þiðreks saga* and the *Nibelungenlied* are the following four points:

1. Hagen's proposal of a hunt, the salting of the food, and the withholding of drink
2. The spearing of Siegfried as he lies drinking at the spring
3. Siegfried's felling of his murderer with a shield or sword cast (?)
4. His dying reproach of his murderers

[46]Heusler, "Die Quelle der Brünhildsage," *Kleine Schriften,* I, 70. The germ of this relationship may again be found in the "Ältere Not," in which Kriemhilt singled out Giselher and greeted him affectionately on his arrival in Hunland (*Þiðreks saga* II.299.3–4; *Nibelungenlied* 1737).

[47]Helmut de Boor, "Eine Spur der 'älteren Not'?" *BGDSL* (Tübingen), 77 (1955), 248–51, located the salted food motif in Heinrich von dem Türlin's *Krône* and derived it from the "Ältere Not." If the detail really does originate in a *Nibelungenlied* source, it is more likely to belong to the "Brünhildenlied."

Adventure 16 concludes with an agreement among the hunters that the slaying will be attributed to brigands, perhaps an anticipation of the version later foisted on Kriemhilt. In Adventure 17 Siegfried is placed on Kriemhilt's threshold, where he is discovered by a chamberlain.[48] On being informed, Kriemhilt immediately realizes the identity of the dead knight and cries aloud. An inspection of the body reveals that he has been murdered. The deposition of Siegfried's corpse on the threshold seems clearly an effort to moderate the raw motif preserved in *Þiðreks saga*, according to which the murdered man is left in his wife's bed. The discovery of the body by a chamberlain instead of Kriemhilt herself may be understood in the same way and her instantaneous realization completes the pattern of inklings and monitions which began with the departure for the hunt. Her shriek, though absent from *Þiðreks saga*, is an old feature guaranteed by *Skamma* 29–30 (*Vǫlsunga saga* 81.18–19) and *Guðrúnarkviða* I.16.[49] The motif of the undamaged shield is identical down to the details of phraseology in the two sources:

owê mich mînes leides!   nu ist dir dîn schilt
mit swerten niht verhouwen;   du list ermorderôt.
wesse ich wer iz het getân,   ich riet' im immer sînen tôt.

(Woe is me! Now your shield lies undamaged by swords; you lie there murdered. If I knew who had done it, I would bring about his death.) [*Nibelungenlied* 1012.2–4]

hér stendr þinn gulbuinn skiolldr hæill oc æcki er hann spilltr oc þinn hialmr er hvergi brotinn. hui vartu sua saʀ þu mant væra myrðr. vissi ek hveʀ þat hæfði gort þa mætti þat væra hans gialld.

(Here stands your gold-ornamented shield whole and undamaged and your helmet is not broken anywhere. How did you get such wounds? You must have been murdered. If I knew who had done it, I would repay him.) [*Þiðreks saga* II.267.23–268.1]

---

[48]See Heusler, *Nibelungensage und Nibelungenlied*, pp. 92 and 128, and Kralik, p. 148. Interesting legal notes on the return of Siegfried's corpse to Kriemhilt are provided by Fritz Mezger, "The Publication of Slaying in the Saga and the Nibelungenlied," *ANF*, 61 (1946), 208–24.
[49]Heusler, *Nibelungensage und Nibelungenlied*, p. 129.

At this point the *Nibelungenlied* initiates the mourning of Siegfried, to which Sigemunt is summoned together with Siegfried's
followers (1014–35). This is a characteristic instance of anticipation for the purpose of expanding the text and absorbing the
additional cast of characters. Gunther's false condolences (1041)
and the bier test (1043–45) are similarly the responsibility of the
Nibelungenlied poet, the latter perhaps inspired by Hartmann
von Aue's *Iwein*. Hagen's manifest guilt causes him to allege
murder by brigands, whom Kriemhilt tartly identifies (1046). This
allegation corresponds to the boar motif in *Þiðreks saga*
II.268.1–5: "Then Hǫgni replies: 'He was not murdered. We were
hunting a wild boar and this same wild boar gave him his fatal
wound.' Then Grimhild replies: 'You, Hǫgni, were that wild boar
and no one else.'" The boar version has been considered original
because it corresponds to a motif in the chanson de geste *Daurel
et Beton*, claimed by Samuel Singer and others as the source
underlying both *Nibelungenlied* and *Þiðreks saga*. I doubt that
this source is necessary (below Chapter 6), but the boar remains
better integrated into the imagery of the tale and the *Nibelungenlied* poet, who is more given to innovation than the compiler of
Þiðreks saga, may well have suppressed it in favor of human
murderers in the form of brigands, all the more so because after
Siegfried's display of venary heroics it would seem most implaus-
ible that a mere boar could lay him low. The final details in Adventure 17, the mourning of Gernot and Giselher, the pomp and
masses, and Kriemhilt's final view of the corpse, are the poet's
embroidery. *Þiðreks saga* II.268.7–9 merely alludes to such ob-
sequies: "And Grimhild calls her men and has Sigurd's corpse
taken and prepared with great splendor."

    Adventure 18 is given over to Sigemunt's departure with Sieg-
fried's men and Kriemhilt's decision to remain, the former dictated by the need to relieve the scene of supernumeraries and the
latter by the need to keep Kriemhilt in place for Etzel's wooing
and the wish to reaffirm her bonds with her younger brothers. The
final stanza (1100) takes leave of an exultant Brynhild:

> Prünhilt diu schœne   mit übermüete saz.
> swaz geweinte Kriemhilt,   unmære was ir daz.
>
> (Beautiful Brynhild held sway with arrogance. Whatever Kriemhilt
> mourned was a matter of indifference to her.)

This stanza corresponds to Brynhild's final appearance in *Þiðreks saga* II.268.6–7: "Þæir ganga nu brot af loptino oc in i hollina oc ero nu kat*ir* oc brynilldr æigi ukatare" ("They go now from the bedchamber and into the hall and are in good cheer and Brynhild is no less cheerful"). The motif is old in the legend and reflects Brynhild's triumphant laughter in *Brot* 10 and *Skamma* 30.[50] Thus very probably the burial in Adventure 17 and her exultation at the end of 18 (in whichever order) mark the conclusion of the source shared with *Þiðreks saga*. Adventure 19, with its account of Siegfried's treasure, serves only to anticipate the preoccupations of Part II and effect a transition.

We may now complete the outline of the common source underlying the account of Siegfried's death in *Þiðreks saga* and the *Nibelungenlied*. To the four points already listed above can be added the following seven:

5. Siegfried's body is cast into Kriemhilt's bed.
6. Kriemhilt cries aloud.
7. She infers from the undamaged shield that Siegfried has been murdered.
8. Hagen alleges that he was killed by a boar.
9. Kriemhilt identifies Hagen as the boar.
10. Brynhild triumphs.
11. Kriemhilt arranges Siegfried's burial.

The remaining task is to reconstruct the total extent of the German source on which Part I of the *Nibelungenlied* and the Sigurd sections of *Þiðreks saga* are based:

1. Kriemhilt has an ominous dream in which her falcon or hawk is rent. The bird is interpreted as her future husband. (The dream is preserved in the *Nibelungenlied* 13–14 and partially in *Vǫlsunga saga* 61.13–21 = *Meiri* or "Traumlied.")
2. Sigurd is of uncertain parentage and grows up in the wilds. His youthful exploits include the slaying of a dragon and the acquisition of a treasure. (This account is contained in *Þiðreks saga* I.299–315, minus the acquisition of the treasure. Reference to Siegfried's youthful exploits is made in the *Nibelungenlied* 21 and the supplementary stanza C 21. The acquisition of a treasure is recounted by Hagen in the *Nibelungenlied* 87–99 and the slaying of the dragon in the *Nibelungenlied* 100. The dragon adventure is also alluded to by Kriemhilt in the *Nibelungenlied* 899–902. Siegfried's doubtful parentage survives in the *Nibelungenlied* only in the vassal fiction and his solitary youth only in

[50]Ibid., p. 93.

the habit of riding out alone or in small companies, e.g., stanzas 59, 88, 180, 341, and 485. As we will see below (Chapter 7), a full version of Siegfried's wayward youth in the "Brünhildenlied" is suggested by correspondences between *Þiðreks saga* and *Das Lied vom Hürnen Seyfrid*.)

3. Siegfried rides out alone and encounters Brynhild. (Since the prior betrothal is lost in the *Nibelungenlied*, the only remnant of this passage is *Þiðreks saga* I.315.9–10.)

4. He wins Brynhild with a display of force against her family or guardians. (The only direct evidence of this scene is chapter 168 of *Þiðreks saga*, to the extent it may be interpreted as a wooing episode. Siegfried's display of force is also signaled by *Oddrúnargrátr* 18. It appears to be transferred to the wooing of Kriemhilt in the *Nibelungenlied* 110–14.)

5. Siegfried comes to Burgundy and accomplishes great feats with the Burgundian brothers. (The motif persists in *Vǫlsunga saga* 64.19–22, 65.32–66.2, 75.22–23 = *Meiri*, in *Norna-Gests þáttr*, chap. 7, perhaps in Siegfried's joint adventures with Dietrich in *Þiðreks saga*, chaps. 200–224, and is the basis of the Dano-Saxon war in the *Nibelungenlied*, Adventure 4.)

6. Siegfried aids Gunther in the winning of Brynhild because he knows the location and the way. (This motif is verified by *Þiðreks saga* II.38.14, the *Nibelungenlied* 331, 378, and elsewhere, and *Skamma* 3.6.)

7. Siegfried reconciles Brynhild to the new match with representations of Gunther's greatness. (That persuasion, not conquest, was the original mode in the German version is suggested by *Þiðreks saga* II.39.14–17, the *Nibelungenlied* 420–22, and *Vǫlsunga saga* 75.28–76.5 = *Meiri*.)

8. A double wedding is celebrated, uniting Brynhild with Gunther and Kriemhilt with Siegfried. (The double wedding cannot be argued with absolute conviction since it is wanting in *Þiðreks saga* II.37.18–38.4. It is, however, the majority version, supported by the *Nibelungenlied* 628, and elsewhere, and *Grípisspá* 43 = *Meiri*. It is perfectly possible that *Þiðreks saga* represents the original situation and that Siegfried was wed to Kriemhilt before accompanying Gunther on the wooing expedition. We must then decide with Heusler ("Die Quelle der Brünhildsage," p. 88) that the double wedding was arrived at independently by the *Nibelungenlied* and *Meiri* poets. But it is equally possible that the double wedding was the common version and that the translator of *Þiðreks saga* separated the weddings in accordance with the Norse legend.)

9. Brynhild resists her husband, and Siegfried, disguised as Gunther,

is called on to subdue and deflower her, taking her ring with him on his departure. (The deflowering is explicit in *Þiðreks saga* II.42.11–12 and implicit in the protests of the *Nibelungenlied* poet in 655–56 and 667, in Kriemhilt's accusation in 840, and in the deflected motif of Siegfried's alleged boast in 855, 857, and 867.)

10. Brynhild grieves over having the lesser husband and charges Kriemhilt with duplicity. She vows vengeance. (This motif is lost in *Þiðreks saga*, but retained in *Vǫlsunga saga* 70.19–71.3 = *Meiri* and in altered form in the *Nibelungenlied* 618–24.)

11. Brynhild challenges Kriemhilt in the hall over a matter of precedence. (The queens dispute the highseat in *Þiðreks saga* II.259.10–260.1 and the right to enter church first in the *Nibelungenlied* 838–43. The seating dispute in the hall is probably original because the hall quarrel is confirmed by *Meiri*. The *Nibelungenlied* poet transferred the quarrel to the church perhaps to make the scene grander and more colorful or perhaps because precedence at church was culturally more meaningful to him in a way we no longer understand. Having effected this change, he was obliged to transpose the quarrel over precedence and the quarrel over the relative merits of the husbands. Since the latter could not take place during the church service, it was allowed to precede the contested entrance at the church door.)

12. The queens quarrel over the relative distinction of their husbands. (This is a universal feature: *Vǫlsunga saga* 69.15–23 = *Forna*; *Vǫlsunga saga* 71.4–23 = *Meiri*; *Snorra Edda*, ed. Finnur Jónsson, p. 131.1–7; *Þiðreks saga* II.260.1–8; *Nibelungenlied* 815–29.)

13. Kriemhilt charges that Siegfried was Brynhild's first lover and displays the ring that Siegfried took from her to prove the contention. (This motif is also universal: *Vǫlsunga saga* 69.23–70.5 = *Forna*; *Vǫlsunga saga* 72.3–6 = *Meiri*; *Snorra Edda*, p. 131.7–9; *Þiðreks saga* II.260.8–261.16; *Nibelungenlied* 839–40 and 846–47.)

14. Brynhild complains to Hagen and Gunther that Siegfried slept with her and exposed the fact to Kriemhilt. She threatens not to sleep with Gunther unless Siegfried is killed. (The first item is retained in *Þiðreks saga* II.262.3–26 and is reworked in the *Nibelungenlied* 851–54. The sexual threat is preserved in *Vǫlsunga saga* 79.14–16 = *Meiri* and stanza 797 of redaction A of the *Nibelungenlied*.)

15. Hagen and Gunther determine to kill Siegfried. (The decision is implicit in the replies given Brynhild by Hǫgni and Gunnarr in *Þiðreks saga* II.262.14–16 and 23–26. It is more fully described in the *Nibelungenlied* 864–76, but complicated by the poet's efforts to extricate Gunther from his share in the complicity.)

16. Hagen devises the stratagem of a hunt during which salted provisions are consumed and drink is withheld. (The stratagem is pre-

served best in *Þiðreks saga* II. 263.19–264.9 and 264.20–24. The hunters' common meal is retained in the *Nibelungenlied* 963, but the idea of salted food is lost. The withholding of drink is reinterpreted as a misshipment of wine by Hagen in 965–68.)

17. As Siegfried slakes his thirst at a spring, Hagen spears him from behind. (The accounts are similar in *Þiðreks saga* II.266.9–14 and the *Nibelungenlied* 981.)

18. Siegfried fells Hagen with a cast of his shield. (*Þiðreks saga* omits this detail, but it is preserved in the *Nibelungenlied* 985. In *Skamma* 22–23 = *Vǫlsunga saga* 80.18–22 Gotþormr is cut down by a cast of Sigurd's sword.)

19. Siegfried reproaches his murderers with his dying words. (*Þiðreks saga* II.266.15–21 and *Nibelungenlied* 989–90 and 992.)

20. The murderers throw Siegfried's corpse into Kriemhilt's bed. (This motif is found intact in *Þiðreks saga* II.267.11–19, but is mitigated in the *Nibelungenlied* 1003–4, where the corpse is merely deposited on Kriemhilt's threshold.)

21. Kriemhilt cries aloud. (This motif is lost in *Þiðreks saga,* but is documented by *Skamma* 29–30 = *Vǫlsunga saga* 81.18–19 as well as the *Nibelungenlied* 1009.)

22. Kriemhilt infers from the undamaged shield that Siegfried has been murdered. (The phrasing is similar in *Þiðreks saga* II.267.23–268.1 and the *Nibelungenlied* 1012.)

23. Hagen alleges that Siegfried has been killed by a boar. (The motif survives in *Þiðreks saga* II.268.1–3, but the boar is supplanted by brigands in the *Nibelungenlied* 1045.)

24. Kriemhilt retorts that she knows perfectly well who the boar is. (*Þiðreks saga* II.268.3–5 and, with the necessary adjustments, the *Nibelungenlied* 1046.)

25. Brynhild is triumphant. (*Þiðreks saga* II.268.6–7 and the *Nibelungenlied* 1100.)

26. Kriemhilt buries Siegfried. (*Þiðreks saga* II.268.7–9 and the *Nibelungenlied* 1050–72.)

CHAPTER 6

The Composition of
the *Nibelungenlied* Part I

The source outline proposed in the previous chapter has been established from the texts without a point-by-point analysis of the competing schemes offered by Boer, Panzer, Heusler, Droege, Wesle, Hempel, Kralik, Schneider, Wais, and Bumke.[1] Such a running debate would prove cumbersome, but two contributions may not be relegated to footnotes. In the first place, I have clearly returned to the position taken by Heusler in "Die Quelle der Brünhildsage." It is therefore important to review Heusler's theory and account for the differences between his analysis and mine. In the second place, we must come to terms with Bumke's study because it is the most recent and remains in force as long as no counter arguments are brought.[2]

I begin with a review of Heusler's findings. His point of departure is the view held by Wilhelm Braune and others that the Siegfried story existed in written form as a brief preface to the "Ältere Not." This idea he rejects on the grounds that the story is too full to allow for such compression and that the proportions of *Þiðreks saga* suggest the independent transmission of the two legends, the tale of Brynhild and Siegfried in an oral lay and the fall of the Burgundians in a written epic. This independent trans-

---

[1]The titles of these studies may be found in the Selected Bibliography at the end of the volume.

[2]Joachim Bumke, "Die Quellen der Brünhildfabel im *Nibelungenlied*," *Euphorion*, 54 (1960), 1–38. Some objections have been raised by Henry Kratz, "The Proposed Sources of the *Nibelungenlied*," *Studies in Philology*, 59 (1962), 615–30.

mission is indicated by certain inconsistencies pertaining to both plots. For example, the "Ältere Not" described Giselher as too young to participate in Siegfried's murder, whereas the Brynhild story, as reflected by *Þiðreks saga* II.266.21 and 267.1, represents him as being full grown. A second inconsistency is the differing conception of Hagen. According to the German Brynhild legend as documented by *Þiðreks saga*, Hagen was Gunther's vassal. In the "Ältere Not," according to the testimony of *Þiðreks saga* II.282.8–11 and 324.6–20, he was the half brother of the Burgundian brothers, begotten on their mother by an elf.

That the Brynhild legend was communicated to the compiler of *Þiðreks saga* in a short form is suggested in the first instance by its dimensions in relation to the section that derives from the "Ältere Not" (263 lines compared with 880 in Unger's edition). But Heusler believed that a surer measure was to be found in the relative number of characters and scenes. In *Atlakviða* he counted ten characters, in *Þiðreks saga* (roughly equivalent to the "Ältere Not") twenty-five, and in Part II of the *Nibelungenlied* sixty. As for the number of distinct scenes, he counted fourteen in *Atlakviða*, sixty-seven in *Þiðreks saga* up to the moment when Hǫgni beheads Attila's son, and two hundred two in the equivalent section of the *Nibelungenlied*. The Brynhild legend shows an altogether different progression. *Sigurðarkviða in forna* may be calculated to have had six characters and fifteen scenes, the corresponding sections of *Þiðreks saga* six characters (with Giselher and Oda perhaps dropped from the German source) and nineteen scenes (with perhaps four others dropped from the source) and the *Nibelungenlied* twenty-three characters (plus another half dozen unnamed) and one hundred forty-five scenes up the quarrel of the queens. Clearly the epic expansion in the Brynhild legend occurred not at the level of the German lay underlying *Þiðreks saga*, but only in the *Nibelungenlied*.[3]

Heusler next explores whether the Brynhild lay underlying *Þiðreks saga* is an adequate source for Part I of the *Nibelungen-*

[3]For a critique of Heusler's arguments see Heinrich Hempel, *Nibelungenstudien*, I (Heidelberg: Winter, 1926), 210–14. The same arguments were vigorously supported by Hermann Schneider, *Germanische Heldensage*, I (Berlin and Leipzig: de Gruyter, 1928; rpt. 1962), 86–88.

lied. He finds no evidence against such an assumption. Whatever differences exist can be explained as the innovations of the *Nibelungenlied* poet or as reflections of lateral sources. A relatively late date for the main source is indicated by the martial games and the falcon dream (with its echoes of Der Kürenberger), both of which Heusler claimed for the "Brünhildenlied." The length of the poem Heusler calculated at about five hundred long lines, this form being suggested by matching passages in *Þiðreks saga* II.267.25–268.1 and the *Nibelungenlied* 1012:

	Þu mant væra myrðr.
vissi ek hver*R* þ*at* hæfði gort	þa mætti þat væra h*ans* gialld.

(You must have been murdered. If I knew who had done it, I would repay him.)

	du list ermorderôt.
wesse ich wer iz het getân,	ich riet' im immer sînen tôt.

(You lie murdered. If I knew who had done it, I would bring about his death.)

The Norse is translated almost verbatim from the German source, which appears virtually unchanged in the *Nibelungenlied* lines with their archaic rhyme. The original therefore must also have been in rhyming long lines.

The most important deviation of the "Brünhildenlied" from Norse legend lies in the substitution of martial games for the flame wall in the wooing of Brynhild. Siegfried's forest death is adumbrated in *Forna*, but must have been more fully realized in the German original, to which Heusler attributes the motif of partial invulnerability, the boar hunt, the slaking of the hunters' thirst at a spring, the spear thrust, and the dying hero's reproach of his murderers. This version then persists in the "Brünhildenlied." In a number of ways the "Brünhildenlied" was more primitive than the *Nibelungenlied*. Siegfried was still the waif of uncertain parentage. His blood brotherhood with the Burgundians was retained according to the evidence of *Þiðreks saga* II.39.19–40.1

and 41.6–9 and, in Heusler's view, faint echoes in the *Nibelungenlied* 127 and 335. His marriage to Kriemhilt preceded the wooing of Brynhild, the double wedding constituting an innovation arrived at independently by the *Nibelungenlied* and *Meiri* (*Grípisspá* 43). Gunther has three humiliating wedding nights, then enlists Siegfried to deflower Brynhild. The quarrel of the queens takes place not before the church, but in the hall, and Brynhild actively instigates Siegfried's murder. Gernot and Giselher participate in the hunt and the hunters' thirst is caused by salted provisions. Siegfried's corpse is cast into Kriemhilt's bed and the day concludes with triumphant good cheer. In general, the poet's concerns were more evenly divided between the heroines Brynhild and Kriemhilt; to this extent the "Brünhildenlied" represented a middle position between the emphasis on Brynhild in the *Edda* and the emphasis on Kriemhilt in the *Nibelungenlied*.

Alongside the "Brünhildenlied" Heusler assumed that the *Nibelungenlied* poet knew a poem about Siegfried's youthful winning of the treasure and some tradition about his slaying of the dragon. A "Lied vom Nibelungenhort" accounts for the confusion in the *Nibelungenlied* on the score of his home. He is sometimes at home in "Niderlant" and sometimes in "Nibelunge lant"; the latter location is taken over from the poem that recounted his acquisition of the Nibelung treasure. In addition to these supplementary sources, Heusler considered the possibility of an alternate version of the "Brünhildenlied." Such a source was suggested to him by traces of jealousy toward Siegfried in Brynhild's behavior (*Nibelungenlied* 618–24 and 511.4), traces that imply a prior relationship and disappointment on her part. A second possible supplement to the "Brünhildenlied" might be found in Siegfried's dying words in the *Nibelungenlied,* in which the reproaches, found also in *Þiðreks saga,* are combined with solicitous words on behalf of his wife, corresponding to his dying sentiments in *Skamma*. Heusler concluded, however, that this mixture of tones was already present in the "Brünhildenlied" and did not require the positing of an additional source. A final question concerns the reconciliation of Kriemhilt with her brothers. Invention on the part of the *Nibelungenlied* seems improbable because of the correspondence in *Guðrúnarkviða* II. On the other hand, a reconciliation is difficult to imagine in the framework of the "Brünhildenlied" or any analogous piece.[4]

The final portion of Heusler's paper is devoted to Samuel Singer's observation of correspondences between the chanson de geste *Daurel et Beton* and the *Nibelungenlied,* affecting passages that deal with Siegfried's murder and Kriemhilt's mourning.[5] Heusler agreed with Singer in assigning the priority to *Daurel et Beton* and attributed the borrowing to the "Brünhildenlied" since the correspondences to *Daurel* are visible in both *Þiðreks saga* and the *Nibelungenlied.* There are, according to Heusler's analysis, specifically nine points at which the influence seems palpable:[6]

[4]Werner Richter, "Beiträge zur Deutung des Mittelteils des Nibelungenliedes," *ZDA,* 72 (1935), 18–21, argued that the reconciliation was not invented.

[5]"Eine Episode des Nibelungenliedes," *Neujahrsblatt der Literarischen Gesellschaft in Bern auf das Jahr 1917* (Bern, 1916), pp. 97–101. This paper is not available to me, but the substance was repeated in Singer's "Die romanischen Elemente des Nibelungenliedes," *Germanisch-romanisches Mittelalter* (Zurich and Leipzig: Max Niehans Verlag, 1935), 233–54 (specifically 248–51). Singer believed that the borrowing proceeded from France to Germany and Heusler concurred. Ernst Tegethoff, "Spuren germanischer Heldensage in südfranzösischen Märchen," *Zeitschrift für Deutschkunde,* 38 (1924), 243–53, Dietrich von Kralik, *Die Sigfridtrilogie,* I (Halle: Niemeyer, 1941), 845–60, and Kurt Wais, *Frühe Epik Westeuropas und die Vorgeschichte des Nibelungenliedes,* I, Mit einem Beitrag von Hugo Kuhn: *Brunhild und das Krimhildlied,* Beihefte zur Zeitschrift für romanische Philologie, 95 (Tübingen: Niemeyer, 1953), pp. 42–52, assumed a German priority. Friedrich Panzer, *Studien zum Nibelungenliede* (Frankfurt am Main: Verlag Moritz Diesterweg, 1945), pp. 5–42, assumed that the *Nibelungenlied* was based on *Daurel et Beton.* Joachim Bumke, "Die Eberjagd im Daurel und in der Nibelungendichtung," *GRM,* 41 (1960), 105–11, adduced an episode in Apuleius' *Metamorphoses* as the source for *Daurel et Beton,* thus undermining the thought of a loan from Germany. In the same issue of *Germanisch-romanische Monatsschrift* (pp. 111–22) Franz Rolf Schröder pointed out that the correspondence between the *Nibelungenlied* and Apuleius' *Metamorphoses* had already been observed by Walter Anderson, "Zu Apuleius' Novelle vom Tode der Charite," *Philologus: Zeitschrift für das classische Alterthum,* 68 (1909), 537–49 (specifically 545–46). Schröder's own view was that a ballad derived from a proto-*Daurel* was the source for the *Nibelungenlied* and *Þiðreks saga.* A further note in this ongoing controversy is that a source for the episode in Apuleius may be found in Achilles Tatius' *Clitophon and Leucippe* (2.34), trans. S. Gaselee (Cambridge, Mass.: Harvard University Press, Loeb Classical Library, 1969), pp. 118–20. The motif surfaces again in the German chapbook *Die schöne Melusine: Die Geschichte von der schönen Melusine die eine Meerfei gewesen ist,* ed. Fedor von Zobeltitz, Die alten Volksbücher, 2 (Hamburg: Alster-Verlag, 1925), p. 29.

[6]The line references are to *Daurel et Beton: Chanson de geste provençale,* ed. Paul Meyer (Paris: Librairie de Firmin Didot, 1880).

1. The hero takes leave of his wife (*Daurel* 326–35 and 357–59; *NL* 919).

2. The woman has a premonition of her husband's death and warns him, but he replies confidently (*Daurel* 300–309 and 328–31; *NL* 920–24).

3. The dying man utters solicitous words about wife and child (*Daurel* 411–17; *NL* 995–97).

4. A hunting companion condemns the murder (*Daurel* 463–67; *NL* 991 and 1000).

5. The widow swoons (*Daurel* 490; *NL* 1009 and 1066).

6. The townsmen join in the mourning (*Daurel* 492–97 and 516–19; *NL* 1013, 1025, 1045, 1051, 1062, and 1064–65).

7. After her first outburst of grief, the widow accuses the murderer and exposes the corpse (*Daurel* 505–13; *NL* 1041–46).

8. The widow predicts or implores that her husband will be avenged by his son or relatives (*Daurel* 509; *NL* 1046).

9. Three days intervene before the burial (*Daurel* 530; *NL* 1056).

Heusler accepted these correspondences as substantial and explained them through the influence of the written chanson de geste on the oral composer of the "Brünhildenlied."

In evaluating Heusler's theory as a whole, we must begin hysteron proteron by first disposing of *Daurel et Beton,* which, sometimes in the ghostly form of a lost proto-version, has long haunted the source study of the *Nibelungenlied.* To what extent do Heusler's nine points involve real correspondences?

1. Siegfried's farewell to Kriemhilt (919) is more likely to be modeled on Rüdeger's farewell to Gotelint in the "Ältere Not" than on a French chanson de geste. The phrasing of 919.1 ("Di sîne triutinne / kust' er an den munt"—"He kissed his beloved on the mouth") finds its explanation in the text underlying the *Nibelungenlied* 1710.1 ("Mit kusse minneclîche / der wirt dô dannen schiet"—"With a loving kiss the king departed") and *Þiðreks saga* II.295.12–13 ("Oc margreiv*enn* kyssir sina frv Gvdelin*n* aðr h*ann* riði brott"-"And the margrave kisses his wife Guðilinda before riding off"). Even without this "internal" model, we would need to consider that conjugal farewells under the shadow of death are an epic commonplace since Hector and Andromache in Book 6 of the *Iliad.*

2. The similarity between Esmenjart's and Kriemhilt's warnings is not great. Esmenjart inquires why her husband trusts Gui and warns that he will kill Beuve (302–4). Kriemhilt issues her warning in the form of two monitory dreams (921 and 924). As we have seen above (Chapter

5, n. 45), these premonitions are modeled primarily on the dream that Uote invoked in the "Ältere Not" to discourage the journey to Hunland (*Nibelungenlied* 1509; *Þiðreks saga* II.283.15–26). *Þiðreks saga* preserves the passage in fuller form, specifically relating the dream to a prediction of death (II.283.23–25: "oc meiri von þikki mer ef þer faret at margr maðr lati fyr *þat* sitt lif"—"And I rather expect that if you go, many a man will lose his life"). This answers to the context of Kriemhilt's dream (924.1–2: "Neinâ, herre Sîfrit! / jâ fürhte ich dînen val. / mir troumte hînte leide, etc."—"Alas, Lord Siegfried, I fear your fall. I had a bad dream last night, etc."). There is no need to resort to *Daurel*.

3. The correspondence in the heroes' dying words is not so great as the comparisons have suggested. Beuve's solicitude is not so much for his wife as, paradoxically, for his treacherous companion Gui: he would have surrendered Esmenjart to him long ago if he had only known of his passion (407–9)! As things stand, he promotes Gui's welfare by urging him to seek her hand in marriage from Charlemagne (412). He also asks Gui to care for his son (414), but this corresponds to nothing in the *Nibelungenlied,* in which Siegfried merely expresses regret that his son should have murderers as relatives (995).

4. The condemnation of the murder by a hunting companion is found only in *Daurel* (463–67) and by no stretch of the text in the *Nibelungenlied.* In 991 the hunters grieve over Siegfried, and in 1000 they eagerly and fearfully accede to the fiction that brigands slew him.

5. That the widow swoons in both epics is hardly decisive. The motif clearly caught the *Nibelungenlied* poet's fancy and is used in 1070 as well as 1009 and 1066. It seems unlikely that the "Brünhildenlied" borrowed it from one line of *Daurel;* it partakes more of the elaborations in the *Nibelungenlied.*

6. The universal mourning is similarly indecisive. Mass participation is one of the most obvious tendencies in the *Nibelungenlied* and need not be explained by a particular literary source.

7. The widow's accusation in the *Nibelungenlied* differs substantially from *Daurel* in that it is prefaced by the bier test based on the superstition that the wounds of the slain man will open anew when his murderer approaches. This motif is commonly assumed to derive from Hartmann's *Iwein.*[7] The accusation was of course present in the "Brünhildenlied" without the bier test, but only in the metaphorical

---

[7]E.g., Heusler, *Nibelungensage und Nibelungenlied* (Dortmund: Ruhfus, 1965), p. 80, and Friedrich Panzer, *Das Nibelungenlied* (Stuttgart: Kohlhammer, 1955), pp. 360–61.

form of Hagen's claim that Siegfried was slain by a boar and
Kriemhilt's retort that he was the boar. Precisely this form of the
accusation is missing in *Daurel*.[8]

8. The vengeance motif is again quite distinct in the two texts. Esmenjart states (509): "Beton is alive and will know how to avenge him." In
the *Nibelungenlied* Kriemhilt expresses only a ritual wish (1046.2):
"May God permit his kin to avenge it." If she means anything specific, the words must of course refer to her own vengeance.

9. The interval of three days before the burial is too formulaic to carry
much weight.

I can find nothing compelling in Heusler's correspondences and
conclude with Hermann Schneider that we are dealing only with
general similarities of motif.[9] Panzer's alternative view that
Daurel influenced the *Nibelungenlied* directly is at odds with
Philipp August Becker's dating of the chanson de geste no earlier
than 1220.[10] In addition to these difficulties, there is an intrinsic
unlikelihood in Heusler's proposition that an oral German lay
should have borrowed from a written French text.[11] With Bumke
("Die Eberjagd," p. 110), I find it easier to embrace the skepticism voiced by Schneider and Becker.

We may now turn to Heusler's reconstruction of the "Brünhildenlied" without regard to *Daurel et Beton*. He did not outline it
in detail, but a comparison of "Die Quelle der Brünhildsage" and
his book of the same year *Nibelungensage und Nibelungenlied*
(pars. 13–16) allows the following summary:

1. Kriemhilt's falcon dream
2. The oaths of blood brotherhood binding Siegfried to the Burgundian princes
3. Siegfried's marriage to Kriemhilt
4. Siegfried's participation in the wooing of Brynhild
5. The martial games
6. Gunther's three disconsolate wedding nights
7. Siegfried's deflowering of Brynhild on Gunther's behalf

---

[8]See Bumke, "Die Eberjagd," p. 110 and n. 22.

[9]"Deutsche und französische Heldenepik," *ZDP*, 51 (1926), 206–7, and *Germanische Heldensage*, I, 88. Richter, p. 46, concurred.

[10]Becker, "Zur Jagd im Odenwald," *BGDSL* (H), 70 (1948), 420–31 (specifically 430–31), and Panzer, *Studien zum Nibelungenliede*, pp. 189–93.

[11]Karl Droege, "Zur Geschichte der Nibelungendichtung und der Thidrikssaga," *ZDA*, 58 (1920–1921), 40, and "Das ältere Nibelungenepos," *ZDA*, 62
(1925), 204.

8. The queens' quarrel and the revelation of Siegfried's indiscretion
9. Brynhild's instigation of Siegfried's murder
10. Hagen's provision of salted food
11. The participation of all the brothers in the hunt
12. Siegfried's murder at the spring
13. Siegfried's corpse cast into Kriemhilt's bed
14. The festive triumph of Brynhild and the murderers
15. Siegfried's burial

Heusler found this plot not quite adequate to account for everything in the *Nibelungenlied* and therefore had recourse to several other traditions that must have been known to the *Nibelungenlied* poet: (1) Siegfried's winning of the treasure (a separate poem), (2) his slaying of the dragon (an unformed tradition), and (3) his prior betrothal to Brynhild (an alternate version of the "Brünhildenlied"). It will be readily apparent that the outline of Heusler's source closely resembles my own, but six areas of disagreement remain.

My outline (at the end of Chapter 5) includes an account of Siegfried's youthful adventures and prior betrothal to Brynhild (points 2–5). Heusler's exclusion of these points forces him to posit three additional sources for the *Nibelungenlied,* a separate poem on the winning of the treasure, a separate tradition on the slaying of the dragon, and an alternate "Brünhildenlied" with the prior betrothal. Since both *Þiðreks saga* and the *Nibelungenlied* give evidence of these traditions, I see no difficulty in attributing them to the common source. That a fairly full version of Siegfried's youthful exploits was part of the "Brünhildenlied" will emerge from an analysis of *Das Lied vom Hürnen Seyfrid* in the next chapter. Especially awkward is the exclusion of the prior betrothal because it is so persistently implied in the *Nibelungenlied* and clearly stated in *Þiðreks saga* II.38.20–39.3. The awkwardness is redoubled when we observe that *Þiðreks saga* II.38.14 and the *Nibelungenlied* 378.3 have a verbatim correspondence in Siegfried's declaration that he knows the way to Brynhild's residence. The correspondence can come only from a common source and this source can be only Heusler's primary "Brünhildenlied." The narrative gap in Heusler's scheme between the falcon dream and Siegfried's arrival at the Burgundian court cries out for content. We may assume that it accommodated

some account of Siegfried's first adventures as well as his prior
betrothal to Brynhild.

Despite Polak's objection that Siegfried's simple plea on
Gunther's behalf is too prosaic a wooing motif to be original, it is
supported directly by *Þiðreks saga* and indirectly by the
Nibelungenlied and *Meiri* (Chapter 4, par. with n. 28 and Chapter
5, par. after n. 22). Since there is no sign of the martial games
outside of the *Nibelungenlied*—Heusler can invoke only metrical
evidence in favor of their antiquity—I prefer to believe that they
are the poet's innovation based on Panzer's *Brautwerbermärchen*.[12] Heusler placed Siegfried's wedding to Kriemhilt before
the wooing expedition on the evidence of *Þiðreks saga*. I prefer
the double wedding on the dual evidence of the *Nibelungenlied*
and *Meiri (Grípisspá* 43). It is difficult for me to believe that this
is a coincidence. Heusler's view was to some extent conditioned
by his rejection of the evidence of German influence on *Meiri*
("Die Quelle der Brünhildsage," p. 81). This evidence seems to
me strong and suggests that not only the double wedding, but also
the prior betrothal in *Meiri* was a concession to German legend.
The prior betrothal is thus vindicated for the "Brünhildenlied" on
this count as well. The single weddings in *Þiðreks saga* are a
secondary feature attributable to the Norse redactor on the basis
of the Norse tradition prior to *Meiri*.

The remaining points of disagreement may be stated more
briefly. In point 10 I attribute to the "Brünhildenlied" a scene in
which Brynhild grieves over her marriage on the evidence of
Meiri and the *Nibelungenlied* (Chapter 5, par. with n. 30). The
murder council I envisage as point 15 is only a slight variation on
Heusler's point 10 (Brynhild's instigation of the murder). My
points 21–24 on Kriemhilt's reaction to her husband's death involve motifs that Heusler also attributed in part to the "Brünhildenlied," but from the evidence of *Daurel*. I consider that they
are adequately documented by *Þiðreks saga* and the *Nibelungen-*

[12]Léon Polak, *Untersuchungen über die Sigfridsagen*, Diss. Berlin (Berlin:
Universitäts-Buchdruckerei, 1910), p. 108; Heusler, "Die Quelle der
Brünhildsage," *Kleine Schriften*, I, ed. Helga Reuschel (Berlin: de Gruyter,
1969), 83, and *Nibelungensage und Nibelungenlied*, p. 84. Friedrich Panzer, *Studien zur germanischen Sagengeschichte*, II: *Sigfrid* (Munich: Beck, 1912), 182,
believed that the martial games were dropped by *Þiðreks saga*. See also Klaus von
See, "Die Werbung um Brünhild," *ZDA*, 88 (1957–1958), 12.

lied and may be attributed to the common source on this basis. Items 2 (the blood brotherhood) and 11 (the participation of all the brothers in the hunt) in Heusler's reconstruction need not be contested; they are not plot segments, but inherent details which may or may not have been narratively realized.

It will be apparent from my results that, far from disagreeing with Heusler, I have proposed a more radical version of his solution. That is, I have tried to eliminate his lateral sources and concentrate the total story in his "Brünhildenlied."[13] This has chiefly involved making provision for Siegfried's youthful exploits and prior betrothal. The weakness in Heusler's scheme was in fact not the single "Brünhildenlied" as such, but its apparent inadequacy in accounting for everything in the *Nibelungenlied*. Heusler's critics (Sperber, Kralik, Schneider, Bumke) did not so much attack his "Brünhildenlied" as they sought to flesh out his additional sources. Criticism might have taken a different turn if Heusler had not allowed such latitude; his successors would have been obliged to come to terms more precisely with his "Brünhildenlied" rather than capitalizing on the loose ends that remained outside the framework of this source. The fundamental question is: Can everything in the *Nibelungenlied* and *Þiðreks saga* be derived from a single source? If so, the simplest solution has a claim to being the best. Only if it can be shown that the "Brünhildenlied" probably did not accommodate the necessary details should the single source be rejected and a multiplication of sources undertaken. The case of the "Ältere Not" is instructive. This hypothetical poem is adequate to explain Part II of the *Nibelungenlied* and no recourse has been taken to supplementary sources, but it is clearly not adequate to explain "Niflunga saga" in *Þiðreks saga,* for which some additional source must be posited, whether Heusler's unformed Saxon tradition, Hempel's Saxon lay, or Wisniewski's chronicle. I find no such compulsion in Part I of the *Nibelungenlied* or the equivalent sections of *Þiðreks saga.*

Since Kralik the *Nibelungenlied* has been explored for inconsistencies that might suggest a variety of sources imperfectly

---

[13]Wilhelm Lehmgrübner, *Die Erweckung der Walküre* (Halle: Niemeyer, 1936), p. 57, commented on the advantage of a single source.

harmonized by the last poet. The variety is predicated to some extent on the three *Sigurðarkviður* of the *Edda*, but this model is misleading.[14] The three *Sigurðarkviður* were presumably not orally competing versions in circulation at the same time. Both *Skamma* and *Meiri* were late literary recastings, one in an elegiac and the other in a quasi-epic mode, one and perhaps both motivated by German influence in the twelfth and thirteenth centuries. They do not prove a plurality of simultaneous versions. The case for plural sources in the *Nibelungenlied* therefore must rest not on the known circulation of variants, but on the internal demands of the text. Kralik so overperceived these demands that his elaborate solutions were judged unnecessary, but his method was refined twenty years later by Joachim Bumke in an essay as tight and finished as Kralik's was diffuse and open-ended.[15] Bumke sought to document two competing sources on the basis of observable inconsistencies in the *Nibelungenlied*. The first source was equivalent to Heusler's ''Brünhildenlied,'' the second had the following action (p. 29):

> Gunther persuades Siegfried to help him overcome Brynhild in the martial games, a task that he accomplishes with the aid of the *Tarnkappe*. Siegfried does not substitute for Gunther in bed and does not deflower Brynhild. One day when the queens vie in the praise of their husbands, Brynhild claims Gunther's wooing as the greatest deed. Kriemhilt then reveals that Siegfried assisted Gunther in the games. Brynhild complains to Gunther and threatens to withhold her marital favors. In addition she perhaps alleges that Siegfried slept with her. The murder council convenes. Gunther seeks to dissuade, but Hagen argues for Siegfried's death because of his sexual infringement (''suln wir gouche ziehen?''—''should we maintain seducers?''). Gernot offers to accomplish the deed. A sham war is declared and Kriemhilt betrays Siegfried's vulnerable spot. One of the four commits the murder, perhaps Gernot, but Siegfried kills his murderer with a dying stroke.

---

[14]Hans Sperber, ''Heuslers Nibelungentheorie und die nordische Überlieferung,'' *Festschrift Max H. Jellinek, zum 29. Mai 1928 dargebracht* (Vienna and Leipzig: Österreichischer Bundesverlag, 1928), pp. 123–38, and Bumke, ''Die Quellen,'' p. 1.

[15]Bumke, ''Die Quellen,'' pp. 1–38.

There are several general problems in Bumke's reconstruction, not the least of which is that the version corresponds to nothing we have direct evidence of in Germany or Scandinavia. The most important internal flaw is that Siegfried's murder is predicated on the allegation that he slept with Brynhild despite the fact that he does not enter her bed and therefore has no opportunity. Brynhild would have to persuade Gunther of a rape and the legend nowhere provides for such a narrative twist. We have seen above that the quarrel of the queens everywhere ends with the revelation of a sexual betrayal, but against the evidence of five sources (*Forna, Meiri, Snorra Edda, Þiðreks saga,* and the *Nibelungenlied*) Bumke's reconstruction ends the quarrel with the revelation of a deception on the athletic field. Bumke also enlists motifs for his German source which are documented only in Scandinavia and not in Germany. Brynhild's praise of Gunther's wooing feat is a high point of the quarrel only in *Snorra Edda* and *Vǫlsunga saga*, not in *Þiðreks saga* or the *Nibelungenlied*. Gernot as murderer is derived from *Skamma,* as is Siegfried's last-ditch killing of his assailant. On the other hand, some details in the reconstruction look like the *Nibelungenlied* poet's idiosyncrasies. The sham war surely belongs only in the context of the original Dano-Saxon war of Adventure 4. Gunther's reluctance to murder Siegfried grows out of the *Nibelungenlied* poet's solicitude for his royal character and reputation and is found nowhere in the older sources.[16] Such delicacy is possible in the *Nibelungenlied*, in which Siegfried's guilt is uncertain, but is unlikely to have emerged with the escalated charge of rape that Bumke's reconstruction implies.

Bumke arrived at his separation of sources by studying the *Nibelungenlied* at three crucial junctures: wooing deception, quarrel, and murder. We may therefore retrace his findings one episode at a time. Siegfried's participation in the wooing of Brynhild has a dual motivation. On the one hand he is the strong helper who is required to aid Gunther in the enterprise, on the

---

[16]On such modifications of the legend in the *Nibelungenlied* see Heusler, *Nibelungensage und Nibelungenlied,* pp. 59–60 and 87–94, and Hans Naumann, "Stand der Nibelungenforschung," *ZD,* 41 (1927), 14–15.

other he is a guide who knows the way to Brynhild's realm. The latter motif belongs to Heusler's "Brünhildenlied," the former must belong to the same source as the martial games in which his help is required. Brynhild's stipulation is that she will marry the victor in the games, but contrary to this stipulation, she seems reluctant to marry and convenes a last-minute council. Again the narrative is twofold. On the one hand Brynhild offers herself as a prize to the victor, on the other she is reluctant to marry. The reluctant bride belongs to the "Brünhildenlied," the wooing games to the second source. The conquest of Brynhild is similarly doubled. On the one hand she is subdued on the athletic field, on the other in bed. The sexual conquest belongs to the "Brünhildenlied," the athletic conquest to the second source. (The *Tarnkappe* was originally associated with the athletic contests and was transferred, with some implausibility, to the bed scene by the *Nibelungenlied* poet.)

Bumke argues further that the quarrel of the queens in the *Nibelungenlied* rests on double sources. The quarrel at the tourney concerns the relative merits of the husbands while the quarrel at church concerns the status of the women. The latter motif is found in *Þiðreks saga* and belongs to the "Brünhildenlied." The former is found only in the Norse versions and is assigned by Bumke to the second source, where it was connected with the martial games. In this source the issue was the victory in the games and the identity of the victor. A quarrel over the respective superiority of the husbands was well adapted to reveal the true victor. A quarrel over status between the two queens was equally well adapted to reveal that Brynhild was sexually compromised, as was the case in the "Brünhildenlied."

The final stage involves the circumstances surrounding Siegfried's murder. Bumke notes that in 867 Hagen urges Siegfried's death because he boasted of possessing Brynhild. Ortwin offers to carry out the deed despite Siegfried's overpowering strength (869). This motif is connected with the following scene in which Hagen proposes to circumvent Siegfried's strength with a stratagem (873–74). Siegfried's boast cannot belong to the "Brünhildenlied" because in this source Siegfried deflowered Brynhild with Gunther's blessing. The murder council, based as it is on the idea of Siegfried's sexual transgression, was therefore not part of the "Brünhildenlied" and is hence not found in *Þið-reks saga;* it must be assigned to the second source. In the implementation of the murder, we again find two competing ideas, the war stratagem and the hunting stratagem. The hunting stratagem is guaranteed for the "Brünhildenlied" by *Þiðreks saga* and the war stratagem can therefore be allocated to the second source. Finally, Bumke finds, along with other inconsistencies, indications of a double origin for the shield with which Siegfried fells Hagen after receiving his fatal wound. The shield is shattered by the blow, but still serves as a bier on which to bring Siegfried's body home. Bumke resolves the contradiction by suggesting that in one source Siegfried succumbed without retaliation. In this version Hagen was the murderer. In the other version Siegfried succeeded in killing his murderer before succumbing. The murderer was someone other than Hagen, since his presence is required for the continuation, and the murder weapon was surely something other than a shield. The first version corresponds to the "Brünhildenlied," the second version must come from some other source, in which Siegfried was killed during a military campaign and would naturally have had his weapons along.

Without doubt Bumke made a clear case for dual sources and succeeded in establishing two carefully differentiated sequences. Though some doubt attaches to the internal logic of the second source as it finally emerges, the argumentation that leads to it is precise. The remaining question is whether we cannot after all account for everything just as logically with one source.

In the wooing sequence Bumke distinguishes between Siegfried as helper in the games and Siegfried as guide to Brynhild's realm. This is a real distinction, and I too must resort to a second source in a certain sense. That is, I believe that the poet of the *Nibelungenlied* did not find the games in the "Brünhildenlied." Here Bumke has achieved a real advantage over Heusler's standpoint. But in my opinion, a whole alternate lay is not necessary to account for the games. They were taken by the *Nibelungenlied* poet from a story akin to Panzer's folktale and added to the sexual conquest out of the same narrative delight that inspired Siegfried's feats in the Saxon war and his antics during the hunt. They represent not a whole lost version, but an ornamental borrowing to expand and enliven the story. All the inconsistencies that Bumke observes (Siegfried as helper as well as guide, Brynhild's contravention of her own agreement, the senseless use of the *Tarnkappe*[17]) derive from the superimposition of the games, not from the interweaving of two incongruent plots.

The separation of two quarrel sequences is less satisfactory. The contests over the respective merits of the husbands and the status of the queens belong together in all the sources—*Þiðreks saga* and the *Nibelungenlied* as well as *Snorra Edda* and *Vǫlsunga saga*. There is no reason to separate them. They were presumably joined in the "Brünhildenlied" as they were everywhere else. As for the discrepancies in the murder sequence, they, like those in the wooing sequence, can be explained as disturbances introduced by the *Nibelungenlied* poet. The "boast" can be traced without difficulty to the "Brünhildenlied," in which Siegfried divulged the deception of Brynhild to his wife and brought about her public humiliation. This divulging of the secret was translated into a "boast" by the *Nibelungenlied* poet in his uncertainty as to how he should preserve the motivation for Siegfried's murder once Brynhild's deflowering had been suppressed. The council scene as it stood in the "Brünhildenlied" has been conflated with Brynhild's incitation in *Þiðreks saga,* but since it survives in the Norse sources as well as in the *Nibelungenlied,* there is no reason to doubt its existence in the "Brünhildenlied."

The war stratagem is so closely allied to the Saxon war of Adventure 4 that it seems more likely to be an extension of this episode than a reflection of a lost source. Just as the *Nibelungenlied* poet duplicates the bed conquest with an athletic conquest, so too he duplicates the hunting stratagem with a war stratagem to enrich the tale. The presence of weapons on the hunt is not out of the question since Siegfried kills his prankish bear with a sword (962).[18] As for the shield anomalies, Homer also nods.[19] In sum, it does not appear to me that Bumke's second source is a compel-

[17]Bumke, "Die Quellen," pp. 8–10.
[18]Observed by Kratz, p. 628.
[19]Panzer, *Das Nibelungenlied,* p. 446, lists the shield problem with a variety of other inconsistencies in the text. Such inconsistencies are commonplace and do not imply dual sources.

ling assumption. Part of it is lodged in the "Brünhildenlied" and part in the *Nibelungenlied* poet's own innovations.

The ultimate justification for the effort expended on the reconstruction of lost sources is a better appreciation of the extant texts. The version in *Þiðreks saga* has no great claim to artistic merit and imposes no heavy critical burden, but the *Nibelungenlied* is an important text from the first great flowering of German literature and requires evaluation. Our understanding of the literary scene around 1200 turns in some part on our understanding of the *Nibelungenlied* and the literary questions it poses. One such question concerns the extent and nature of the poet's originality. Another involves the reworking of traditional material and the tendencies that underlie the poet's ascertainable revisions; his changes remain the best key to his narrative concerns and literary profile. A third question involves the possibility of an overall interpretation. The evidence of originality and planned change has disproportionate weight in establishing such an interpretation. Indeed, interpretation is often tantamount to observing how the changes comment the action. The poet's position emerges from his response to the traditional tale. This response is of course not limited to the cases of innovation and revision; the poet may also be judged to approve what he retains from the tradition. But a clear view of his retentions also depends on a detailed separation of old and new elements.

Some years ago I analyzed Part II of the *Nibelungenlied* in an effort to establish the "Ältere Not" and the poet's revision of this older epic.[20] I concluded that fifteen of the Adventures in Part II were largely traditional and five almost wholly new (26, 29, 30, 32, 37). In Part I the source was thinner and the poet's obvious interest in balancing the dimensions of the two parts brought about a much more substantial expansion of the story. Here we find that eleven of the Adventures have a traditional core (1–4, 6–8, 10, 14, 16–17), while eight are by and large new (5, 9, 11–13, 15, 18–19). In addition, the more traditional Adventures are very liberally expanded beyond their original compass. Some of the capital revisions are the invention of a princely youth for Sieg-

---

[20]"The Epic Source of Niflunga saga and the Nibelungenlied," *ANF*, 88 (1974), 1–54.

fried, the suppression of his betrothal to Brynhild, the transference of several motifs in this wooing to the wooing of Kriemhilt, the elaboration of the Dano-Saxon war and its renewal in Adventure 15, the casting of Siegfried's wooing in terms of *Minnedienst*, the recasting of Brynhild's wooing as a martial contest, the suppression of Siegfried's sexual infringement, and his hunting heroics. It will be noted that Siegfried is the beneficiary of almost all these alterations. Kriemhilt profits to a lesser extent and Brynhild's role is significantly reduced.

Several of the changes have long been understood as "courtly" modifications: a fitting youth and military record for Siegfried, his role as *Minnediener*, Kriemhilt's corresponding emergence as courtly maiden par excellence, and the removal of the double blot involved in Siegfried's prior betrothal and subsequent deflowering of Brynhild. But some changes run counter to this trend and build on the image of the rambunctious folktale hero who lives on in *Þiðreks saga* and must have belonged to the *Nibelungenlied* poet's source. Siegfried's original personality shows through in the wild and woolly escapades reported by Hagen and in Adventure 8. The poet chose not to suppress this contradictory streak for the sake of preserving courtly consistency, but availed himself of it to develop the rakish and athletic qualities of his hero even further. The result can be seen in the provocations of Adventure 3 and the military, athletic, and hunting hyperbole of Adventures 4, 7, and 16. The contradiction in Siegfried might well persuade us that consistent characterization was not in the poet's mind and teach us not to be unduly perplexed by the disjunctions in the conduct of Kriemhilt and Hagen between Parts I and II.

Before proceeding to a fuller tabulation of old and new elements, it may be useful to review the poet's reliance on tradition Adventure by Adventure. For fear of losing focus, we must content ourselves with the major points. In Adventure 1 the falcon dream belongs to the tradition (documented by *Vǫlsunga saga*) and gave rise to the conversation between mother and daughter modeled on the *Eneide*. This particular model was attracted by the maiden's reluctance to wed, a motif transferred to Kriemhilt from Brynhild's traditional status as warrior virgin. In Adventure 2 the references to Siegfried's youthful exploits and his courting of fair women may echo his youthful feats in other sources and his

prior betrothal to Brynhild. The royal circumstances and the protracted dubbing ceremony are new. In Adventure 3 Kriemhilt's
rejection of suitors is a motif transferred from Brynhild, as in
Adventure 1. The alarm over Siegfried's dangerous prospects at
Worms may be connected with the arduous wooing of Brynhild
related in the source and partially retained in *Þiðreks saga* 168. In
Adventure 4 the Dano-Saxon war is an extensive elaboration of
foreign campaigns referred to in *Vǫlsunga saga* and *Norna-Gests
þáttr*.

The victory celebration in Adventure 5 is new and Siegfried's
introduction to Kriemhilt is modeled on her introduction to Etzel
in the "Ältere Not." In Adventure 6 Siegfried's knowledge of
Brynhild's location and the course to be steered can be explained
from a prior visit. His small retinue retains the original dimensions of the wooing expedition and is reminiscent of the solitary
exploits of his youth. The vassal fiction is an extension of his
unknown parentage in the source and his representations on
Gunther's behalf derive directly from the wooing scene in the
source as reproduced by *Þiðreks saga*. On the other hand, the
conception of Kriemhilt's hand as a reward for his support of
Gunther is a combination of *Brautwerbung* and *Minnedienst*
ideas. The wistful departure from Worms is borrowed from the
"Ältere Not." Adventure 7 is a continuation of 6 and extends
several of its themes: Brynhild and Siegfried recognize each other
because of the prior visit and the vassal fiction is further elaborated. Brynhild's conquest in bed retains the situation in the
source minus the deflowering. By contrast, the martial games are
new and several of the peripheral motifs are taken from the "Ältere Not" (the teichoscopy, the disarming of the guests, and the
identification of Siegfried from afar). Adventure 8 echoes in some
fashion the wooing sequence of *Þiðreks saga* 168.

Adventure 9 has no traditional core and is pieced together from
borrowed feathers. The dispatching of messengers to announce
the success of the wooing at Worms is modeled on the dispatching
of messengers to Hunland in the "Ältere Not." Siegfried's eager-
ness to serve as emissary in order to see Kriemhilt recalls the
allaying of his wrath inspired by the thought of Kriemhilt in Adventure 3. His special report to her and the humorous inflection of
the *botenbrôt* pick up motifs from Adventure 4 (225–42). Adven-

ture 10 is again traditional. Brynhild's tears belong to an old scene in which she bewails her marriage. Her refusal to sleep with Gunther anticipates a traditional motif in her later incitation of Gunther to murder Siegfried. The double wedding duplicates *Meiri (Grípisspá)* and has a good chance of being traditional. The subduing of Brynhild in bed is confirmed for the tradition by *Þiðreks saga,* as are the ensuing festivities. The form of the festivities is, however, a retake of Adventure 4 and may have been suggested ultimately by the banquet in the "Ältere Not." The exercise of liberality echoes Adventure 5.

Adventure 11 is a pastiche of motifs taken largely from the "Ältere Not." The offer of the Burgundian brothers to share their land with Siegfried is modeled on Etzel's similar offer in the "Ältere Not" (*Þiðreks saga* II.281.15–17). The preoccupation with Kriemhilt's retinue also looks ahead to a passage in the older source (stanza 700 = 1283). Hagen's intervention against her choice of retinue anticipates the animosity he exhibits in seizing her treasure and the whole antagonism that underlies the "Ältere Not." Sigemunt's cession of his crown to Siegfried is a motif borrowed from Etzel's aging and need of a caretaker for his realm in the "Ältere Not" (*Þiðreks saga* II.281.9–14). Sigelint's death similarly echoes Helche's death and the birth of sons to both Brynhild and Kriemhilt (a blind motif) was suggested by the birth of Kriemhilt's son Ortliep in Hunland. Adventure 12 is no less a pastiche. Brynhild's invitation of Kriemhilt and the dispatching of messengers are modeled on Kriemhilt's invitation of her brothers in the "Ältere Not." The council to ponder the invitation duplicates the analogous council at Worms (stanzas 757–62 = 1457–72). An exact correspondence is the retinue of one thousand (760 = 1472). The messengers are rewarded in the customary manner echoing 243 and 558. Hagen's lively interest in Siegfried's treasure prepares the way for his seizure in Adventures 19 and 20. Adventure 13 contains nothing more than conventional ceremony and attaches to no specific models.

Adventure 14 returns to the traditional story. The three phases of the quarrel rehearse the three traditional issues: comparison of husbands, dispute over precedence, and revelation of the deception. The allegation that Siegfried boasted of a sexual conquest is the deflection of a real infringement in the source, from which the murder council was also taken over with some elaboration. Adventure 15, with its sham declaration of war, embroiders on the Dano-Saxon hostilities of Adventure 4. Adventures 16 and 17 blend old and new. In 16 Hagen's proposal of a hunt, his mis-shipment of wine, his slaying of Siegfried at the spring, Siegfried's retaliation, and his dying reproaches belong to the source. On the other hand, the farewell scene is modeled on the Burgundian farewells of the "Ältere Not," while the nonparticipation of Ger-not and Giselher, Siegfried's additional hunting exploits, Hagen's knowledge of a spring, the dash to the spring, and Siegfried's courtesy are the poet's independent additions. In 17 the deposi-tion of Siegfried's corpse on Kriemhilt's threshold, her shriek, the verdict of murder based on the undamaged shield, the allegation of murder by brigands, Kriemhilt's identification of Hagen and Gunther as the murderers, and Siegfried's burial belong in some manner to the source. New features are the summoning of Sige-munt to participate in the mourning, the bier test, the mourning of Gernot and Giselher, the funerary pomp, and Kriemhilt's final view of the corpse. Adventures 18 and 19 are largely an effort to effect a transition between Part I and Part II. Only the exultant Brynhild of stanza 1100 has traditional standing. Sigemunt's de-parture is dictated by the necessity of removing him from the scene and Kriemhilt's decision to remain by the necessity of keeping her in place for Etzel's wooing.

Adventure 19 consists chiefly of an interesting effort to set the stage psychologically for the coming action. The reconciliation, or at least the appearance of one, makes it possible for the Bur-gundians to consider Kriemhilt's remarriage and reestablishment with an independent power base. Her retrieval and distribution of treasure foreshadow her later strategy. Hagen's seizure of this treasure focuses the antagonism of Part II. The agreement be-tween Hagen and Gunther not to reveal the location of the trea-sure prepares the way for the traditional withholding of that se-cret as it was found in the "Ältere Not" and retained in Part II. Kriemhilt's double sorrow over the loss of husband and treasure buttresses the double motivation for her revenge in Part II and the passage of thirteen years allows time for the reconciliation to appear well established.

By way of a final summary I shall now tabulate the poet's major innovations by Adventure. There is of course considerable latitude for arbitrariness in this tabulation since the line between major and minor innovations is impossible to draw. My hope is only to convey some approximate sense of the procedure. Those items that are more nearly invented are italicized to distinguish them from borrowings from known sources (indicated in parentheses).

1. conversation between mother and daughter (from the *Eneide*)
2. *dubbing ceremony*
4. greatly elaborated military campaign (perhaps from *Cligés*)
5. *victory celebration*
   Siegfried's introduction to Kriemhilt (imitation of "Ältere Not")
6. *Kriemhilt's hand as a reward for Siegfried's service*
   departure scene (imitation of "Ältere Not")
7. teichoscopy (imitation of "Ältere Not")
   disarming of guests (imitation of "Ältere Not")
   identification of Siegfried (imitation of "Ältere Not")
   martial games (from the *Brautwerbermärchen*)
9. dispatching of messengers (imitation of "Ältere Not")
   special report to Kriemhilt (imitation of Adventure 4)
10. reception festivities (imitation of Adventure 4)
    extravagant liberality (imitation of Adventure 5)
11. offer of a share in the realm for Siegfried (imitation of "Ältere Not")
    selection of Kriemhilt's retinue (imitation of "Ältere Not")
    Hagen's intervention against Kriemhilt (anticipates "Ältere Not")
    Sigemunt's cession of his crown to Siegfried (imitation of "Ältere Not")
    Sigelint's death (imitation of "Ältere Not")
    birth of sons (imitation of "Ältere Not")
12. Brynhild's invitation of Kriemhilt and Siegfried (imitation of "Ältere Not")
    dispatching of messengers (imitation of "Ältere Not")
    council to ponder the invitation (imitation of "Ältere Not")
    retinue of one thousand (imitation of "Ältere Not")
    rewarding of messengers (imitation of stanzas 243 and 558)
    Hagen's interest in the treasure (anticipates Adventures 19 and 20)

13. reception (imitation of Adventures 4 and 10)
    feasting and ceremony (imitation of Adventures 5 and 10)
15. *sham Saxon war* (inventive extension of Adventure 4)
16. farewell scene (imitation of "Ältere Not")
    Gernot and Giselher refrain from the hunt
    Siegfried's hunting exploits
    Hagen's location of the spring
    the dash to the spring
    Siegfried's courtesy
17. *Sigemunt summoned to the mourning*
    the bier test (perhaps from *Iwein*)
    the mourning of Gernot and Giselher
    the funerary pomp
    Kriemhilt's final viewing of the corpse
18. *Sigemunt's departure*
    Kriemhilt's decision to remain
19. *Kriemhilt's reconciliation with Gunther*
    the retrieval of Siegfried's treasure
    Kriemhilt's distribution of treasure (imitation of "Ältere
      Not")
    Hagen's sinking of the treasure (imitation of "Ältere Not")
    Hagen's and Gunther's agreement not to reveal the loca-
      tion (imitation of "Ältere Not")
    Kriemhilt's double sorrow (imitation of "Ältere Not")
    the passage of thirteen years

The most striking result of this tabulation is the emergence of
the "Ältere Not" as the most important source for the poet's
expansions in Part I. Those who side with Panzer (against Boer,
Heusler, Polak, de Boor, Hempel, Schneider, Lohse, and Wisniewski) in rejecting the "Ältere Not" will naturally be skeptical
and seek to find some other explanation, but the evidence of
borrowing, for example in the journey to Islant in Adventure 7
and the invitation sequence in Adventure 12, is so strong that it is
difficult to evade the concept altogether. I have noted twenty-one
instances of such borrowing in a total of fifty innovations; some
may be illusory, but further instances have no doubt escaped my
attention. The conclusion seems to me inescapable that in his
attempt to bring Part I up to epic strength the poet took grafts
from the written epic that stood model for Part II.

The "Ältere Not," though clearly the most important, was not the only literary source. Our poet also made use of Heinrich von Veldeke's *Eneide*, possibly Chrétien's *Cligés* (or a lost German version by Konrad Fleck), the bride quest in Panzer's folktale, and perhaps Hartmann's *Iwein*. These loans, along with the mining of the "Ältere Not," are most conspicuous in the first thirteen Adventures. Beginning with Adventure 15 (the sham declaration of war) the poet appears to free himself from his literary dependence and improvise more on his own, as the more abundant italicization in Adventures 15–19 above indicates. The sham war may well be redundant as a false prelude to the hunt, but it is not without a certain ingenuity in reconciling the theme of invulnerability with Siegfried's murder. Nor is Kriemhilt's culpability in revealing the vulnerable spot without psychological interest, no matter how taxing on the reader's credence.[21] Siegfried's hunting feats, footrace, and misplaced courtesy in Adventure 16 are perhaps incongruous, but they can be justified as pathos and testify to the scenic talents that Bumke placed at the center of our understanding of the *Nibelungenlied* poet's craftsmanship.[22] The emotional management of the burial in Adventure 17 is both full and independent, while the anticipatory shaping of the antagonism between Hagen and Kriemhilt bridges the concerns of Part I and Part II skillfully. In the latter stages of Part I the poet appears to have grown into his task. He has become more self-reliant, more engaged in the emotional life of his characters, more aware of the necessity for psychological adjustments. We may surmise that the superiority of Part II, generally agreed on by the critics, lies not entirely in the advantage of an epic model, but in the poet's cumulative experience and his ability to learn as he wrote.

[21]On the folktale context see Panzer's description of "Das Märchen vom bedingten Leben" in *Studien zur germanischen Sagengeschichte*, II, 254–70.

[22]"Die Quellen," pp. 30–38. See also Heusler, *Nibelungensage und Nibelungenlied*, p. 115; Naumann, pp. 13–14; Hugo Kuhn, "Über nordische und deutsche Szenenregie in der Nibelungendichtung," *Edda, Skalden, Saga: Festschrift zum 70. Geburtstag von Felix Genzmer*, ed. Hermann Schneider (Heidelberg: Winter, 1952), pp. 279–306; rpt. in his *Dichtung und Welt im Mittelalter* (Stuttgart: Metzler, 1959; rpt. 1969), pp. 196–219; and Carl S. Singer, "The Hunting Contest: An Interpretation of the Sixteenth Aventiure of the *Nibelungenlied*," *GR*, 42 (1967), 163–83.

CHAPTER 7

Das Lied vom
Hürnen Seyfrid

Das Lied vom Hürnen Seyfrid (HS), a poem of 179 stanzas preserved in twelve prints from the sixteenth and seventeenth centuries, has only a tangential relationship to our theme since Brynhild no longer appears in it. It has, however, long figured in the discussion as a clue to the form of the legend prior to the *Nibelungenlied.* Much of the discussion has been highly speculative, but the *HS* has relevance at least to the traditions of Siegfried's youth. I begin with a summary of the poem.

Seyfrid is the son of King Sigmund in Niderland, but he is so unruly that he is banished from the court. He takes service with a village smith, but his behavior shows no signs of improvement: he hammers the iron apart, drives the anvil into the earth, and beats apprentice and master until the smith wishes to be well rid of him. Accordingly he sends him to a dragon lair on the pretext that he should fetch coal, fully expecting that the dragon will resolve his problem. On the way Seyfrid encounters a whole brood of dragons, tears up trees, lays about him with his club until all the dragons are dead, then builds a fire and heaps the bodies on the flames. As they melt, he sticks a finger into the liquid and discovers that when it has cooled, his finger has become horny. He promptly smears his whole body with the liquid, except between the shoulders. The poet notes that this untreated spot was the cause of his death, as can be read in other poems. Seyfrid next goes to the court of King Gybich and does service for eight years to win the hand of his daughter. In the meantime he discovers the Nybling treasure in a cave, in which it has been locked by the dwarf Nybling. On his death Nybling leaves the treasure (fated to be the cause of slaughter among the Huns that only Dietrich and Hiltebrandt escape) to his three sons.

The narrative now returns abruptly (stanza 16) to the city of Worms on the Rhine, where King Gybich resides with three sons and his daughter. One day the daughter is standing in a window and is carried off by a flying dragon to a cliff. Here he keeps her imprisoned for four years despite tears and pleas. As we learn later (125), he is a handsome youth who was transformed when a woman cursed him for his faithless love, but he is destined to return to human shape after five years, at which time he holds out the unvarnished prospect of taking her virginity (26). This congress seems also to imply eternal damnation for her (27) and in her distress she invokes the Virgin Mary.

With another abrupt transition (33) we are told of a prince named Seyfrid, so strong that he hung lions in the trees by their tails for sport. When he comes of age, he goes out hunting one morning and pursues a dragon track. A retrospective stanza (38) tells us that he had long done knightly combat and had the service of five thousand dwarves in return for his killing of a dragon against which they were defenseless. One look at the present dragon, however, is enough to make him opt for prudent withdrawal. As he is about to ride off, the dwarf Euglein (Eugel) approaches (42) and greets him. Seyfrid applies to him for information on his parentage, about which he is suddenly pictured as being ignorant (47) because he was sent far off into the forest to be raised by a smith. Eugel informs him that his mother was Siglinge and his father Sigmund and advises him to be off before the dragon discovers his presence. At the same time, he informs him of the captive maiden Krimhilt, the daughter of King Gybich. Seyfrid replies that he knows her well since they loved one another in her father's land (51). He then swears three oaths not to depart without her. Eugel seeks to dissuade him, but is forced to act as helper when Seyfrid seizes him by the hair and smites him against the rock.

The dwarf now communicates the information that the key to the dragon's cave is in the possession of the giant Kuperan. Seyfrid challenges the giant, who emerges from his house brandishing the emblem of his ilk, a steel staff. He swings ineffectually and when he bends down to dislodge the staff from the earth, Seyfrid gets in a series of quick cuts. Kuperan finally flees into his house, and Seyfrid is about to finish him off when he remembers that Krimhilt's release depends on the acquisition of the key. Having bandaged his wounds, the giant sallies forth again, this time armed with byrnie, sword, helmet, shield, and another steel staff. After an exchange of provocations, the fighting is renewed and Seyfrid inflicts sixteen wounds. Kuperan sues for peace and offers to deliver byrnie, sword, and self. Seyfrid stipulates his aid in releasing the maiden and they seal the agreement with oaths, but the giant disregards the oaths at the first chance and lays Seyfrid low with a blow from behind. He is saved only by the intervention of Eugel, who covers his body with a "cloak of mist" and leaves Kuperan searching vainly for his vanished victim.

When Seyfrid comes to his senses, the fighting recommences. Once again Kuperan is saved only by Seyfrid's knowledge that his death would mean the loss of Krimhilt (97). Kuperan opens the mountain and they ascend laboriously to reach Krimhilt. She welcomes the hero and the giant informs him of a hidden sword capable of dispatching the dragon, but while Seyfrid is distracted, Kuperan once more delivers a sneak blow. A new struggle ensues and ends with Seyfrid's plunging the giant off the cliff (114). Eugel and attendant dwarves materialize unexpectedly to provide food and drink for the hero and his maiden, but before they can begin, the dragon arrives. Seyfrid attacks with the sword signaled by Kuperan and the dwarves flee, with the exception of Eugel. Two of Nybling's sons (Eugel's brothers) remove their treasure from the mountain (134). Seyfrid takes cover from the dragon's heat and discovers the treasure, imagining that the dragon has gathered it there. He takes no further interest in the treasure, and Krimhilt now warns him of sixty additional dragons, but when he returns to the fray, they fly off in apparent panic. Despite the heat and flames, Seyfrid prevails and sends the fragments of the dragon after those of Kuperan (148). He then falls into a Tristan-like swoon and recovers only to find Krimhilt in a similar state, but Eugel provides the requisite herb and she recovers her senses. Eugel now tells how the dragon subjected a thousand dwarves and offers their services in return for their liberation (153–54). He and his brothers entertain the couple and offer to accompany them home, but Seyfrid declines. Before parting, Eugel prophesies that Seyfrid will be murdered after eight years of marriage, that his wife will avenge him with great slaughter, and that she too will die.

At the last moment Seyfrid is reminded of the treasure. He thinks both of Kuperan and the dragon, but supposes that the treasure was gathered by the latter against the day of his transformation into a human. In any case, he has a claim to it and loads it on his horse, but on the road it occurs to him that his life is measured and the treasure useless. He therefore sinks it in the Rhine (167) without knowing that it belongs to Nybling's heirs. Nor does Eugel know the fate of

the treasure. King Gybich is informed of his daughter's release and
rides out to meet Seyfrid with a great retinue. His marriage to
Krimhilt is celebrated on a grand scale for fourteen days. Thereafter
he becomes such a pillar of the realm that envy sets in and Gunther,
Hagen, and Gyrnot plot his death. Hagen stabs him at a cold spring
in the Odenwald (177). Readers who wish to hear more are referred
to "Sewfrides hochzeyt" (179), in which his eight years of marriage
are related.

Rather than review the inconclusive scholarly controversy surrounding the *HS*, I propose to summarize the most obvious
points.[1] My premise is that we do not need to account for much
lost material; almost everything in the *HS* can be explained from
the "Brünhildenlied," the *Nibelungenlied* (redaction m), and the
heroic tale *Rosengarten A*.

The introduction of Seyfrid as the son of Sigmund in Niderland
clearly derives from the *Nibelungenlied* and his exile for unruly
behavior is just as clearly an effort to bridge the discrepancy
between the courtly youth of the *Nibelungenlied* and the
obstreperous youth familiar from *Þiðreks saga*.[2] The latter tradition is developed in detail in the first eleven stanzas of the *HS*; all
the important motifs here may be found in *Þiðreks saga* and can
therefore be attributed to a common source. The most obvious
candidate is the "Brünhildenlied," which also accounts for the
correspondences between *Þiðreks saga* and the *Nibelungenlied*.

---

[1]Orientations may be found in the editions of Wolfgang Golther, *Das Lied vom
Hürnen Seyfrid*, Neudrucke deutscher Literaturwerke 81–82 (Halle: Niemeyer,
1911); and K. C. King, *Das Lied vom Hürnen Seyfrid* (Manchester: Manchester
University Press, 1958). See also Elisabeth Bernhöft, *Das Lied vom Hörnenen
Sigfrid: Vorgeschichte der Druckredaktion des XVI. Jahrhunderts* (Rostock: Carl
Boldtsche Hofbuchdruckerei, 1910); Friedrich Panzer, *Studien zur germanischen
Sagengeschichte*, II: *Sigfrid* (Munich: Beck, 1912), 1–35; Hendrik Willem Jan
Kroes, *Untersuchungen über das Lied vom Hürnen Seyfrid, mit Berücksichtigung
der verwandten Überlieferung* (Gouda: G. B. van Goor Zonen, 1924); Hermann
Schneider, *Germanische Heldensage*, I (Berlin and Leipzig: de Gruyter, 1928;
rpt. 1962). 115–21; Willy Krogmann, "Der Hürnen Sewfrid" in *Die deutsche
Literatur des Mittelalters: Verfasserlexikon*, IV (Berlin: de Gruyter, 1953), 180–
92; Friedrich Panzer, *Das Nibelungenlied: Entstehung und Gestalt* (Stuttgart:
Kohlhammer, 1955), pp. 293–95 and 307; Gerhard Philipp, *Metrum, Reim und
Strophe im "Lied vom Hürnen Seyfrid,"* Göppinger Arbeiten zur Germanistik,
171 (Göppingen: Alfred Kümmerle, 1975), pp. 151–64. My own views are closest
to those expressed by Krogmann and Panzer, *Das Nibelungenlied*.

[2]Bernhöft, pp. 25–26.

The motifs in question are the following:
1. Seyfrid takes service with a smith.
2. He drives the anvil into the earth.
3. He beats the smith's apprentice(s).
4. The smith wishes to be rid of him and sends him to a dragon's lair on the pretext of burning or fetching coal.
5. He hews down or tears up trees.
6. He clubs the dragon(s) to death with a tree.
7. He cooks or burns the dragon(s).

At this point *Þiðreks saga* and *HS* diverge. In the former, Sigurd concocts a stew, puts his finger in it, and then cools the finger in his mouth. In the latter he puts his finger in the molten dragon flesh and notices that when it cools, the skin turns horny. The common feature is the contact of finger and dragon flesh. In one case it produces an understanding of the birds, in the other invulnerability. The bird motif in *Þiðreks saga* matches the *Edda*. The invulnerability motif matches the *Nibelungenlied* (stanza 100). It seems likely, then, that *HS* and *Nibelungenlied* represent the German original, while the translator of *Þiðreks saga* introduces the bird motif as a concession to the Eddic version and to connect the dragon episode with the killing of the smith (Chapter 4, n. 16). This view is verified by *Þiðreks saga,* in which the narrative goes on to retrieve the bath in dragon's blood momentarily suspended to allow for the bird motif. It follows that the "Brünhildenlied" contained the bath in dragon's blood and the invulnerability that we find in *HS* 10–11 and the *Nibelungenlied* 100.

The author of *HS* then turns briefly to *Rosengarten A* 1–3 to record the arrival of Seyfrid at Gybich's court (the name Gybich for Dancrat in the *Nibelungenlied* betrays the use of *Rosengarten*) and the wooing of his daughter (*HS* 11–12).[3] The acquisition of Nybling's treasure in 13–14 is a synopsis of the *Nibelungenlied* 87–99. *HS* 16 reverts to *Rosengarten A* 1 with close verbal parallels ("Ein Stadt leyt bey dem Reyne" = "Ein stat lît an dem Rîne"). The abduction of Krimhilt by a flying dragon (17–32) was told in Adventures 6–9 of redaction m of the *Nibelungenlied*.[4]

---

[3]Ibid., pp. 43–44. *Rosengarten A* was edited by Georg Holz, *Die Gedichte vom Rosengarten zu Worms* (Halle: Niemeyer, 1893), pp. 3–67.

[4]Only the table of contents survives. For the text see Helmut de Boor, "Die Bearbeitung m des Nibelungenliedes," *BGDSL* (Tübingen), 81 (1959), 176–95.

Whether *HS* took the story from this redaction or an independent version is immaterial. The motif may ultimately have been suggested by *Rosengarten A* 329: "er [Siegfried] ersluoc uf eime steine / einen trachen vreissam" ("he slew a fearsome dragon on a rock"). This hint could have been developed along stereotypical lines. Seyfrid is then reintroduced in stanza 33 with the note "Das er die Löwen fieng / Und sie dann zů gespötte / Hoch an die baumen hieng" ("that he caught lions and then for sport hung them on the trees"). These lines echo *Rosengarten A* 3:

> der pflac sô grôzer sterke,   daz er die lewen vienc
> und sie mit den zegeln   über die mûren hienc.

> (He possessed such great strength that he caught lions and hung them over the walls by their tails.)

Here the loans from *Rosengarten* conclude.

What follows is Seyfrid's departure for the hunt (34):

> Er wolt eyns morgens jagen
> Und reyten zů dem than
> Mit Habich und mit hunden

> (One morning he wanted to hunt and ride to the woods with hawk and hounds.)

The passage echoes Sigurd's departure for his encounter with Brynhild in *Vǫlsunga saga* 58.8–10: "Ok einn dag er fra þvi sagth, at Sigurdr reid a skog vid hundum ok haukum ok miklu fiolmenni" ("And one day it is told that Sigurd rode to the woods with hounds and hawks and a great company"). But we must assume that hunting is a commonplace and is normally accompanied by hawks and dogs. The remainder of the *HS* can be derived in large part from the *Nibelungenlied*. The reminiscence in stanza 38 of a prior dragon slaying and the service of five thousand grateful dwarves blends the later theme of hostility between dwarves and dragons with Alberich's service to Siegfried in the *Nibelungenlied* 99 and Adventure 8. Eugel's role as Seyfrid's helper against the dragon extends the idea. His information on Seyfrid's parentage was once taken as a reflection of Sigrdrífa and the *Erlösungssage,* but K. C. King, with de Boor's concurrence, was skeptical and the idea may be considered to be abandoned.[5] The motif of unknown parentage may be taken as a reflex of the "Brünhildenlied" and remains unreconciled with Seyfrid's princely status in Niderland, derived from the *Nibelungenlied.* A dwarf as dispenser of wisdom requires no special explanation. Seyfrid's persuasion of Eugel by means of a firm grasp on his hair reflects Siegfried's mock *zuht* in bearding Alberich in the *Nibelungenlied* 497.

The story of Kuperan in *HS* may have had some separate status in tradition, but the *Nibelungenlied* is again an adequate background. Each time Siegfried deals with Alberich in the *Nibelungenlied,* he must also confront attendant giants, twelve in the first episode (94–95) and one in the later episode (489–92). The latter is armed similarly to Kuperan, including the requisite steel staff. The dwarves' provision of food and drink for hero and released maiden may also have its origin in the serving of *lûtertranc* during Siegfried's visit to his Nibelungs (504). The dwarves' removal of their treasure from the mountain (134) is a rather pointless loan from the *Nibelungenlied* 89, with the confusion compounded because of the poet's view that treasures normally belong to dragons and his projection of this view on Seyfrid. Eugel's prophecy on Seyfrid's fate, the sinking of the treasure in the Rhine, and the final details on Seyfrid's marriage, murder, and avenging are a thumbnail synopsis of the remaining sections of the *Nibelungenlied.*

It should be apparent that the *HS* begins with details from Siegfried's youth found in the "Brünhildenlied," adds a few touches from *Rosengarten A,* and for the rest embroiders freely on the *Nibelungenlied.* It offers nothing to conflict with the source already established for *Þiðreks saga* and the *Nibelungenlied.* Indeed, it supports the likelihood that the "Brünhildenlied" included a fair amount of detail on Siegfried's childhood.

[5]King, pp. 91–96, and de Boor's review in *BGDSL* (T), 81 (1959), 228.

CHAPTER 8

The Literary Fortunes
of Brynhild

The full story of Brynhild is divulged only in *Vǫlsunga saga*. Without this text we would be thrown back on the impenetrable version of *Skamma*, a few hints in the Eddic elegies, and the shadowy silhouette that survives in *Þiðreks saga* and the *Nibelungenlied*. The Brynhild who lives in popular imagination as the prototypical Germanic heroine does so only by virtue of her standing in *Vǫlsunga saga*.

In the pages of the saga her tale is amply detailed. She once intervened in a battle, presumably as a warrior maiden, and killed Odin's favorite Hjálm-Gunnarr. In retribution he stuck her with a "sleep-thorn" and determined that she should be condemned to marry. In return she swore an oath to marry only the man who knew no fear. She is eventually awakened from her slumber by the hero Sigurd, to whom she imparts wise counsel and to whom she betrothes herself on his departure. Sigurd next comes to the home of the chieftain Heimir, who is married to Brynhild's sister Bekkhild; Bekkhild plies the needle while Brynhild treads the battlefield in helmet and byrnie. Sigurd is hospitably welcomed and remains as an honored guest. In the meantime, Brynhild returns to Heimir, who, we learn, is her foster father as well as her brother-in-law, and takes up residence in a bower with her maidens. Here she busies herself weaving in gold Sigurd's deeds—the slaying of the serpent, the winning of the treasure, and the death of Reginn. One day Sigurd rides into the forest to hunt. His hawk escapes and perches by a window on a high tower. As he retrieves the hawk, he sees Brynhild through the window

and becomes lovesick. Inquiries reveal her identity as Brynhild
the daughter of Buðli and the fact that she is interested only in
warlike pursuits. Sigurd nonetheless vows to woo her and suc-
ceeds in overcoming her reluctance. They renew their oaths.

The story turns to Gjúki's court, where Gudrun dreams of a
hawk she would give anything not to lose. A lady-in-waiting takes
this to signify that she will love her husband deeply. Gudrun
proposes to consult Brynhild to learn his identity. In the course of
their conversation Brynhild reveals that her betrothed will be
beguiled by Grimhild's potion, will marry Gudrun, and will die
soon after. Gudrun will then marry Atli, lose her brothers, and kill
her husband. The first part of the prophecy is duly fulfilled and
Sigurd marries Gudrun. Then Grimhild proposes Brynhild as a
wife for Gunnarr and suggests that Sigurd take part in the wooing.
They ride off to Hlymdalir and learn from Heimir that Brynhild's
hall is enclosed by a flame wall and that she will accept only the
suitor who crosses it. When Gunnarr fails, he exchanges shapes
with Sigurd as Grimhild had instructed them and Sigurd clears the
flames. In the guise of Gunnarr he sues for her hand and over-
comes her resistance by reminding her of her oath to marry the
man who crosses the flame wall. They spend three nights together
separated by the sword Gramr, Brynhild leaves her daughter Áslaug, conceived in the previous meeting with Sigurd, with Heimir,
and her marriage to Gunnarr is celebrated at Gjúki's court.

One day the queens quarrel in the bath and the deception is
revealed. Brynhild turns pale and departs in silence. The next day
Gudrun tries to comfort her, but more harsh words pass between
them. Gunnarr makes a similar attempt and is bitterly reproached. Finally Sigurd seeks her out in an effort to reconcile
her, and she gives vent to the love and hatred she feels for him.
Then she threatens Gunnarr with desertion unless he kills Sigurd
and Sigurd's son. Hǫgni protests, but Gunnarr persists and
suggests that they delegate Gotþormr since he is not bound by
oaths. He bids Brynhild take heart, but she warns him that he will
not share her bed until the deed is done. The brothers incite
Gotþormr and he delivers the fatal thrust as Sigurd lies sleeping
by Gudrun. Brynhild laughs aloud as she hears Gudrun gasp, but
Gunnarr sees through her false joy. Now everyone is puzzled that
she should grieve with tears over what she demanded with a light

heart. She recounts an ominous dream forecasting Gunnarr's death, reproaches him for betraying his sworn brother, and reveals that Sigurd kept his faith by placing a sword between them. Finally she rehearses the circumstances of her wooing and declares her intention to die. Gunnarr seeks to dissuade her and asks for Hǫgni's help, but Hǫgni considers that they will be well rid of her. Brynhild distributes her gold and stabs herself with a sword, but before dying she prophesies the future and instructs Gunnarr to build a pyre on which she and Sigurd will lie with a sword between them as once before.

Our survey of the legend has taught us that this story is not from a unified source. It is composed from a variety of poems and a variety of concepts. There is general agreement that the warrior maiden who contravenes Odin's will and is awakened from her magic sleep by Sigurd was not originally Brynhild, but a woman named Sigrdrífa, whom the author of *Vǫlsunga saga* (perhaps following the lead of *Helreið Brynhildar* and *Fáfnismál* 42–43) identified as Brynhild. The first episode of the story is therefore a very late speculation and is poorly integrated inasmuch as Sigurd proceeds to betrothe himself to Brynhild at Heimir's residence without recognizing her from their previous encounter.

But the encounter at Heimir's has also revealed itself as a secondary accretion taken over by the author of *Vǫlsunga saga* from *Sigurðarkviða in meiri,* which in turn drew on a German version of the story. This is the nub of the problem. Because the prior betrothal of Brynhild and Sigurd is fully described only in the Norse *Vǫlsunga saga* and is only partially or dimly hinted at in the German versions (*Þiðreks saga* and *Nibelungenlied*), it has always been assumed that the prior betrothal was peculiar to the Norse version. In fact, it is a specifically German motif and acquired currency in the north only because the *Meiri* poet sought to harmonize the Norse and German variants and because the author of *Vǫlsunga saga* accepted his harmonization. The primary result of the preceding investigation has been to distinguish these two variants of the Brynhild legend, a Norse variant without a prior betrothal between Brynhild and Sigurd and a German variant with the prior betrothal. Closest to the Norse prototype is *Sigurðarkviða in forna,* but we must bear in mind that *Forna* may not be a particularly old poem; it already shows signs of the eroticization that is characteristic of the German version.

Nor is the German variant preserved in unmixed form. The Norse redactor of *Þiðreks saga* seems to have been irresolute about the prior betrothal he found in his German exemplar. He began by suppressing it as a concession to the Norse version, but later felt obliged to retrieve it. The *Nibelungenlied* poet suppressed it without regrets, leaving only tantalizing indications of the first meeting between Brynhild and Siegfried. Thus the prior betrothal survives intact only in *Vǫlsunga saga*'s adaptation of *Sigurðarkviða in meiri,* but this amalgam provides no clear view of Brynhild's character in the German original (the "Brünhildenlied") because it reinterpreted her in terms of the Norse Brynhild inherited from *Forna.*

The existence of two variants implies in effect the existence of two Brynhilds, the Brynhild who swore to have the greatest man only to be deceived by that very man and the Brynhild who was betrothed to Siegfried and subsequently lost him to Kriemhilt. The existence of two separate variants also precludes the penetration to a unified prototype. The simpler form without the prior betrothal may well be older, but there is no way to document the priorities. On the whole we will do better to study the two extant Brynhilds without trying to derive them from a common ancestor.

The prehistory of the Norse Brynhild is lost in the lacuna of Codex Regius, and we cannot be certain about the circumstances of her wooing and the details of her motivation. In *Vǫlsunga saga* 68.13–16 Sigurd (disguised as Gunnarr) holds her to her promise in the following words: "You have accomplished many great deeds, but now remember your promise that if this fire were crossed, you would marry the man who did it." These words come from a passage most likely to originate in *Forna,* but they may also represent an admixture from *Meiri.* Establishing the exact source is, however, an academic question. Since there is reason to believe that *Meiri* adhered closely to *Forna* in this part of the story, it does not make a great deal of difference whether the precise words come from one poem or the other.

All other hints about Brynhild's hopes and expectations derive from passages in *Vǫlsunga saga* directly attributable to *Meiri.* In 71.6–7 she says to Gudrun: "I would be happy if you did not have the more distinguished husband." In 73.13–17 she says to Gunnarr: "I made a vow at home in my father's house that I would love only the man who was born to be the most distinguished and that man is Sigurd. Now I am an oath breaker since I do not have him and for that reason I will bring about your death." In her concluding dialogue with Sigurd she says (77.7–9): "I swore an oath to marry the man who crossed my flame wall and I wish to keep that oath or die." Although these words belong to *Meiri*, they presumably elaborate an idea received from *Forna*. They are in any case the best evidence we have of Brynhild's original motivation in the Norse variant. The essential point is that she has vowed to have the most distinguished man and that the right suitor will be identified by his ability to cross the flame wall. When Sigurd accomplishes the feat, but plays her into the hands of a lesser man, her will is contravened.

The consequences of her disappointment in the Norse original are less clear. In *Skamma* and presumably *Meiri* she committed suicide, but it is not certain that she did so in *Forna*, which concludes with her declaration of Sigurd's innocence. If the end of the poem is complete as it stands, we must imagine a version of the story in which she lives on. This possibility alters the picture considerably. We are accustomed to thinking of Brynhild as a broken woman for whom suicide is the only remaining option. Perhaps we must revise this concept and imagine a victorious Brynhild, grief-stricken but triumphant, a woman who has avenged the deception that deprived her of the man she wanted and has survived intact. She may not have been a romantic victim from the outset, but rather a tragic heroine comparable to such male counterparts as Angantýr, who has the ill fortune to make good his inheritance at the expense of killing his brother (*Hlǫðskviða*), or Hildebrand, who must kill his son in order to win the necessary victory (*Hildebrandslied*). Angantýr and Hildebrand grieve over their losses, but they live on to enjoy their wealth or standing.

Hans Kuhn has argued that Brynhild did not originally commit suicide.[1] The evidence for such a suicide is indeed very thin. There is no hint of it in *Þiðreks saga* or the *Nibelungenlied* and therefore no reason to attribute it to the "Brünhildenlied." *Meiri* probably did have the suicide, but judging from *Vǫlsunga saga*'s

[1]"Brünhilds und Kriemhilds Tod," *ZDA*, 82 (1948–50), 191–99; rpt. in his *Kleine Schriften*, ed. Dietrich Hofmann, II (Berlin: de Gruyter, 1971), 80–87.

dependence on *Skamma, Meiri* appears to have had a less fully developed version of it. The chances are that *Meiri* simply imitated the conclusion of *Skamma* and therefore offers no independent confirmation of the suicide. We are left with the impression that the suicide was peculiar to *Skamma* and, far from being generalized as a rudiment of the story, should rather be regarded as an idiosyncratic deviation from the common version. Perhaps it was modeled on Gudrun's suicide in Atli's flaming hall, but pyre and sword are compellingly reminiscent of Dido's fate and the conclusion of *Skamma* may owe something to Virgil's prototypical victim of blind passion.[2] The dramatic suicide of *Skamma* has tended to obscure the other Brynhild, who was cheated, took revenge, and survived to exult. The exultation is far better attested than the suicide and is documented by *Brot* 10, *Þiðreks saga* II.267.11–16, and the *Nibelungenlied* 1100.

In any era dominated by a romantic outlook, the erotic strain is likely to be emphasized to the exclusion of other factors. This is true of the thirteenth and nineteenth centuries equally. Thus the *Skamma* and *Meiri* poets developed an eroticism conceivably never dreamt of by the *Forna* poet. As recently as 1953 Klaus Fuss was able to reduce Brynhild's emotional life to sexual fascination.[3] But in the first instance it appears not to have been the man who fascinated Brynhild, but her own claim to distinction. Fuss's phrasing suggests that she was overcome by sexual passion, but more likely she was overcome by a more encompassing ambition and she desired Sigurd only to ratify her will. Sigurd's pale personality in most versions of the story may indeed derive from his lack of status in the original, in which he was no more than a creation of Brynhild's desire. We may also consider her in the context of the strong-willed women elsewhere in Icelandic literature, most particularly her literary descendant Guðrún Ósvífrsdóttir in *Laxdæla saga*. Guðrún contrives the death of the man she loves, triumphs, and mourns in silence, but goes on to

---

[2]To my knowledge, Dido's suicide is recorded in medieval Iceland only in *Hauksbók (Breta sǫgur)*, ed. E. Jónsson and F. Jónsson (Copenhagen: Thiele, 1892–1896), p. 232 (normalized): "En er hon spurði, at víst var, at hann vildi eigi til hennar koma, þá fyrirfór hon sér sjálfri..." ("But when she learned that it was certain that he did not want to come to her, she took her life...").

[3]"Brynhild," *ZDP*, 72 (1953), 110.

cut a commanding figure the rest of a long life. Perhaps the pattern was suggested by a Brynhild not fatally overwrought by sexual passion, but merely insistent on her own terms.

The appropriateness of the heroic rather than the romantic paradigm to explain Brynhild is supported by the curious references to her career as a shield maiden. Alsviðr informs Sigurd (*Vǫlsunga saga* 59.9–10): "She wishes to wage war and achieve all manner of famous deeds." Brynhild confirms this wish to her suitor (60.5–8): "I am a shield maiden and I wear a helmet among warrior kings and to these kings I wish to render service and I am eager to do battle." When Sigurd woos on Gunnarr's behalf, Brynhild sits before him (*Vǫlsunga saga* 68.7–8) "and has a sword in her hand and a helmet on her head and wears a byrnie." Her response to the suit is (*Vǫlsunga saga* 68.11–13): "I was in battle with the King of Novgorod and our weapons were reddened in men's blood and this is still my desire." As we have seen above, the poet of *Helreið Brynhildar* capitalized on this theme to equate Brynhild with Sigrdrífa and create a warrior youth for her. How far back in time does the shield-maiden motif reach? Brynhild's appearance in armor and reference to warlike activity with the King of Novgorod belong to a context in which the *Forna* and *Meiri* layers cannot be separated. But it is difficult to imagine that her militarism originated with the *Meiri* poet, who was intent on making her over into a romance heroine weaving in a bower and ultimately succumbing to her love for Sigurd. The idea must therefore be at least as old as *Forna*.

Brynhild's force of arms and her stern will must be related in some way. On the face of it, there is equal likelihood that her warriorlike qualities gave rise to a story of deception and bloody revenge or that her adamant personality in the revenge story suggested the concept of a warrior maiden. But if we bear in mind that we are dealing with a fully developed narrative, not with a series of loose motifs, the revenge story must take precedence. Brynhild's days as a warrior maiden are not anchored in the plot and could not have existed apart from the story. We must therefore imagine that the Norse variant originated as a story of Brynhild's determination to have the greatest man, her deception, and her subsequent revenge. She was a figure in the tradition of the Langobardic queen Rosimund, who washed away a cruel in-

sult in the blood of her husband Alboin.[4] A military career was
felt to be in the spirit of such action and was added in perhaps on
the analogy of the Norse valkyrie concept or some such figure as
Hervǫr, who spent her youth engaged in warfare.[5]

Brynhild's physical prowess is in any case deeply imbedded in
the legend because it appears in the German variant as well, albeit
in different form. Here Brynhild figures as a supernaturally strong
virgin who can only be subdued by Sigurd and whose strength
subsides to a normal level once she is deprived of her virginity
(Þiðreks saga II.41.14–18 and Nibelungenlied 682.1). The athletic
powers that she demonstrates during the bridal games in the
Nibelungenlied probably did not enter the legend prior to this
text, but this new motif was presumably attached to the legend
because of Brynhild's known capacities. Her martial stature,
either in the form of physical strength or deeds of arms, is thus a
shared feature in north and south and antedates the separation of
the variants. A particular aspect of her supernatural qualities are
the sybilline gifts with which she is endowed. These also bridge
the variants and may be found in Chapter 168 of the German
Þiðreks saga, in which she recognizes Sigurd's presence sight
unseen and informs him of his ancestry, and in more elaborate
form in the Norse story. Already in Brot 16 she prophesies the
future and this prophecy is further developed in Skamma. In
Meiri Brynhild's clairvoyance is extended to provide an interpretation of Gudrun's monitory dreams. Both her physical strength
and her prophetic powers may be understood as objectifications
of her innate attributes. We may imagine that she was in the first
instance a powerful personality with an overriding will and that
later poets, awed by her temper, read some additional magic into
the story.

What sets the legend of Brynhild apart from all other Germanic
tales of forceful women, with the possible exception of Guðrún
Ósvífrsdóttir who was modeled on her, is the element of will.
Even among the male heroes only Egill Skallagrímsson has some
affinity to her as a paradigm of determination, but in his case will

[4]Paul the Deacon, Historia Langobardorum, Scriptores rerum germanicarum,
ed. Georg Waitz (Hannover: Hahn, 1878), II.28 (pp. 104–6).
[5]Jón Helgason, ed., Heiðreks saga, Samfund til udgivelse af gammel nordisk
litteratur (Copenhagen: J. Jørgensen & Co., 1924), chaps. 4–5 (pp. 14–33).

can assume the form of cranky contentiousness or simple covetousness. Only in Brynhild is it stylized on a grand scale. This
celebration of will is unique in Germanic prose and poetry. Elsewhere action is a reflex of the social code, not of character. Gudrun acts to avenge her brothers. Kriemhilt acts to avenge her
husband. Hildebrand acts because he is trapped and finds no
acceptable exit from the situation. Gunnarr accepts the deadly
invitation to Hunland because he is expected to do so. Rosimund
acts to avenge an intolerable public affront. Hlǫðr acts to
vindicate what he and probably others perceive to be his right.
Only Brynhild acts without social pressure; she acts to satisfy
herself. Other Germanic heroes and heroines are caught in a web
of expectations, their own and others', which they must satisfy as
best they can. It is possible to imagine some unstated reluctance
in their stories. But Brynhild is solely abandoned to her wishes.
Her emotional isolation is reflected in her remoteness from society. Germanic heroes and heroines regularly appear in the context
of their families and are characteristically trapped in a situation
that compels them to act against family obligations or interests.
Hildebrand must kill his son. Angantýr must kill his brother.
Rosimund and Signý must contrive the deaths of their husbands
and Kriemhilt the death of her brothers. Gudrun must dispatch
her sons Hamðir and Sǫrli to their deaths. Gunnarr must abandon
his family to the bears and the wolves. Everywhere the immediate
social context of the family focuses the tragedy. But Brynhild
appears originally to have had no family. In Þiðreks saga she
resides alone in a castle with her retainers. In the Nibelungenlied
she is an independent princess on a remote island; the only signs
of family are vague references to relatives in stanzas 476 and 526
and an adventitious uncle to whom she entrusts her realm in
stanza 523. In Icelandic literature she does acquire a family: a
father Buðli, a brother Atli, a sister Bekkhild, and a foster father
Heimir. But here too she resides apart, in a tower or behind her
magic flame wall, and the family looks like a late speculative
attempt to domesticate her in the style of other heroic stories.

    Living in a social vacuum, Brynhild became emotionally con-
centrated. The story would have been quite different had the
arena been a desire for land, power, possessions, or honor.

Perhaps in desiring the best man, Brynhild desired all these things as well, but in the absence of any hint to this effect, it was possible to interpret her motivation as a desire to satisfy her erotic needs. No other major figure in Germanic literature was open to such an interpretation. Love never impinges on the actions of heroes, whose stance is regularly to ignore erotic considerations that might tend to compete with more serious imperatives. Rosimund dismisses whatever marital affection she may have felt for Alboin. Gudrun becomes truly spirited only in the prosecution of her vengeance and, like Rosimund, she represses any affection she may have for Atli and their children. The original Brynhild of the Norse variant may have behaved similarly and may have responded to the thwarting of her ambition by plotting the death of her ordained husband without apparent qualms. But even in the earliest text (*Brot* 15) her grief over her loss emerges with painful clarity.

This is the point of departure for the romantic variant of Brynhild's career. At some point a poet shifted the emphasis slightly and focused not on Brynhild's abstract wish to fulfill herself, but on her desire for a particular man. Ambition was transmuted into passion. Brynhild was no longer imagined to be in control of her destiny and able to punish those who crossed her; she was cast instead as a victim of erotic betrayal. That victor and victim lie so close together in this story is a fascinating paradox. On one side of the coin Brynhild is the most dominant and triumphant figure in Germanic legend. On the other she is a hapless woman. The Norse variant developed the dominant figure first. The German variant developed the sexually betrayed woman and used the prior betrothal to emphasize her victimization. Ultimately, the Norse poets chose to follow this lead. The *Skamma* poet conceived of the suicide to further intensify the sexual crisis and the *Meiri* poet systematically harmonized the Norse and German variants.

The difficulty in dealing with the German variant stems from Brynhild's badly faded image in the German texts. Her martial maidenhood is foreign to both *Þiðreks saga* and the *Nibelungenlied* and her athleticism in the latter looks like an overly explicit resurrection of the theme. It converts her forceful and somewhat mysterious personality into truculence and muscle.[6] The magic wooing in the northern variant appears as a prosaic arrangement in *Þiðreks saga* 227 and as the taming of a bully in the *Nibelungenlied*. Still more disenchanting is the second phase of Brynhild's subjection, her unceremonious deflowering in *Þiðreks saga* and Siegfried's wrestling conquest in the *Nibelungenlied*. It is tempting to think that this denigration of Brynhild in the German variant is connected with her status as victim. The powerful and independent queen whom we must posit for the original story must have encountered cultural or literary resistance in the south. The southern milieu, or a particular poet, responded negatively to such an overwhelming apparition and proceeded to neutralize her by making her a slave of passion and devising crasser forms of humiliation—jilting, physical subjection, and defloration.

In Germany there is no trace of the moving conflict between love and hate within Brynhild, a theme sounded in *Brot* 15 and expounded at length in the dialogue between Brynhild and Sigurd in *Meiri*. In the *Nibelungenlied* Brynhild's mastery in contriving Siegfried's murder is largely transferred to Hagen. Nor does she exhibit any reaction to his death, only a heartless disregard for Kriemhilt in stanza 1100. In *Þiðreks saga* she prosecutes her design with special malice in a last-minute incitation of Hǫgni, greets the returning assassins with unmixed gratification and the gratuitous suggestion that they deposit the corpse in Grimhild's bed, then celebrates the questionable triumph with them. Clearly the German texts consciously dismantled the once proud figure of Brynhild and undertook, particularly in the *Nibelungenlied*, a corresponding justification of Kriemhilt, who, to the extent she was developed at all in the northern variant, was viewed as an intruder into Brynhild's prerogatives. Symbolic of the shift in sympathies is stanza 593 of the *Nibelungenlied*, which does not shun the invidious comparison and specifies that Kriemhilt was more beautiful than Brynhild.

[6]Friedrich Neumann, "Schichten der Ethik im Nibelungenliede," *Das Nibelungenlied in seiner Zeit* (Göttingen: Vandenhoeck & Ruprecht, 1967), p. 15: "Kurz: über Brünhild, die den Weitsprung wagt und den Stein stösst, die mit Gunther and Siegfried ringt, haben Kleriker, Ritter und Ritterfrauen gelacht. Grade der Gegensatz zum herrschenden Ideal der Frau musste erheiternd wirken."

The late Icelandic reaction to the German denigration of Brynhild is interesting. Assuming that the poets of both *Skamma* and *Meiri* were familiar with some form of the German story, it is evident that neither participated in the detraction that characterized this version. On the contrary, both systematically reinstated Brynhild. *Skamma* retains her slander of Sigurd (stanza 19) and her triumph mixed with grief (stanzas 30–31) from *Forna*, but enters into no derogation of her character. Instead, it provides an extended apologia for her action (stanzas 33–41) and above all it introduces the suicide to expiate Brynhild's guilt and grief. This is a proud end with no concession to the humiliated Brynhild of southern tradition, who survives in a depraved state of exultation. As a suicide she remains the dignified executor of her own fate.

The problem of maintaining Brynhild's honor was more complex in *Meiri* since the poet incorporated a series of German episodes in his revision: Kriemhilt's dream, the prior betrothal, the hall quarrel, and the discussion of broken oaths between Brynhild and Sigurd. But despite this harmonization, nothing was admitted that might tend to compromise Brynhild, neither the translation of personal stature into brute strength, nor the humiliation of physical subjection, nor, as far as we can tell, the cruel triumph over Gudrun. In contrast to the German tradition, this poet took Brynhild's role as victim seriously. Rather than humbling her, he chose to explore her psyche. This intention is clearest in his transformation of the German wooing dialogue (*Þiðreks saga* 227) into a last reckoning between the lovers. In the German scene she is a passive figure who accedes to her betrayer's practical advice. In *Meiri* she morally dominates Sigurd, declares her love and hatred openly, and forces him to accede to her view. In both *Skamma* and *Meiri* Brynhild becomes comprehensible. In *Skamma* she explains herself in a long monologue and in *Meiri* in a series of dialogues with Gudrun, Gunnarr, and Sigurd. She is neither degraded nor reduced; on the contrary, her role grows and she is analyzed with increasing care. At no point is there a suggestion that her action was perverse or inexplicable. In the south her personality was judged to be barren, but in the north it became wonderfully fertile.

Iceland did not of course remain untouched by the German

disapprobation of Brynhild. In *Skamma* 44 Gunnarr appeals to
Hǫgni to placate her and Hǫgni replies (*Vǫlsunga saga* 83.17–19):
"Let no one dissuade her from dying, for she has profited neither
us nor anyone since she came here." Hǫgni appears to voice the
German reservations (cf. *Skamma* 19) and open the subsequent
debate on Brynhild's character. The debate is prosecuted in the
Eddic elegies, poems which are still later and in which the southern distaste for Brynhild has left a clearer mark. In *Guðrúnarkviða*
I Gudrun's sister Gullrǫnd condemns her in drastic terms as *þjóð-
leið* (universally detested) and the "greatest of husband killers"
(stanza 24). But here too Brynhild is allowed to speak her piece;
she attributes the disaster to Atli (as in *Skamma*) and regrets ever
having seen Sigurd. And even in the context of Gudrun's lament
she is allowed to participate in the mourning of Sigurd, something
she does not do in *Þiðreks saga* or the *Nibelungenlied*. The same
uncertainty about her role prevails in *Helreið Brynhildar*. The
witch on her path to the underworld reproaches her for visiting
another woman's husband and greets her as a murderess, but
Brynhild is free to reply and account for her actions in an extended monologue. The gist of the monologue in the final stanza is
a vindication of her place next to Sigurd, in rough analogy to the
common pyre of *Skamma*. *Helreið* has consequently been understood in general terms as an apologia. It is clear that even in these
latest documents the one-dimensional German view of Brynhild
did not pass unchallenged. Her claims continued to be respected.

The reasons for the split between the northern and southern
perceptions of Brynhild can be only a matter of speculation. Was
the heroic model alive and productive longer in the north than in
the south and could it be construed in Brynhild's favor? Did the
forceful women of Icelandic saga tradition serve as literary role
models for the Eddic Brynhild? Did the refinements, the social
stratification, and the more vigorous Christianity of the south
confine a woman's image with additional proprieties and thus
foreclose the understanding of such a self-willed heroine? Had the
gentle heroine of romance already obtruded so fully on the literary imagination that there was no place for the active woman of
heroic legend? Whatever the reason, Germany bequeathed to us a
vindictive Amazon subordinated to her rival Kriemhilt, while Iceland bequeathed a spirited heroine with a clear consciousness of

herself, equally impressive in the fullness of her ambition and the anguish of her disappointment, an object of wonder to all who told her story. The Brynhild of *Skamma,* and more particularly of *Meiri,* is the most complete psychological portrait, male or female, in Icelandic literature. Her legend inspired these poets to widen and enrich their literary resources in an admiring effort to account for such a singular phenomenon.

Selected Bibliography

The following list is a minimum guide to the literature on the Nibelung problem. It does not include everything that I have found useful (the footnotes are rather more inclusive), but is limited to a hundred items with which a serious student of the problem should be familiar. The works are chosen because they are fundamental contributions, or because they shed light on some important aspect of the problem, or because they are devoted to Brynhild in particular. A much fuller bibliography may be compiled by consulting Per Wieselgren's "Bibliographische Übersicht" in his *Quellenstudien zur Vǫlsunga saga,* pp. 394–413 (marred by incomplete references and inaccuracies) and Roswitha Wisniewski's "Bibliographie zur deutschen Heldensage 1928–1960" in the second printing of Hermann Schneider's *Germanische Heldensage,* pp. 474–511. In addition, I have provided a list of articles surveying Nibelung research.

Critical Studies

Beyschlag, Siegfried. "Das Motiv der Macht bei Siegfrieds Tod." *GRM,* 33 (1952), 95–108. Rpt. in *Zur germanisch-deutschen Heldensage: Sechzehn Aufsätze zum neuen Forschungsstand.* Ed. Karl Hauck. Bad Homburg vor der Höhe: Hermann Gentner Verlag, 1961. Pp. 195–213.
———. "Deutsches Brünhildenlied und Brautwerbermärchen." In *Märchen, Mythos, Dichtung: Festschrift zum 90. Geburtstag Friedrich von der Leyens.* Ed. Hugo Kuhn and Kurt Schier. Munich: Beck, 1963. Pp. 121–45.
Boer, Richard Constant. "Sigrdrifumál und Helreið." *ZDP,* 35 (1903), 289–329.

——. *Untersuchungen über den Ursprung und die Entwicklung der Nibelungensage*. 3 vols. Halle: Verlag der Buchhandlung des Waisenhauses, 1906–1909.

Boor, Helmut de. *Die färöischen Lieder des Nibelungenzyklus*. Germanische Bibliothek: Untersuchungen und Texte, 12. Heidelberg: Winter, 1918.

——. "Kapitel 168 der Thidrekssaga." In *Edda, Skalden, Saga: Festschrift zum 70. Geburtstag von Felix Genzmer*. Ed. Hermann Schneider. Heidelberg: Winter, 1952. Pp. 157–72.

——. "Die Bearbeitung m des Nibelungenliedes (Darmstädter Aventiurenverzeichnis)." *BGDSL* (Tübingen), 81 (1959), 176–95.

Brandl, Alois. "Medea und Brünhilde." In his *Forschungen und Charakteristiken*. Berlin and Leipzig: de Gruyter, 1936. Pp. 24–27.

Bumke, Joachim. "Sigfrids Fahrt ins Nibelungenland: Zur achten aventiure des Nibelungenliedes." *BGDSL* (Tübingen), 80 (1958), 253–68.

——. "Die Quellen der Brünhildfabel im *Nibelungenlied*." *Euphorion*, 54 (1960), 1–38.

Droege, Karl. "Zur Geschichte des Nibelungenliedes." *ZDA*, 48 (1906–1907), 471–503.

——. "Die Vorstufe unseres Nibelungenliedes." *ZDA*, 51 (1909), 177–218.

——. "Zur Geschichte der Nibelungendichtung und der Thidrekssaga." *ZDA*, 58 (1920–1921), 1–40.

——. "Das ältere Nibelungenepos." *ZDA*, 62 (1925), 185–207.

——. "Zur Thidrekssaga." *ZDA*, 66 (1929), 33–46.

——. "Zur Siegfrieddichtung und Thidrekssaga." *ZDA*, 71 (1934), 83–100.

Finch, R. G. "The Treatment of Poetic Sources by the Compiler of *Vǫlsunga saga*." *Saga-Book of the Viking Society*, 16 (1962–1965), 315–53.

——. "Brunhild and Siegfried." *Saga-Book of the Viking Society*, 17 (1966–69), 224–60.

Fromm, Hans. "Kapitel 168 der Thidrekssaga." *DVLG*, 33 (1959), 237–56.

Fuss, Klaus. "Brynhild." *ZDP*, 72 (1953), 110–24.

Gildersleeve, Virginia C. "Brynhild in Legend and Literature." *MP*, 6 (1909), 343–74.

Golther, Wolfgang. "Ueber die Sage von Siegfried und den Nibelungen." *ZVL*, 12 (1898), 186–208 and 289–316.

Heinrichs, Heinrich Matthias. "Sivrit—Gernot—Kriemhilt." *ZDA*, 86 (1955–1956), 279–89.

Heinzel, Richard. "Ueber die Nibelungensage." In *Sitzungsberichte der*

252 Bibliography

Kaiserlichen Akademie der Wissenschaften, phil.-hist. class, 109 (1885), 671–718.

Helm, Karl. "Siegfried und Xanten." *BGDSL*, 65 (1941), 154–59.

Hempel, Heinrich. *Nibelungenstudien: Nibelungenlied, Thidrikssaga und Balladen*. Germanische Bibliothek: Untersuchungen und Texte, 22. Vol. I (no more published). Heidelberg: Winter, 1926.

———. "Sächsische Nibelungendichtung und sächsischer Ursprung der Þiðrikssaga." In *Edda, Skalden, Saga: Festschrift zum 70. Geburtstag von Felix Genzmer*. Ed. Hermann Schneider. Heidelberg: Winter, 1952. Pp. 138–56. Rpt. in his *Kleine Schriften*. Ed. Heinrich Matthias Heinrichs. Heidelberg: Winter, 1966. Pp. 209–25.

———. "Sigurds Ausritt zur Vaterrache." In *Beiträge zur Runenkunde und nordischen Sprachwissenschaft (Festschrift Gustav Neckel)*. Ed. Kurt Helmut Schlottig. Leipzig: Harrassowitz, 1938. Pp. 155–69. Rpt. in his *Kleine Schriften*, pp. 184–94.

———. "Niederdeutsche Heldensage." *Die Nachbarn: Jahrbuch für vergleichende Volkskunde*, 3 (1962), 7–30. Rpt. in his *Kleine Schriften*, pp. 134–52.

Heusler, Andreas. "Die Lieder der Lücke im Codex Regius der Edda." In *Germanistische Abhandlungen Hermann Paul dargebracht*. Strasbourg: Trübner, 1902. Pp. 1–98. Rpt. in his *Kleine Schriften*. Vol. II. Ed. Stefan Sonderegger. Berlin: de Gruyter, 1969. Pp. 223–91.

———. "Altnordische Dichtung und Prosa von Jung Sigurd." In *Sitzungsberichte der Preussischen Akademie der Wissenschaften*, phil.-hist. class (1919), pp. 162–95. Rpt. in his *Kleine Schriften*. Vol. I. Ed. Helga Reuschel. Berlin: de Gruyter, 1969. Pp. 26–64.

———. "Die Quelle der Brünhildsage in Thidreks saga und Nibelungenlied." In *Aufsätze zur Sprach- und Literaturgeschichte Wilhelm Braune dargebracht*. Dortmund: Ruhfus, 1920. Pp. 47–84. Rpt. in his *Kleine Schriften*, I, 65–102.

———. *Nibelungensage und Nibelungenlied: Die Stoffgeschichte des deutschen Heldenepos*. Dortmund: Ruhfus, 1920. 2d ed., 1923; 3d ed., 1929; rpt. 1946, 1955, 1965.

Holzapfel, Otto. *Die dänischen Nibelungenballaden: Texte und Kommentare*. Göppinger Arbeiten zur Germanistik, 122. Göppingen: Alfred Kümmerle, 1974.

Hungerland, Heinz. "Zeugnisse zur Vǫlsungen- und Niflungensage aus der Skaldendichtung." *ANF*, 20 (1904), 1–43 and 105–42.

Jónsson, Finnur. "Sigurðarsaga og de prosaiske stykker i Codex Regius." *Aarbøger for nordisk oldkyndighed og historie* (1917), pp. 16–36.

———. "Sagnformen i Sigurðarkviða en skamma." *ANF*, 34 (1918), 278–84.

———. "Sagnformen i heltedigtene i Codex Regius." *Aarbøger for nordisk oldkyndighed og historie* (1921), pp. 1–104.

Kralik, Dietrich von. *Die Sigfridtrilogie im Nibelungenlied und in der Thidrekssaga.* Vol. I (no more published). Halle a. d. Saale: Niemeyer, 1941.

Kratz, Henry. "The Proposed Sources of the Nibelungenlied." *Studies in Philology,* 59 (1962), 615–30.

Kroes, H. W. J. "Die Kampfspiele des Nibelungenliedes (NL 389–481)." *Neophilologus,* 29 (1944), 161–64.

Kuhn, Hans. Review of *Quellenstudien zur Vǫlsungasaga,* by Per Wieselgren. *Deutsche Literaturzeitung,* 59 (1938), 1385–87.

――――. "Brünhilds und Kriemhilds Tod." *ZDA,* 82 (1950), 191–99. Rpt. in his *Kleine Schriften.* Ed. Dietrich Hofmann. Vol. II. Berlin: de Gruyter, 1971. Pp. 80–87.

――――. "Das Eddastück von Sigurds Jugend." *Miscellanea Academica Berolinensia,* 2 (1950), 30–46. Rpt. in his *Kleine Schriften,* II, 88–101.

Kuhn, Hugo. "Über nordische und deutsche Szenenregie in der Nibelungendichtung." In *Edda, Skalden, Saga: Festschrift zum 70. Geburtstag von Felix Genzmer.* Ed. Hermann Schneider. Heidelberg: Winter, 1952. Pp. 279–306. Rpt. in his *Dichtung und Welt im Mittelalter.* Stuttgart: Metzler, 1959 and 1969. Pp. 196–219.

Lehmgrübner, Wilhelm. *Die Erweckung der Walküre.* Hermaea, 32. Halle: Niemeyer, 1936; rpt. 1973.

Lohse, Gerhard. "Xanten und das Nibelungenlied." *Bonner Jahrbücher,* 153 (1953), 141–45.

――――. "Rheinische Nibelungendichtung und die Vorgeschichte des deutschen Nibelungenliedes von 1200." *Rheinische Vierteljahrsblätter,* 20 (1955), 54–60.

Lunzer, Justus. "Kleine Nibelungenstudien." *ZDA,* 69 (1932), 71–89, 225–37, and 277–95.

Magoun, Francis P., Jr. "The Iceland Voyage in the 'Nibelungenlied.'" *MLR,* 39 (1944), 38–42.

Mayer, Chr. Aug. "Brünhilde: Eine Untersuchung zur deutschen Heldensage." *ZVL,* 16 (1905), 119–71.

Mogk, Eugen. "Die germanische Heldendichtung mit besonderer Rücksicht auf die Sage von Siegfried und Brunhild." *Neue Jahrbücher für das klassische Altertum, Geschichte und deutsche Litteratur und für Pädagogik,* 1 (1898), 68–80.

Mohr, Wolfgang. "Entstehungsgeschichte und Heimat der jüngeren Eddalieder südgermanischen Stoffes." *ZDA,* 75 (1938), 217–80.

――――. "Wortschatz und Motive der jüngeren Eddalieder mit südgermanischem Stoff." *ZDA,* 76 (1939), 149–217.

――――. "Giselher." *ZDA,* 78 (1941), 90–120.

――――. Review of *Die Sigfridtrilogie,* by Dietrich von Kralik. *Dichtung und Volkstum,* 42 (1942), 83–123.

――――. Review of *Frühe Epik Westeuropas*, by Kurt Wais. *Anzeiger für deutsches Altertum*, 68 (1955–56), 7–20.

Neckel, Gustav. "Zur Vǫlsunga saga und den Eddaliedern der Lücke." *ZDP*, 37 (1905), 19–29.

――――. "Zu den Eddaliedern der Lücke." *ZDP*, 39 (1907), 293–330.

――――. *Beiträge zur Eddaforschung mit Exkursen zur Heldensage.* Dortmund: Ruhfus, 1908.

――――. "Aus der nordischen Nibelungendichtung." *GRM*, 1 (1909), 349–56.

――――. "Die Nibelungenballaden." In *Aufsätze zur Sprach- und Literaturgeschichte Wilhelm Braune dargebracht.* Dortmund: Ruhfus, 1920. Pp. 85–137.

――――. "Sigmunds Drachenkampf." *Edda*, 13 (1920), 122–40 and 204–29.

Neumann, Friedrich. "Schichten der Ethik im Nibelungenlied." In *Festschrift Eugen Mogk zum 70. Geburtstag.* Halle: Niemeyer, 1924. Pp. 119–45. Rpt. in his *Das Nibelungenlied in seiner Zeit.* Göttingen: Vandenhoeck & Ruprecht, 1967. Pp. 9–34.

――――. *Das Nibelungenlied in seiner Zeit.* Göttingen: Vandenhoeck & Ruprecht, 1967.

Panzer, Friedrich. *Studien zur germanischen Sagengeschichte.* Vol. II: *Sigfrid.* Munich: Beck, 1912.

――――. "Siegfriedmärchen." In *Aufsätze zur Sprach- und Literaturgeschichte Wilhelm Braune dargebracht.* Dortmund: Ruhfus, 1920. Pp. 138–47.

――――. *Studien zum Nibelungenliede.* Frankfurt am Main: Moritz Diesterweg, 1945.

――――. "Nibelungische Ketzereien. 1. Das russische Brautwerbermärchen im Nibelungenlied." *BGDSL*, 72 (1950), 463–98. Rpt. in *Zur germanisch-deutschen Heldensage: Sechzehn Aufsätze zum neuen Forschungsstand.* Ed. Karl Hauck. Bad Homburg vor der Höhe: Hermann Gentner Verlag, 1961. Pp. 138–72.

――――. "Nibelungische Ketzereien. 2. Lectulus Brunhildę." *BGDSL*, 73 (1951), 95–123.

――――. "Nibelungische Ketzereien. 3. Thidrekssaga und Nibelungenlied, Irrungen und Wirrungen. 4. Das 'Traumlied' in der Völsungasaga." *BGDSL*, 75 (1953), 248–72.

――――. "Nibelungische Problematik: Siegfried und Xanten, Hagen und die Meerfrauen, Magyaren und Hunnen." In *Sitzungsberichte der Heidelberger Akademie der Wissenschaften*, phil.-hist. class, 38 (1953–1954), no. 3, pp. 7–32.

――――. *Das Nibelungenlied: Entstehung und Gestalt.* Stuttgart: Kohlhammer, 1955.

Polak, Léon. *Untersuchungen über die Sigfridsagen.* Diss. Berlin 1910.
Berlin: Universitäts-Buchdruckerei von Gustav Schade, 1910.

Richter, Werner. "Beiträge zur Deutung des Mittelteils des Nibelungenliedes." *ZDA,* 72 (1935), 9–47.

Sayce, Olive L. "Abortive Motivation in Part I of the Nibelungenlied."
MA, 23 (1954), 36–38.

Schneider, Hermann. *Germanische Heldensage.* Vol. I. Grundriss der
germanischen Philologie, 10/1. Berlin and Leipzig: de Gruyter, 1928;
rpt. 1962.

———. "Verlorene Sigurddichtung." *ANF,* 45 (1929), 1–34.

———. "Siegfried." *Forschungen und Fortschritte,* 12 (1936), 3–4.

———. *Die deutschen Lieder von Siegfrieds Tod.* Weimar: Hermann
Böhlaus Nachfolger, 1947.

Schröder, Franz Rolf. *Nibelungenstudien.* Rheinische Beiträge und
Hülfsbücher zur germanischen Philologie und Volkskunde, 6. Bonn
and Leipzig: Kurt Schroeder, 1921.

———. "Die nibelungische Erweckungssage." *ZD,* 44 (1930), 433–49.

See, Klaus von. "Die Werbung um Brünhild." *ZDA,* 88 (1957), 1–20.

———. "Freierprobe und Königinnenzank in der Sigfridsage." *ZDA,* 89
(1958–59), 163–73.

Symons, Barend. "Untersuchungen ueber die sogenannte Völsunga saga." *BGDSL,* 3 (1876), 199–303.

———. "Sigfrid und Brunhild: Ein Beitrag zur Geschichte der Nibelungensage." *ZDP,* 24 (1892), 1–32.

Sperber, Hans. "Heuslers Nibelungentheorie und die nordische Überlieferung." In *Festschrift Max H. Jellinek zum 29. Mai 1928 dargebracht.* Vienna and Leipzig: Österreichischer Bundesverlag, 1928. Pp.
123–38.

Stroheker, K. F. "Studien zu den historisch-geographischen Grundlagen
der Nibelungendichtung." *DVLG,* 32 (1958), 216–40.

Sveinsson, Einar Ólafur. *Íslenzkar bókmenntir í fornöld.* Vol. I (no more
published). N.p.: Almenna Bókafélagið, 1962.

Sydow, C. W. von. "Sigurds strid med Fåvne: En studie rörande hjäl-
tesagans förhållande till folkdiktningen." *Lunds Universitets
Årsskrift,* N.F., Avd. 1, 14 (1918), no. 16, 1–51.

———. "Brynhildsepisoden i tysk tradition." *ANF,* 44 (1928), 164–89.

Ussing, Henrik. *Om det indbyrdes forhold mellem heltekvadene i ældre
Edda.* Copenhagen: Gad, 1910.

Vries, Jan de. *Studiën over Færøsche Balladen.* Haarlem: H. D. Tjeenk
Willink & Zoon, 1915.

———. "Het Korte Sigurdlied." In *Mededeelingen der Koninklijke Nederlandsche Akademie van Wetenschappen,* Afd. Letterkunde, N.R.,
Part 2 (1939), no. 11, pp. 1–75 (367–441).

Wais, Kurt. *Frühe Epik Westeuropas und die Vorgeschichte des Nibelungenliedes*. Mit einem Beitrag von Hugo Kuhn: *Brunhild und das Krimhildlied*. Vol. I (no more published). Beihefte zur Zeitschrift für romanische Philologie, 95. Tübingen: Niemeyer, 1953.

Wapnewski, Peter. "Rüdigers Schild. Zur 37. Aventiure des Nibelungenliedes." *Euphorion*, 54 (1960), 380–410.

Wesle, Carl. "Brünhildlied oder Sigfridepos?" *ZDP*, 51 (1926), 33–45.

Wieselgren, Per. "Vǫlsungasaga und Liederlücke." *ANF*, 50 (1934), 70–89.

———. *Quellenstudien zur Vǫlsungasaga*. Acta et Commentationes Universitatis Tartuensis, B XXXIV.3. Tartu: K. Mattiesens Buchdrukkerei, 1935.

Zeller, Rose. *Die Gudrunlieder der Edda*. Tübinger germanistische Arbeiten: Studien zur nordischen Philologie, 26. Stuttgart and Berlin: Kohlhammer, 1939.

Surveys of Research

Beyschlag, Siegfried. "Das Nibelungenlied in gegenwärtiger Sicht." *WW*, 3 (1952–1953), 193–200.

———. "Die Erschliessung der Vorgeschichte der Nibelungen: Zu Kurt Wais, Frühe Epik Westeuropas und die Vorgeschichte des Nibelungenliedes (Tübingen 1953)." *GRM*, 35 (1954), 257–65.

Bohning, Elizabeth Edrop. *The Concept 'Sage' in Nibelungen Criticism: The History of the Conception of 'Sage' in the Nibelungen Criticism from Lachmann to Heusler*. Bethlehem, Pennsylvania: Times Publishing Company, 1944.

Engert, Horst. "Nibelungenprobleme in neuer Beleuchtung." *ZD*, 38 (1924), 352–64 and 415–24, and 39 (1925), 685–704 and 763–70.

Fischer, Hermann. *Die Forschungen über das Nibelungenlied seit Karl Lachmann*. Leipzig: Verlag von F. C. W. Vogel, 1874.

Fleet (Thorp), Mary. "The Recent Study of the Nibelungenlied." *JEGP*, 52 (1953), 32–49.

Hoffmann, Werner. "Zur Situation der gegenwärtigen Nibelungenforschung: Probleme, Ergebnisse, Aufgaben." *WW*, 12 (1962), 79–91.

———. "Die englische und amerikanische Nibelungenforschung 1959–62." *ZDP*, 84 (1965), 267–78.

Kroes, H. W. J. "Neues zum Nibelungenlied." *Neophilologus*, 40 (1956), 269–77.

Moelleken, Wolfgang W. "Methodik der Nibelungenliedinterpretation." *German Quarterly*, 39 (1966), 289–98.

Naumann, Hans. "Stand der Nibelungenforschung." *ZD*, 41 (1927), 1–17.

Neumann, Friedrich. "Das Nibelungenlied in der gegenwärtigen Forschung." *DVLG*, 5 (1927), 130–71.

———. "'Nibelungenlied' und 'Klage.'" In *Die deutsche Literatur des Mittelalters: Verfasserlexikon*. Ed. Karl Langosch. Vol. III. Berlin: de Gruyter, 1943. Pp. 513–60. Vol. V (1955). Pp. 705–720.

———. *Das Nibelungenlied in seiner Zeit*. Göttingen: Vandenhoeck & Ruprecht, 1967. Pp. 122–82.

Olrik, Axel. "Nyere tysk literatur om Sigurd og Brynhild." *Dania*, 1 (1890–1892), 287–300.

Piquet, F. "Où en est l'étude du 'Nibelungenlied'?" *Revue germanique*, 18 (1927), 215–38 and 316–37.

Rosenfeld, H.-Fr. "Nibelungensage und Nibelungenlied in der Forschung der letzten Jahre." *NM*, 26 (1925), 145–78.

Schneider, Hermann. "Forschungsbericht. Die Quellen des Nibelungenliedes. Zu Friedrich Panzers Studien zum Nibelungenlied 1945." *Euphorion*, 45 (1950), 493–98.

Thorp, Mary. *The Study of the Nibelungenlied: Being the History of the Study of the Epic and Legend from 1755 to 1937*. Oxford: Clarendon, 1940.

Vancsa, Kurt. "Die Forschungen zum Nibelungenlied 1960–63: Eine kritische Übersicht." *Jahrbuch für Landeskunde von Niederösterreich*, 36 (1964), 881–88.

Index of the Principal Motifs

General Index

General Index

Publications Relating to the Fiske Icelandic Collection
in the Cornell University Libraries

*Volumes I–XXII were first published by the Cornell University Library; later volumes were published by Cornell University Press. Volumes I–XXXVI have been reprinted by Kraus Reprint Co.

XXX. *The Vinland Sagas.* Ed. with an introduction, variants, and notes by Halldór Hermannsson. 1944.

XXXI. *The Saga of Thorgils and Haflidi.* Ed. with an introduction and notes by Halldór Hermannsson. 1945.

XXXII and XXXIII. *History of Icelandic Prose Writers: 1800–1940.* By Stefán Einarsson. 1948.

XXXIV. *History of Icelandic Poets: 1800–1940.* By Richard Beck. 1950.

XXXV. *The Saga of Hrafn Sveinbjarnarson: The Life of an Icelandic Physician of the Thirteenth Century.* Tr. with an introduction and notes by Anne Tjomsland. 1951.

XXXVI. *The Age of the Sturlungs: Icelandic Civilization in the Thirteenth Century.* By Einar Ól. Sveinsson. Tr. by Jóhann S. Hannesson. 1953.

XXXVII. *Bibliography of the Eddas: A Supplement to ISLANDICA XIII.* By Jóhann S. Hannesson. 1955. (Out of print.)

XXXVIII. *The Sagas of Icelanders (Íslendinga Sögur): A Supplement to IS-LANDICA I and XXIV.* By Jóhann S. Hannesson. 1957.

XXXIX. *The Hólar Cato: An Icelandic Schoolbook of the Seventeenth Century.* Ed. with an introduction and two appendices by Halldór Hermannsson. 1958.

XL. *Bibliography of Modern Icelandic Literature in Translation, including Works Written by Icelanders in Other Languages.* Compiled by P. M. Mitchell and Kenneth H. Ober. 1975.

XLI. *Halldór Hermannsson.* By P. M. Mitchell. 1978.

XLII. *Old Norse Court Poetry: The Dróttkvætt Stanza.* By Roberta Frank. 1978.

XLIII. *The Legend of Brynhild.* By Theodore M. Andersson. 1980.

CATALOGUES

Catalogue of the Icelandic Collection Bequeathed by Willard Fiske. Compiled by Halldór Hermannsson. 1914.*

———: *Additions 1913–26.* 1927.

———: *Additions 1927–42.* 1943.

Catalogue of Runic Literature forming a Part of the Icelandic Collection Bequeathed by Willard Fiske. Compiled by Halldór Hermannsson. Oxford: Oxford University Press, 1917. (Out of print.)

*This volume and the additions were reprinted in 1960 by Cornell University Press.

Library of Congress Cataloging in Publication Data

Andersson, Theodore Murdock, 1934–
  The legend of Brynhild.

  (Islandica; 43)
  Bibliography: p.
  Includes index.
  1. Germanic literature—Themes, motives. 2. Brunhild. 3. Helden-
sage. I. Title. II. Series.
PN831.A5   830'.09   80-16008
ISBN 0-8014-1302-8